Qualitative Methods for Practice Research

POCKET GUIDES TO
SOCIAL WORK RESEARCH METHODS

Series Editor
Tony Tripodi, DSW
Professor Emeritus, Ohio State University

JEFFREY LONGHOFER
JERRY FLOERSCH
JANET HOY

Qualitative Methods for
Practice Research

OXFORD
UNIVERSITY PRESS

OXFORD
UNIVERSITY PRESS

Oxford University Press is a department of the University of Oxford.
It furthers the University's objective of excellence in research,
scholarship, and education by publishing worldwide.

Oxford New York
Auckland   Cape Town   Dar es Salaam   Hong Kong   Karachi
Kuala Lumpur   Madrid   Melbourne   Mexico City   Nairobi
New Delhi   Shanghai   Taipei   Toronto

With offices in
Argentina   Austria   Brazil   Chile   Czech Republic   France   Greece
Guatemala   Hungary   Italy   Japan   Poland   Portugal   Singapore
South Korea   Switzerland   Thailand   Turkey   Ukraine   Vietnam

Oxford is a registered trademark of Oxford University Press in the UK
and in certain other countries.

Published in the United States of America by
Oxford University Press
198 Madison Avenue, New York, NY 10016

© 2013 by Oxford University Press, Inc.

Library of Congress Cataloging-in-Publication Data
Longhofer, Jeffrey L. (Jeffrey Lee)
Qualitative methods for practice research / Jeffrey Longhofer,
Jerry Floersch, Janet Hoy.
p. cm. — (Pocket guides to social work research methods)
Includes bibliographical references and index.
ISBN 978-0-19-539847-2 (pbk. : alk. paper)
1. Social service—Research—Methodology. 2. Qualitative research.
I. Floersch, Jerry. II. Hoy, Janet. III. Title.
HV11.L588 2013
001.42—dc23
2012000410

Printed in the United States of America
on acid-free paper

Contents

Acknowledgments

We have so many to thank. First, for many years Morteza Ardebili patiently mentored Jeffrey and Jerry as they struggled to understand and integrate critical realism—to help us live comfortably beneath the surface. We cannot find words enough to thank our editors at Oxford University Press, Maura Roessner and Nicholas Liu, and the several anonymous reviewers for their focused and thorough comments. We thank, too, our many teachers, colleagues, and students. Without Richard Edwards, Rutgers University Interim Executive Vice President for Academic Affairs, and former dean of the Rutgers School of Social Work, this book would not exist. He offered Jeffrey and Jerry an academic home to imagine and create new possibilities for clinical social work. We would also like to thank the Acting Dean at the Rutgers School of Social Work, Kathleen Pottick, for her always generous insights and observations about our work and for her commitment to clinical social work. There are others we'd like to personally name: Donald Stull, Ann Kuckelmann-Cobb, Elizabeth Hansen, Scott Wehman, Anna Janicki, and Vera Camden. Finally we thank the many with whom we've had the great pleasure of collaborating in research and our many clients for bringing to us more than their concerns and personal projects but also their insights into the nature of our work.

Portions of chapter 2 have been reproduced from *Qualitative Social Work* with the kind permission of Sage Publications.

Introduction

The school nurse calls at work. She's just seen his five-year-old son. "It's a terrible earache. He is crying, feverish, and lethargic." The young and worried single father leaves work, something he rarely does, yet fears losing his job. This will be the second time in six months. It is now almost two years since his wife and sister had been killed in a tragic auto accident. It's just now the two of them. They'd recently moved north from a small city in the south. They are alone, living in a small, cramped, studio apartment in a mostly poor neighborhood of African Americans, without family and friends. Dad has an associate's degree in computer science but cannot find a job in his field. He's paying loans on a college education that seems like a underwater mortgage. They are both seeing a social worker and dad recently decided to take an anti-depressant. Tyshawn often seems to react to stress in bodily ways (i.e., hives, headaches) and dad has noticed that he is often physically ill when things are not going well for dad. And the transition from home to school has been rocky; for some time now dad has noticed that Tyshawn is wetting at night. The social worker has helped them understand that he is often worried; and he once asked the school nurse whether he should call home to see if dad is sad.

The supervisor at work, who tends to fill a space with his body and voice, rolls his eyes in disbelief and takes a long, deep drag on his unfiltered cigarette. "An earache, yeah, go on," he says as he dismissively waves, turns, and lumbers toward the door of an office too small for his volume.

He decides to first try the free clinic. The car has just been repaired but he has reservations about the long drive in rush hour traffic. Tyshawn seems listless and indifferent to his reassurances and questions. The waiting room, filled with people, is dimly lit and jam-packed with unmatched folding chairs. A cacophony of sounds fills the immense room: children hacking or crying, a buzzer that sounds each time the door opens, the grating voice of the receptionist barking names and numbers. One can only imagine what the numbers mean. You could still see high on the vaulted ceiling places where pulleys and tracks had once moved heavy engines. Overpowering antiseptic cleaning solutions mix with the lasting stench of oil and grease from engines. There's something in the pores of the place: stagnant, makeshift, desperate, historical. It has served some other remote purpose—engine repair.

More than an hour passed. He wondered: should they go to the emergency room? The hospital is an hour away, even in light traffic. It's rush hour. Soon, Tyshawn is stretched out on his lap. He's sleeping in fits and starts, interrupted by the raspy voice of the receptionist calling out over the din of the crowd populated with other terribly sick children with their anxious parents. Little by little Tyshawn's father feels his privacy invaded by the place, by the too-closeness of the chairs, by the incessant calling of names, by the relentless sound of the buzzer, by the hacking and crying. He's worried and anxious.

Finally, after two hours, a nurse calls out Tyshawn's name and directs the father and son to a cramped examination room crowded with steel gray furniture imported from another time and place. Another 15 minutes pass and a harried young internist with a heavy accent appears. Without introduction the internist does a quick examination and abruptly declares that Tyshawn is suffering from "acute otitis media." Tyshawn's anxious father asks the doctor, who now has a grip on the door handle, to explain and write it down. All he can make out is something about fluid and pus in the middle ear. He says, brusquely, "this means redness of the eardrum." The physician brushes off the request. He thought for a moment that the doctor was not fluent enough in English to write it down.

It felt like he was falling, along with son, into a huge abyss, a communication cul-du-sac, a feeling that he'd many times experienced in similar situations. The condescension caused him to feel powerless, helpless, and hopeless. The doctor seems to think the infection will clear up but gives them the option to try an antibiotic. He turns, expression-less, and parts without saying goodbye. Tyshawn and his father sit in worried silence, relieved to be away from the din of the waiting room and pass the time with an occasional shared but unspoken expression of agitation and worry, until a nurse comes into the examination room, hands the father a prescription, and gives instructions for using the correct hallway to exit.

Practitioners are responsible for solving specific problems. But now, more than any other time in the history of the profession, social workers are required to know the research behind specific interventions. What evidence exists to address the complex psychosocial factors contributing to Tyshawn's earache? How was this knowledge produced? Today, knowledge is produced and transferred by research stakeholders—researcher, practitioner, and client—vertically: one-way knowledge transfer to the ultimate end-user, the client. Indeed, evidence-based social work research imagines that generalized knowledge trickles down to the practitioner and client (Gray, Plath & Webb, 2009). There is a second way that we envision the transfer of knowledge. Here, the focus is on knowledge of context and particularity, on practitioner wisdom and client experience. However, it too is often perceived as moving in only one direction: from client to practitioner, or practitioner to researcher. Hardwick and Worlsey (2011), for example, argue that "practitioner-led research" (PLR) offers a more comprehensive account of situated knowledge and that such knowledge, produced at sites where users, carers, and organizations relate, should be transferred upward. We argue that one-way transfers, *downward or upward* (i.e., from the expert researcher to the uniformed practitioner or from the wise practitioner to the uninformed researcher), rarely produce collaboration: each group claims *equal but autonomous knowledge*. And as a result, often they do not respect, listen, or understand one another. At best it is a stalemate. At worst it is a standoff: stakeholders refuse to acknowledge different points of view.

This book is for the beginning or experienced practitioner with the desire to adopt a different understanding of knowledge production and transfer. It's about the use of qualitative methods for *knowledge coproduction*. We will explore reasons for practitioner use of qualitative methods to study and understand interactions, events, circumstances, institutions, interventions, or mental states, in Tyshawn's case, among physician, patient, and parent; or in other cases between social workers and their clients. Moreover, we will introduce the reader to quick-start methods for collaborating in qualitative research. The identification of problems and solutions are activities we encounter in our everyday practice. We see these activities as occurring in *open systems* where the variables are many, complex, messy, contradictory, and fluid. In these same open systems we are also faced with *normative, ethical, and evaluative* questions about how our clients are doing, how social, interpersonal, and psychological forces are affecting their lives (and ours), and what can be done to improve the quality of living (Fraser & Honneth, 2003; Honneth, 1996; Houston, 2003, 2008; Putnam, 2002; Sayer, 2011; Smart, 2007; McBeath and Webb, 2002; Webb and McBeath, 1989).

Indeed, because our practice is determined by normative evaluations, social work practitioners and researchers cannot separate *fact* from *value* or reason from emotion (Putnam, 2002; Sayer, 2007, p. 240, 2011; Smith, 2010, pp. 384–433). And because we practice as evaluative beings, that is, we make judgments about things in fluid and contextual ways (Flyvbjerg, 2001; Held, 2006; Sayer, 2011;), we must produce knowledge that allows us to fully explore these dynamics (i.e., fact–value, reason–emotion) as they continuously and recursively unfold in caring relationships (Rossiter, 2011). Social work is interested in what causes suffering and what causes well-being (Houston, 2008; Rossiter, 2011). In short, we are interested in how and why things matter to people (Sayer, 2011), and in this book, we are especially interested in what we are calling engaged scholarship, a form of knowledge production that deepens understanding of what matters most.

WHAT IS ENGAGED SCHOLARSHIP?

We argue that knowledge production that respects the open system of social work requires unique engagement with *all* participants. This is not to be confused with *action research* or *participatory action research* and their myriad permutations; the latter refer mainly to *modes of relating* in the research process (Stahl & Shdaimah, 2008). In a very different way Andrew Van de Ven (2007) has defined engaged scholarship as a

> . . . form of research for obtaining the different perspectives of key stakeholders (researchers, users, clients, sponsors, and practitioners) in

studying complex problems. By involving others and leveraging
their different kinds of knowledge, engaged scholarship can produce
knowledge that is more penetrating and insightful than when scholars or
practitioners work on the problems alone. (p. 9)

Van de Ven does not describe the knowledge-to-practice debate in con-
ventional terms, which largely discusses how knowledge or theory is
transferred downward to practice and includes the numerous gaps
and misapplications caused by mishandled transfers: the uninformed
practitioner who fails to use evidence-based research, for example (this is
sometimes described as fidelity research). Those who articulate and
produce these two types of knowledge, practitioners and researchers,
typically identify one-way gaps between generalized knowledge (e.g.,
evidence-based practice; based on numerous cases) and practice reflexivity (e.g., tacit, situated, or practical wisdom, based on single case studies).
These gaps, many argue, can be bridged through more *efficient transfer* of
knowledge from the researcher to the practitioner. Or when practice
knowledge is considered equal to research, moving knowledge upward
from the practitioner to researcher bridges the gap. Rarely has the debate
led to an alternative: where social work practitioners, researchers, and
clients act as knowledge coproducers (Stahl & Shdaimah, 2008). Where
knowledge is coproduced it is not so easy to accuse one another of
mishandled transfers, or even ignorance.

For Van De Ven (2007) there is a common gap between research or
scholarship and real-life situations encountered by practicing managers
of organizations. Instead of conceptualizing this as a problem of
knowledge transfer, or as two distinct types of knowledge, he under-
stands knowledge-to-practice gaps as a problem of knowledge production. He proposed a strategy to exploit the real differences among those
with *incommensurable* perspectives with the shared goal of arriving at a
richer, more thorough, and more nuanced understanding of the complex phenomenon under investigation. He calls this *arbitrage,* and for
him it "represents a dialectical method of inquiry where understanding
and synthesis of a common problem evolves from the confrontation of
divergent theses and antitheses" (Van de Ven & Johnson, 2006, p. 809).
Van de Ven and Johnson show how relationships that form among
participants are crucial to the success of arbitrage and that success
occurs over time, through repeated iterations. The result is trust and

cooperation among participants. For example, how can various stake-holder perspectives inform research aims and questions? Surprisingly, consensus is not the goal! Instead, it is assumed that conflict is necessary and that stakeholders will often make *different* ontological (what is the nature of reality) and epistemological (how do we make knowledge claims) assumptions; disagreements, therefore, must be creatively, productively, and proactively used and managed.

Van de Ven (2007, p. 268) has described four types of engaged scholarship projects: (1) informed basic science; (2) collaborative research; (3) design or evaluation research; and (4) action or interven-tion research. These are not without precedent in social work (Enthoven, 2010; Houston, 2010). For several decades arguments have been made for basic science and evaluation research. Collaborative research is not unlike what is often described as community participatory research. Nor is action or intervention research new to social work. However, engaged scholarship does not assume, like its cousins (i.e., community participa-tory research and action research), that the end game is consensus or reconciliation of difference; instead, coproduction of knowledge is the goal, and it is accomplished by testing assumptions with collaboratively collected and analyzed data.

This book describes engaged scholarship as a framework for reformulating the knowledge-to-practice debate within open systems. And even though the idea of practitioner, researcher, and client social work research collaboration is not new, we shall integrate these various approaches under engaged scholarship.

WHY ENGAGED SCHOLARSHIP NOW?

From its beginnings in the late nineteenth-century to approximately 1960, social work based practical action on ethical, moral, social, economic, and psychological theories. Prominent theoreticians (e.g., Mary Richmond, Edith Abbott, Jane Addams) were associated with various legitimizing institutions (i.e., public and social welfare programs, schools of social work, and settlement houses), and they often asserted their explanations without the expectations of present-day research norms; students and practitioners were largely expected to believe and act upon assertions. The second era, 1960 to the present, began with a reaction to the "theory only" approach and culminated in a method-ologically positivist, evidence-based (i.e., variables research) movement that assumed a one-way, top-down knowledge producer—the social work researcher.

Here's a brief example. We have an idea at the university that comes from reading the literature and theory related to drug addiction. We develop a method for testing this theory in the field. We go to an agency engaged in working with addicts and propose testing our idea. They agree. We administer a survey or make observations. We return to the university where we analyze, write, publish, and present our results at professional meetings. This is not engaged scholarship.

In this book, we argue that social work is poised for a new era, one where engaged scholarship will redefine the relationships among researchers, practitioners, and clients; in short, as opposed to *equal but autonomous* knowledge producers, engaged scholarship views partici-pants as *different but interdependent*. The "equal but autonomous" posi-tion results in parallel social work universes where practitioners and researchers pursue separate visions about what constitutes knowledge, carrying with it an attitude expressed as "my practice (or research) knowledge is better than yours," or "my methods outshine yours," or "my methods are more scientific than yours." Perhaps it's time for a new approach.

And although the equal but autonomous perspective has become the norm, no one group has managed to assert absolute knowledge claims. Why? Because this often results in power struggles won by those most adept at defending their claim to specific forms of knowledge produc-tion—whose knowledge will be disseminated and how and whose knowl-edge explains what matters most to people. We believe that the current *equal but autonomous* perspective has produced a stalemate where each group (i.e., practitioner and researcher) either acknowledges the other without resistance or opposes the other; in either case, *knowledge produc-tion is limited.* One could argue that in the United States, the three major social work associations—Council on Social Work Education, National Association of Social Workers, and Society for Social Work and Research—are unable or unwilling to collaborate over what matters most to the people served: *equal but autonomous* results in each association believing in and defending the uniqueness of its position. Here's the result. Leaders and members are unwilling to develop *different but interdependent* positions, associations, and meetings from which these hardened positions can be loosened, discussed, and integrated, or where differences can be sharpened for the purpose of advancing knowledge.

Engaged scholarship frames social work research as more than tolerance or recognition of equal positions. It requires dialogue and *arbitrage* (Van de Ven, 2007). It requires respect for knowledge conceived as different but interdependent. With arbitrage, knowledge production must occur in the same universe while recognizing the likelihood that our knowledge claims and methods may sometimes be incommensurable (we will have more to say about this in chapter 1). This should not lead to impasse. Practitioners produce knowledge differently than do researchers. In fact, when ontological and epistemological differences remain hidden, unspoken, or unacknowledged, scientific investigation and practice looks more like a horse race than collaboration. When we openly discuss our sometimes hidden assumptions, we not only acknowledge the limitations and potential of knowledge production, we also open up new possibilities for practice in complex, open, human systems (open systems are discussed in chapter 1).

HOW WE USE ENGAGED SCHOLARSHIP

This is a book about the relationship between theory and practice and qualitative methods across the various domains of clinical social work practice. In the chapters that follow we offer a unique way of understanding how practitioners, scholars, and clients produce and deploy knowledge. And while engaged scholarship is a mode of relating, it is also a philosophical system that begins with a set of guiding assumptions derived from critical realism: open systems, emergence, and causal mechanisms (Van de Ven, 2007, pp. 61–68). The book demonstrates how students, practitioners, and agency directors can use qualitative research to initiate, with research partners, engaged scholarship projects. And because this is not a book aimed at the range of qualitative research methods (or techniques), relevant books and articles will be referenced so you may consider exploring specific methods in greater detail. Moreover, because this is not our aim, we hope to open the social work imagination to new ways of thinking about *why to use existing qualitative methods.* There are many and useful introductions and comprehensive texts on qualitative methods, and we refer to them throughout this work.

This book will be useful to those seeking to learn about the role of qualitative *research in practice*; for practitioners and client advocates seeking to have their voices included in the development of applied knowledge; for faculty teaching qualitative research; and, for researchers wanting to conduct ongoing research in open practice settings. The methods in this book can be used to explore practitioner, client, and practitioner–client interactions. In chapter 1, we provide a concise, although challenging, introduction to the philosophy of social science that underlies this entire book, especially as it relates to our thinking about methods and methodology in open systems. Critical realism is especially suited to engaged scholarship projects (Van de Ven, 2007, pp. 60–61).

In chapter 1, we focus on critical realism. We use critical realism as a way of thinking about open systems and how qualitative methods can be used to investigate the application of theory to social work *practice* in these systems (Willig, 2001, pp. 9–10).[1] It is in this way that we take seriously the idea of a pocket guide. We offer, therefore, not another comprehensive guide to qualitative methods, clearly beyond the scope of a book this size, but a book focused specifically on how to carefully and thoughtfully consider the creative tensions that inevitably exist in open systems between theory and practice: what we call a *phenomenological practice gap* (PPG). We consider the PPG and the problem of knowledge transfer (Van de Ven, 2007, pp. 3–10) within the gap, and in chapter 1 we explain why this is called phenomenological and why a gap. Moreover, we are especially interested in the use of critical realism to think about the many and complex ways that social work researchers confront the world of *fact and value* in dynamically *open systems*: mental health centers, schools, communities and neighborhoods, families, organizations, and in working with individuals. We will argue that seemingly intractable practice conundrums have their roots in the lived experience of practitioner and client interactions, like the one described in the opening paragraphs of this chapter; thus qualitative data collection techniques and analytic strategies are essential research tools for revealing the key components of the role of theory in practice.

In chapter 2, we illustrate how qualitative methods can be used in engaged scholarship projects. How are aims and questions formulated?

How does critical realism apply to a research question? What techniques are used to collect and analyze data? We describe a quick-start method for how thematic, grounded theory and narrative data analytic strategies can be used along with various data collection techniques. In this chapter, the reader will also learn how to use a computer software program to both manage and analyze data. The chapter applies critical realist ideas to problem formulation, collection, analysis, and interpretation of findings.

In chapter 3 we show how ethnography, institutional ethnography in particular, offers an especially effective way of understanding theory-to-practice divides in mental health settings. Ethnography pays attention to natural, real-world settings and to the collection of "near experience" data: in-vivo or in actual time. Here, we use examples from our research in mental health case management and mental health policy implementation to illustrate the fundamentals of qualitative research in open systems. Chapter 4 shows how an engaged scholarship perspective is adapted to the implementation of evidence-based interventions: that is, how to allow context and particularity to inform implementation.

In the conclusion (chapter 5), we bring together our ideas and concepts to describe a way of thinking about reflexive *practice* (praxis). We propose that a truly reflective practice is one based upon careful methodological considerations of the PPG. And using the work of the critical realists, Margaret Archer and Andrew Sayer, we will outline an approach to reflective practice and argue that qualitative methods informed by critical realism and deployed in engaged scholarship contexts will open up the possibility of a new era in social work knowledge coproduction.

In sum, we offer you a way of thinking about qualitative methods in clinical social work and mental health practice. However, it could easily be used and read by anyone interested in studying the dynamics of practice (e.g., nursing and medicine, psychology) in open systems. And while we will offer you some helpful ways of thinking about how to do research, we are most interested in offering you *reasons* to do so. In short, we offer you a rationale for considering qualitative methods and some concrete examples of their use in two mental health practice settings.

Qualitative Methods for Practice Research

1

Engaged Scholarship and Critical Realism

In this first chapter we offer a brief introduction to critical realism, a philosophy of social science that offers social work researchers and their *engaged* collaborators a means not only of understanding practice as it unfolds in open systems, but also of addressing the growing gap between theory and practice and the increasing concern that academic research is irrelevant to the everyday concerns of mental health practitioners.[1] Critical realism also offers social work researchers a way, perhaps the only way at present, of truly engaging the complex dynamic between *fact and value*, between the *is and the ought*, between the *positive and the normative* (Sayer, 2011; Smith, 2010). The latter is especially important in social work because it is a field of practice in which we make evaluations every moment about what to do in the best interest of others: children, families, neighborhoods and communities, schools, individuals and groups, and organizations. We are never engaged only with descriptive aspects (i.e., what is) of human experience. We are always and everyday engaged with what matters (i.e., what ought to be) to people (Sayer, 2011) and with how what matters matters (i.e., moral considerations about what is best to do under particular empirical accounts and conditions). Critical realism may also offer a useful way of thinking about the artificial and sometimes unconstructive conceptual divides between the micro and the macro, the individual and the social, direct practice and social policy.

We first consider distinctions that critical realists make between things we *experience* and things that *cause* what we experience. To accomplish this we return to Tyshawn's experience in the free clinic and his painful earache. We talk about the structures and the underlying and invisible mechanisms that cause his earache. This is especially difficult for some, particularly for those committed to the notion that the only things that are real are the things that can be seen or somehow experienced (i.e., using a special lens or sense-enhancing technology).[2] Here we offer a clear alternative to what we call *variables-based* (Smith, 2010) social work research. We then talk about *open systems* and a very important concept, *emergence*, which will help us learn more about how open systems work and how social work research and mental health practice might benefit from using this concept to overcome both *social and biological reductionism* (i.e., reducing the social and psychological to biology, genes, body, or brain, or reducing the psychological to the social). It seems that we live in yet another age of reductionism, and various forms of biological reductionism (see Healy, 2004; Lewontin, 1983, 2001; Valenstein, 2002a, 2002b) have become increasingly popular and problematic (i.e., to brain, to body, to genes, to neurotransmitters). We turn next to a very brief discussion of the critical realist distinction between necessity and contingency. In social work, in open systems, events always occur *contingently*. We show how and why it is important to grasp this fundamental notion and why it is important in the framing of research questions and the conduct of research. Next we consider the *concept dependent* nature of our knowledge and related critiques of *essentialism*. This latter discussion is especially important in social work and mental health, as an increasing number of scholars and practitioners have found it virtually impossible to reason their way out of unnecessary critiques of human development, child development, infant determinism, attachment theory, and arguments about the nature of the self and subjectivity (i.e., essentialism vs. social constructivism) and social constructions of suffering and pain (Cromby, 2004). We also consider what we call the phenomenological practice gap (PPG). These are the social, psychological, and physical spaces where social workers use theory or attempt to use theory in practice. It describes the necessary and inevitable gaps between theory or models of practice and the actual practices of social workers. It is in these gaps where we live and struggle and where our clients struggle alongside us. And it is in these gaps where our values are often revealed, contested, and formed. Finally, we integrate topics of this chapter by discussing the difference between methods and methodology. This will offer you a clear picture of the philosophical grounds for our discussion of qualitative methods in subsequent chapters.

The Real, the Actual, and the Empirical

Critical realism makes important distinctions *between the world* and *our experience of it* and between several domains: the *real*, the *actual*, and the *empirical* (Bhaskar, 1975). The *empirical* is the domain of experience where *observations of events* are made: Tyshawn's painful earache, his temperature, his sweating, his anxious state. The *empirical* domain refers entirely to experience and impression, to fact and data. Clearly there are events that occur without our experience of them; and sometimes they can be inferred only from their effects. In short, not all things are experienced. To believe otherwise, as Margaret Archer argues, confines "truth about the world to that which can be experienced" (Archer, 2000, p. 45).[3] *Empirical realists (and positivists)*, unlike critical realists, confine understanding of the world to events and to regularities among them and to that which can be observed. With *empirical realism*, however, objects lack powers and unobservable qualities.

The domain of the *real* refers to the structures, powers, mechanisms, and tendencies of objects (Bhaskar, 2008, pp. 236–237; Elder-Vass, 2007). The "real is whatever exists, be it natural or social, regardless of whether it is an empirical object for us, and whether we happen to have an adequate understanding of its nature" (Sayer, 2000, p. 11). Bacteria that cause otitis media, for example, have causal powers that exist in complex relationships with other causal powers (i.e., economic structures that produce poverty) that together contingently (we will have more to say later about the difference between *contingency* and *necessity*) produce effects. In short, the *real* is that which exists: physical (i.e., atomic, chemical, and biological structures), social (i.e., ideologies and social class), and psychological (i.e., mental structures, schemas, unconscious processes and memory, object relations). These objects of science, that is, the things we study, have been called by critical realists "intransitive": entities (structures, causal powers, mechanisms) that exist independently from observation. And some contemporary philosophers call these *brute facts*.[4] The theories (i.e., explanatory accounts, narratives) and discourses we produce about the things we study, however, occupy a different position: they are called by critical realists "transitive." The intransitive dimension relates to ontology (i.e., these are questions we ask about what is, what we take to be real, and what we consider knowable) and the transitive dimension to epistemology (i.e., how we know something). There is a slightly more complicated notion here. For critical realists, our knowledge exists as a real social object in the transitive dimension. As such, our knowledge is about *real objects* in the intransitive dimension; and the intransitive exists independently of mental activity or our thinking about the objects we study. In short, intransitive objects exist and act independently of our knowledge of them (except when we use our knowledge to intervene), so knowledge is irreducible to what it is about and constitutes an object with its own level of social causality.

For social work research and engaged scholarship, we are always confronted with both intransitive objects (i.e., what knowledge is about) and transitive objects (i.e., existing knowledge from which new knowledge is formed). And it is through the transitive (i.e., the philosopher John Searle called these institutional facts) that we establish explanatory relationships with intransitive objects (i.e., brains, minds, narratives, social classes). And with this distinction between the transitive and the intransitive we come to know that the world (i.e., the intransitive) cannot be conflated with our experience of it. Finally, and especially important for our book on qualitative methods and engaged scholarship, this all unfolds in open systems (to be discussed at length later in the chapter). The philosopher of mind John Searle offers another and useful way of thinking about the transitive and intransitive domains. He distinguishes between "brute" and "institutional facts."

Brute and Institutional Facts

Remember that our young patient Tyshawn displays a number of symptoms: fever, drainage, aching ear, and lethargy. The physician looks at these by using various instruments (otoscope, thermometer, stethoscope) and organizes them into a comprehensible pattern, identifies a precise pathogen, and offers a diagnosis. The diagnosis refers to a distinct reality. Searle calls these kinds of facts *brute facts*.[5] What are brute facts? Very simply put, brute facts don't require human institutions to exist. They exist in what the critical realist would call the intransitive (Bhaskar, 2008, pp. 26–30). In medicine, and in the preceding example, these facts are often established via various instruments, technologies, laboratory tests, or other sensory enabling devices (e.g., microscope). That bacteria causes ear infections (i.e., acute otitis media) is a brute fact. Brute facts, in short, do not depend on our attitudes, feelings, ideologies, or myriad social constructions to exist.[6]

That children under the poverty level have higher incidence of ear infections is not a brute fact.[7] Searle would call this an *institutional fact.* What are institutional facts? Brute facts, like streptococcus pneumonia, *exist* and do not require the institutional arrangements that produce poverty. In this chapter and throughout the book, we show how social work research, when it is done well, examines the complex relationships between brute and institutional facts, or what critical realists call the transitive and the intransitive. We might even want to offer this as a clear way of understanding the complex dynamics among and between among the bio/psycho/social. And social work research, especially in mental health practice, should not confuse brute with institutional facts or reduce institutional to brute facts.[8] Moreover, most research and research methodology in social work is aimed at understanding institutional facts in open systems, topics we will return to later.[9]

Structures and mechanisms, moreover, are nonphysical and unobservable (e.g., social structures, mental structures). Social structures that cause some groups to be more susceptible to ear infection than others are not observable. Just as no one sees gravity, no one sees social structures. *Observable effects* are therefore products of *unobservable structures* or mechanisms that we attempt to explain in continuously changing, historical, open social systems. Bodies, brains, and minds (Will, 1980, 1983, 1984, 1986), for example, have *structures:* they have *powers* to produce effects with particular susceptibility to specific kinds of change in open systems, regardless of whether those powers are exercised; just as the body has *potential* powers to produce effects (e.g., the agility of a great athlete or the graceful moves of a dancer or the tragic limits set by genetic diseases), though not always realized, so do the brain and mind (Williams, 1999, 2000a, 2000b, 2003, 2006).[10] "Complex things, then, have powers in virtue of their structures, and we can investigate their structures and in some instances thereby infer something of their powers" (Lawson, 1997, p. 21).[11]

Let's take an example from attachment theory. Attachment theorists argue that the nature and quality of early attachments have lasting effects on our capacities to form and maintain relationships and that these mental structures, or internal working models, can be known only through their effects. And while these most fundamental human attachments or internal object relations (Clarke, 2006, 2011) are not directly observable, they nevertheless produce effects, contingently, in open systems. Nor is it the case that internal working models work invariably. They have powers and liabilities, that is, only under certain circumstances do they have the power to produce effects (but not under all conditions). And under other conditions, countervailing forces (we have more to say about countervailing forces later) work to mitigate against attachment effects.[12] There's another way of thinking about this. Some might argue that attachment relationships produce *contingent* outcomes, not *necessary* ones. What's the implication of this?

For Tyshawn, the bacteria that causes acute otitis media has causal powers by virtue of its molecular structure to produce effects. And his susceptibility to infection is also caused by co-occurring mechanisms, that is, the structures unique to his ear and social class and family dynamics; when combined these differentially distribute risk and resources or act to mitigate vulnerability (Lanphear et al., 1997; Rosenfeld & Bluestone, 2003, p. 510; Vakharia et al., 2010). The molecular structure and mechanisms exist in the *domain of the real* and these particular bacteria and the toxins produced in the molecular structure—along with the generative mechanism of social class—are governed by combined causal mechanisms with fundamental properties that cannot be observed directly but become manifest in the *domain of the actual.*

The *actual* refers to what happens when the powers and liabilities of objects are activated (Collier, 1994, pp. 42–45) and to what happens when these powers, once activated, produce change. In the actual domain events occur whether we experience them or not. It is most important to remember that the actual refers to what happens if and when mechanisms, which belong to the domain of the real, are activated. In the actual domain there are events that are independent of experience; in short, what happens in the actual may go unobserved. In some psychoanalytic theory, for example, it is assumed that the unconscious acts as an invisible yet determining force that is activated only under particular conditions.

Closed versus Open Systems

In social work generally and all practice in mental health settings, we do not work in or encounter *closed systems*. In short, the mind, the interpersonal world, the family, the neighborhood, the school, are all open systems. Closed systems exist only when we can and do take action to control the variables (e.g., controlling the effects of temperature or pressure or other potentially intervening causes in a laboratory experiment). Another condition for closure is history, that is, once the events have occurred, they are no longer susceptible to the influence of new or countervailing events. Closure occurs when there are no *countervailing causes* and the absence of external influences is insufficient to rule out internal countervailing causes (Bhaskar, 1986, p. 69). What is a countervailing force? Imagine a case from clinical social work or mental health practice. You see an adult who is depressed and anxious. You learn that she recently experienced a major loss, the death of a lifelong partner. You also learn that she has a supportive and loving family and many close friends. You also learn, however, that your client has had a longer history of depression. In your initial visit you learn that she is very gradually getting pleasure out of doing new things and that she has not found herself alone or isolated. One could easily describe the presence of these supportive family and friendship networks as a force (i.e., a countervailing force) acting against the tendency that your client has to experience depression and suffer. In short, your client exists in an open system where there is always the potential for many and even sometimes contradictory countervailing forces to act.

The critical realist Roy Bhaskar describes how experiments work to produce closure:

> An attempt to trigger or unleash a single kind of mechanism or process in relative isolation, free from the interfering flux of the open world, so as to observe its detailed workings or record its characteristic mode of effect and/or to test some hypothesis about them (1986, p. 35).

The experiment is inevitably an attempt to artificially create the conditions for closure. When we close a system, artificially (Ron, 2002, p. 135–136), we can then see how laws produce certain effects (e.g., the effect of temperature on an event). And because it is not possible to close human systems (e.g., families, everyday interactions, neighborhoods and communities, economies), many mechanisms, even competing and contradictory ones, are likely to affect outcomes; and these may change day-to-day or even moment-to-moment. George Steinmetz argues that "generative mechanisms or structures have to be studied 'in the wild,'" as it were, and to complicate matters even further, they often appear in "impure forms, mixed up with other mechanisms" (Bhaskar, 1986: 110). In short, when the rats are out of the maze, all bets are off. It is on the wild terrain of open systems that social workers engage their clients, can potentially conduct the work of truly engaged scholarship, and produce research results that speak directly to the dynamics of open and fluid systems. The elements that constitute causal constellations may vary from case to case. And even if we do find recurrent empirical patterns, these can never be assumed to be universal or to be determined by the same set of mechanisms in each case (Steinmetz, 2004, p. 383). Can you imagine controlling all the things that potentially affect the life of an individual or family: economics, unemployment, history of trauma across the generations, gender inequalities and divisions of labor, illness and death, various forms of discrimination, number of children, divorce, shame and guilt, attachment systems, cognitive schema, psychic defenses, and affect regulation? In variables-based research it is imagined that systems can be artificially closed by "controlling" the variables (Doll, 2008, pp. 76–78; Quinn Patton, 2002, pp. 119–120; Sayer, 2010). We must be cautious when we treat or imagine (or fantasize) that human systems can be closed.

Perhaps most important, however, it is not possible to make predictions in open systems (Houston, 2005, pp. 10–11; Keat & Urry, 2011, pp. 20–31).[13] Andrew Sayer writes of open systems:

> Because events are not pre-determined before they happen but depend on contingent conditions, the future is open—things could go in many different ways. Yet when looking back at changes and explaining them, it is easy to imagine that what did happen was always the only thing that could have happened; hindsight can sometimes be of dubious benefit. One of the temptations of social explanation is to suppress acknowledgments of the fact that at any instant, the future is open, things can happen differently, because once something does happen it is closed (Sayer, 2000, p. 15).

Closure in the human sciences is impossible for two reasons, one intrinsic and the other extrinsic, "both of which are ineluctably violated by what people are" (Archer, 1995, p. 70). Archer argues that the "extrinsic condition of closure requires that no new emergent properties are developing outside the system, which can interfere with the exercise of its known emergent powers in unpredictable ways" (p. 70). Human beings and social structures are "typified by innovativeness, a capacity for interpreting the same material conditions, cultural elements, circumstances and situations in different ways and hence for introducing novel patterns or courses of action in response to them" (p. 70). It is because of our capacity for reflection in thought and reflexivity in action that closure is impossible and cannot be controlled for. Archer nicely summarizes this:

> The second and intrinsic condition of closure is that there must be no change or qualitative variation (like the effects of impurities in chemistry experiments) in the entity possessing the causal powers if the mechanism is to operate consistently and produce regular results. Closure thus implies that no new properties can develop *inside* the system or structure in questions, which change it and alter its effects. Yet any social structure is dependent upon people and operative only through people, for positions have to have occupants and situations are things that people find themselves in and their own capacity for self change and social change thus violates the intrinsic condition of closure. Here, if you like, the horse remains in the stable but has a capacity denied to horses of redesigning it from within. (1995, p. 70)

Emergence and Downward Causation

Emergence for critical realism (and others in the philosophy of social science) is related to and results from the powers and liabilities possessed by objects (Elder-Vass, 2007b, 2007c, 2010; Smith 2010). Bodies, brains, and minds, for example, have different *causal powers* to act in certain ways (Barrett, 2009; Bhaskar, 1998; Nellhaus, 2004; Postle, 2006; Smith, 2010). These are not the same causal powers. The body, for example, has the power to produce a brain. Due to genetic and environmental mechanisms (i.e., biopsychosocial) complexly interacting and relating in open systems, bodies produce different brains with different and dynamic minds.[14] Minds, in turn, develop out of complex intersubjective dynamics between reason and emotion (Allen, Fonagy & Bateman, 2008; Damasio, 1994; Fonagy, 2004; Smith, 2010). The human brain, moreover, has the power to produce a mind, just as seeds have powers to germinate, flowers to propagate, or a person has the power to complete a complex mathematical calculation or to labor in the fields. In short, the mind is an *emergent property* of the brain (Ekstrom, 2004; Freeman, 2000; Hibberd, 2008; Moll, 2004; Postle, 2006; Sawyer, 2001; Smith, 2010; Wilkinson, 2004) just as the brain is an emergent property of the body. And each of these—brains, minds, seeds—have powers and liabilities (i.e., powers to do things and not to do things) because of underlying structures and mechanisms (Hedstrom & Ylikoski, 2010):[15] biologic, neurologic, psychologic, and sociologic (Freeman, 2000, pp. 143–173; Houston, 2010, p. 79). Christian Smith (2010, pp. 25–26). writes that emergence

> refers to the process of constituting a new entity with its own particular characteristics through the interactive combination of other, different entities that are necessary to create the new entity but that do not contain the characteristics present in the new entity. Emergence involves the following: First, two or more entities that exist at a "lower" level interact or combine. Second, that interaction or combination serves as the basis of some new, real entity that has existence at a "higher" level. Third, the existence of the new higher-level entity is fully dependent upon the two or more lower-level entities interacting or combining, as they could not exist without doing so. Fourth, the new, higher-level entity nevertheless possesses characteristic qualities (e.g., structures, qualities, capacities, textures, mechanisms) that cannot be reduced to those of the lower-level entities that gave rise to the new entity possessing them. When these four things happen, emergence has happened. The whole is more than the sum of its parts.

Research in the human sciences, and clinical social work in particular, must attend to the emergent properties of things (Collier, 1994; Layder, 1997; Smith, 2010). Otherwise, the world will appear flat and stripped of all complexity and we will tend to see in it only one dimension. In sum, the worlds that we work in do not consist of horizontal but of complex and stratified realities (ontologies).

There are mental structures, for example, such as memory systems or schemas, with their own unique emergent properties and with powers to influence lower level structures or structures from which they emerge. Take depressive mood, for example. Our psychological states (constantly changing in open and human systems and subject to many dynamic, complex, and interacting influences that affect our neurochemistry) may even alter the lower-level structures of the brain. This is sometimes called downward causation (i.e., where the psychological acts downward to cause the lower level structures to change). And while these psychological structures, with their emergent powers, are rooted in biological structures of the brain, they are not reducible to lower-level mechanisms within the brain. Otherwise, we would be left with simple reductionism in its various forms (i.e., biochemical, neurochemical, brain, biology, genetic): we would only have brains and neurochemistry, and minds would not exist with their unique properties, powers, and liabilities (i.e., with their special capacity to cause change in the structures of the brain); or imagine only behavior without minds (some radical behaviorists make such a claim) with unique structures and capacity to produce motivations for behavior. And we would certainly find it difficult to imagine a role for clinical social work (or any social work for that matter) if reality were flat (i.e., not stratified, with each level having unique emergent properties) and the brain were all we had to work on. We'd only need neuroscience and a pharmacopeia of neurochemical agents. Let us take an example from Tyshawn's life. His body and immune system have emergent properties. Not all immune systems are the same. Tyshawn's body and immune system, each with their own unique emergent properties, has liabilities and potentials; and in some cases, immune systems act back on the body, even sometimes to destroy the body (e.g., auto-immune diseases). Sometimes the immune system, with its unique structure and mechanisms, responds to other causal mechanisms: like the stress produced from grief (i.e., the death of Tyshawn's mother or the worry that he feels for his father's safety and well-being). And all of this occurs in open systems.

Contingency and Necessity

The brain, however, only emerges, *contingently*, from the body. In short, relational, social, and physical factors affect the body/brain relationship, which enables and limits the emergence of the brain (Shonkoff & Phillips, 2000). Likewise, the mind emerges contingently from the brain; the self emerges contingently from the mind; and identity emerges contingently from the self (Smith, 2010), and all of this unfolds in complex, *open systems* (Donati, 2011). What do we mean by contingent? Simply put, the body does not *necessarily* produce a brain and mind. The important contrast here is between *necessary* and *contingent*. Let's take two examples, one from biology and virology (the science and study of viruses) and the other from social work. Not all viruses, for example, produce the same effects. In short, different bodies with the same virus may produce different effects. The virus (because it operates in open systems), thus, produces contingent *not necessary* outcomes. Put differently, the virus does not necessarily produce the same outcome for all bodies. Let's take an example from mental health and social work. Some children growing up under exactly the same structural conditions of poverty (i.e., Garbarino, 1999, 2001) show evidence of great resilience and adaptability while others do not. In short, poverty produces only contingent outcomes.

Bodies and brains have the power to produce minds only when other potential powers have been activated (e.g., attachment relationships, social, cultural, and linguistic capital, narratives, etc.). In short, each of these—body, brain, mind, self, and identity—exist in a stratified reality; each emerges from the other, and each may act back on lower levels to produce new configurations (recall that this is called *downward causation*). In order to understand the complexity of personhood and the human experience in social work one cannot work without the concepts of emergence and downward causation (Smith, 2010). For example, the mind emerges in complex interactional dynamics with other human beings (i.e., in attachments and intersubjective dynamics) and may then act back on the brain's neural networks to produce new structures and dynamics (Shonkoff & Phillips, 2000). It is in this way that clinical social work can imagine its way out of various kinds of dualism and reductionism: biological, behavioral, psychological, and social (i.e., micro and macro practice or theory). In sum, we are rooted in our must basic biological structures but we are not reducible to them.

Let us take an example from cognitive psychology, where some refer to schemas as types of mental structures involved in the organization, filtering, and simplification of information or knowledge (Berlin & Marsh, 1993). These structures, or schemas, may refer to many things: the self, relationships and modes of interacting, events, objects in the material world (Nellhaus, 2004; Smith, 2010, p. 350). And they may be related or hierarchically organized. Most important, schematic structures cause us to notice and interpret, act in the world, make decisions, attribute cause, classify, anticipate or predict, accentuate or minimize. Schemas also have a cultural dimension that allows for sharing and economical communication. Some schema may be strongly favored and commonly used and others may become unyielding and self-sustaining structures even with disconfirming or contradictory evidence. Others will be unconsciously expressed in verbal narratives, sometimes called subliteral (Haskell, 2009). How and when they take these different paths will be contingently determined.

In short, mental structures, like schemas, have powers and liabilities that are only contingently (i.e., neither necessary or impossible) activated (e.g., moisture or sun for the seed to germinate and grow or nutrition for a person). And when causal powers are activated there may be additional contingent conditions; for example, seeds may be encouraged to grow with the addition of nitrates and water or limited in some may by the presence of toxins. Or the capacity of a person to work may be affected by the availability of a computer or the lack of appropriate technology and education.

CONCEPT DEPENDENCE, SOCIAL CONSTRUCTIONISM, ESSENTIALISM: BRINGING THE SELF BACK IN

Critical realists offer important insight into how our observations and knowledge are necessarily concept dependent (i.e., theory laden) and are produced through prevailing discourses. This does not mean, however, that our concepts construct reality (Sayer, 2000, pp. 32–35). This offers social work a way out of the relativism often found in various forms of constructivism (Denzin & Lincoln, 2000, pp. 23–26) and social reductionism, or what Margaret Archer (1995) calls *downward conflation:* the reduction of the individual to social forces, discourses, narratives, or structures (see examples of downward conflation in social work: Specht & Courtney, 1995; Heineman, 1981; Hartman, 1990; Mäntysaari, 2005, p. 94; Arnd-Caddigan & Pozzuto, 2008, p. 432). With downward conflation we are faced with an impossible challenge: we are left with conditions for action but with no agents acting. Radical constructivism (sometimes called anti-essentialism) argues that the world or self can never be independent of our knowledge of them; the argument, in its most extreme form says that reality, or the self, cannot be apprehended apart from social constructions of it (i.e., Heineman, 1981). This position, most forcefully argued by Rom Harré, in his work *Personal Being,* suggests that the self is a mere concept resulting from human interaction (1984). For Harré, the self is "rather like acquiring a personal organizer (a mental filofax)" without ontological depth (Archer, 2000, p. 96).[16] Here, as with the sociologists of childhood and the critics of human development (James, Jenks & Prout, 1998), selves are mere constructions in discourse: there are no prelinguistic or nonlinguistic selves, and intersubjectivity either replaces altogether or supersedes intrasubjectivity (Donati, 2011; Smith, 2010).[17] As Archer argues:

> . . . the carer supplements the deficient efforts of the child by treating it as if it had the full complement of skills, "as if it were a fully competent self, seeing and acting upon the world from its own standpoints (and eventually creat(ing) adult human beings." Only after this partnership of supplementation is the child, aged about three, able to begin to develop the capacity for private discourse. Here, it is of course a secondary ability, as are the powers of self-expression and self-reflexivity. Thus reflexive practices like self-criticism and self-exhortation simply borrow from society's conversation about criticism, exhortation and so on. (Archer, 2000, p. 100)

We are, in short, "nothing beyond what society makes us, and it makes us what we are through our joining society's conversation" (Archer, 2000, p. 4). Thus, for the child, there are no prelinguistic sources for the development of a sense of self; bodies and psyches, moreover, have no properties or emergent powers of their own (Cromby, 2004; Smith, 2010; Williams, 2000a). The child, according to this view, simply joins the discursive community, and through participation in the society, the self, emotion, thought, and memory are made possible. Here, ironically, the child, through socialization, is mere material to be mechanically and deterministically worked on by the social order. Instead of giving the child agency, the child is *socially produced*, not through interaction between complex inside and outside worlds (i.e., stratified levels with their own emergent properties, powers, and liabilities), but through a society's discourse about the child. This, Margaret Archer calls downward conflation (i.e., reduction of self to the social, socialization, or discourses about the child). One is left to wonder how with this downward conflation a child's agency is possible, when as noted previously, the "effects of socialization *impress* themselves upon people, seen as malleable 'indeterminate material'" (Archer, 2000, p. 5).

Although social workers may make any number of interventions on behalf of clients, we may still have no measurable effect on them; they may go on being just as they are, regardless of our discourses or analyses; thus, we have neither discursively produced them nor in any meaningful way affected their lives (Archer, 2010a, 2010b). They may still hear voices, they may still be severely depressed, they may still mutilate themselves, and they may still feel intractable pain. It is in this way that external and objective realities exist outside our discourses about them and our discourses may produce little if any effect. This, of course, makes social work, the human sciences, and the human condition infinitely complex, interesting, and sometimes impossibly difficult to manage or change.

Our theories, we hope, influence our clients; they enter into their self-understandings, even when problems never go away or may even worsen. In short, our clients often, though not always, take up our conceptual schemes, yet they do not always, when returning to their everyday lives, feel and act differently with them. Nor do they take them up in uniform ways. This would obviously suggest that our conceptual schemes are independent of their influence. Some social constructivists—especially the recent cottage industry (i.e., historians, sociologists, and anthropologists of science) aimed at finding data to demonstrate that mental illness is discursively invented or imagined—would argue that discourses of the "other" are available to us only through our own mostly pathologizing ones. That is, we know the presence of mental illness only because we come to them already with concepts that delimit, define, and classify them as such (Martin, 2007; Young, 1995; MacLeish, 2010). Thus, we are never sitting with another's discourse, story, or narrative; we sit with our own or some distorted intertextual version, with discourses interpenetrating and ramifying, never able to sort or distinguish self from other, diseased from nondiseased, lives without pain from those with extraordinary suffering.

Disease labels, nosologies, or social constructions (Williams, 1999, p. 806; Young, 1995) do not, as such, constitute or construct the disease itself (see, for example, the anthropologist Alan Young's study of PTSD). To mistake construction for construal produces both conceptual and practical errors.[18]Conceptually, discursive relativism, of the sort defended by those who see sexual desires, race and ethnicity, or mental illness as simple constructions of the social world (i.e., downward conflation), "commits us to the view that it is our different human perspectives, as members of different communities of discourse, which makes things 'true for them'" (Archer, 2000, p. 45). Imagine if the symptoms of mental illness could be turned on and off by a simple switch with alternative narratives or discourse. Furthermore, this would require that we have some way of knowing or establishing a privileged point outside the *pathologizing discourse* with which to name, recognize, understand, interpret, or explain the existence of pathologizing discourses. Here, as Andrew Sayer suggests, we have mistakenly reduced "mediation or construal to production or construction" (2000, p. 34). By this he means that our concepts do not construct or produce our objects of study, our clients, or their social and psychological problems.[19] They mediate or construe them. And "although all observation is conceptually mediated what we observe is not determined solely by concepts, as if concepts could anticipate all empirical questions, or as if theories were observation-neutral" (2000, p. 41).

Essentialism and the Self

Andrew Sayer (1997) has argued that in our discussion of essentialism, social constructivists have missed the importance of understanding that some things have essences whereas others do not. And many social constructions (i.e., race, gender, sexual desire) are finally felt and experienced as essential and intractable difference. What is the significance of this very important insight for clinical social work and for those who conduct research on clinical practice in open systems? In short, even though language, social institutions, and the psyche are constructed, they may also have, once constructed, essences and generative properties. Surely this must be one way that gender and sexualities (i.e., heterosexuality, homosexuality . . .) and race and racism are produced, felt, and experienced. Race, for example, while clearly a social construction, is not always experienced, internalized, or felt as a social construction. Like gender or sexual desire, race may (i.e., contingently) be felt as essential, material, determinate, inescapable, or natural. This may on the surface seem like an unimportant or unnecessarily abstract debate, but it has very significant implications for mental health practitioners, social workers, and social work researchers. If one practices, or conducts research, under the mistaken notion that a client experiences or feels race or sexual desire merely as a social construction (ironically, allied in theory and practice with the Religious Right), one may fundamentally misrecognize what is "real" for that client. Or one may fail altogether to pose the right questions. Or worse, one may shame the client (i.e., "what's wrong with me that you cannot manage, as researcher or practitioner, to grasp the felt and experienced nature of what seems truly real and inescapable"). Likewise, with equally troubling consequences, there are those who see essential difference where it is indeed absent. Both result in misrecognition. And both have equally troubling social and psychological consequences.

Rorty, using Freud, argues against the notion of an essential or continuous sense of self; for him, we are constituted by a variety of "quasi-selves," different internal clusters of belief and desire, among which there is no inner conversational relationship, since they lack the internal coherence "to constitute one unified person who is self-conscious about her own constituents" (Archer, 2000, p. 36). This, Archer correctly observes, is a fundamental misreading of Freud,

> who was underwriting neither the stern voice of the 'super-ego' nor complete indulgence for the 'id,' but describing the balancing act which the 'ego had to accomplish, on the reality principle, in relation to getting by intact in the world. As Shusterman argues, this 'unified self is not a uniform self, . . . nor can it be an unordered collection of egalitarian quasi-selves inhabiting the same corporal machine' (2000, p. 37).

Some properties of the self, moreover, may be seen as more essential than others, especially if a wider range of emotion, thought, or behavior is enabled by the essential feature. Sayer (1997) argues, as well, that the concept essence may often be expected to do two different kinds of work: (1) to "identify the essence of an object in terms of properties which supposedly determine—or are indispensable for—what it can and cannot do; these are its 'generative' properties"; or (2) to identify the "features of an object which enable us to distinguish it from other kinds of objects; these are its distinguishing or identifying properties" (1997, p. 458). Though the two aspects, the generative properties and the distinguishing ones, may coincide, it may also be the case that "scarcely any generative properties of an object may be unique to it and its distinguishing features may not tell us much about what enables it to do whatever it does" (1997, p. 458).

To have a common essence, therefore, objects must have universally shared attributes. Yet when objects share some features they do not necessarily share essential ones; the features may be accidental. Thus, every object has characteristics that coexist or interact but that could "exist apart from those which could not exist without a certain other feature" (1997, p. 459). It is necessary to understand the attributes of an object and how they must exist in combination with other attributes. Their respective generative powers also must be understood. Some psychic agencies, for example, have no powers by themselves to generate effects, and must coexist with other attributes in order for their effects to be seen or felt.[20]

Against the charge that essentialism treats all members of a class (e.g., gender, economic, childhood, mental illness) as identical (homogeneous), Sayer argues that it may be the case that some members of the class share only *some* features. To know this requires empirical investigation; in short, no a priori statement can be made about those features that are essential and those accidental. According to Sayer, the "claim that there are essential properties shared by humans does not necessarily render 'accidental' differences such as those of particular cultures unimportant, indeed, it may be the essential similarities which are trivial" (1997, p. 456). Sayer observes, "since the whole point of attempting to categorize is to specify what, if anything, is common in the midst of diversity, the search for common properties, including essences, presupposes diversity" (1997, p. 456). Here, Sayer uses racism to illustrate the errors in thinking that may result: first, attention must be paid to the tendency to assert nonexistent commonalities or to deny significant differences, where they exist. Second, we must avoid seeing insignificant differences or denying significant commonalities. With racism, Sayer argues, both errors can be found, that is, the assertion of difference where they do not exist and the denial of differences, where they do (e.g., cultural essentialism and stereotyping are common examples). Thus, for critical realism, any theory—social, psychodynamic, behavioral, cognitive, systems—that makes faulty claims about specific kinds of sameness or difference is suspect (1997, p. 457).

THE PHENOMENOLOGICAL PRACTICE GAP

Exploring the relationship between theory and practice has long produced contentious debate, bold knowledge claims, and various forms of dogmatism and reductionism in social and political theory, philosophy, public policy, and social work (Fook & Gardner, 2007; Stuart & Whitmore, 2006, 156–171; Rosen, 2003).[21] Next we offer a way of conceptualizing, not the history of these debates, but some ways of understanding how theory and practice are always and necessarily in a creative and potentially productive tension (Van de Ven, 2007; Fook, White & Gardner, 2006, pp. 3–20; Stuart & Whitmore, 2006, pp. 156–171).

We propose calling the complex and fluid relationship between knowledge and practice "phenomenological practice gaps" (Longhofer & Floersch, 2004). Why phenomenological and why a gap? It is phenomenological because all of social work practice is first grounded in human experience, in human "life worlds." Two questions must be addressed here. First, there is a question about phenomenology. And second, there is a question about why and how a practice gap can be described as phenomenological.

Phenomenology offers important ways of understanding the practice of social workers. First, it emphasizes understanding the *everyday worlds* in which clients and workers live and interact. Husserl described this as a "life world" (Lebenswelt). These are the practical, everyday worlds of lived experience where clients and social workers go about their daily lives, engage in continual back-and-forth interactions, communicate verbally and nonverbally, struggle to make sense of their worlds, and sometimes succeed and sometimes fail at understanding and changing. This world cannot be captured in the case records or notes that social workers take and that are often used by sociologists, historians, and anthropologists to think about the work that social workers do.[22] Moreover, we come to know our worlds through practice (i.e., by working, performing, applying, doing, enacting, implementing, intervening, failing). And while social workers engage the world in varying ways to understand what "is" (i.e., systems, communities, families, individuals, minds), they insist at the same time that we be aware of our knowing presence (we will have more to say about this in the final chapter of this book) and our influence on what it is we are trying to know (Flyvbjerg, 2001; Dreyfus, 1986).

In mental health research and practice, we are primarily interested in how we understand relationships among clients and workers, psychiatrists and patients; how suffering and pain are experienced; how relationships are affected by suffering; how human flourishing is enabled; and how the body experiences illness. Phenomenology thus explores the role of our *subjective experience* in coming to know phenomena in our various worlds of practice (i.e., between the knower, the practitioner, and the known, and the client). Phenomenology attends to "phenomena" and the relational dimension of consciousness; and because consciousness must always be directed toward something (i.e., practice realities), both material and immaterial things, it is always consciousness of our social work practices and of our complex relationships and roles as researchers and practitioners.

Inevitably there are gaps between theory and practice, and because knowledge, especially in human and open systems, is never a mere reflection of the objects studied, there can never be correspondence between our concepts and their referents, that is, the things they refer to (Fook, White & Gardner, 2006, pp. 228–240). And if they were the same, mirror images of one another, there would be no need to produce knowledge about them or to be concerned about the gaps. Some have argued that *reflective practice (and reflective practitioners)* is necessarily grounded in careful documentation of the gaps between theory and practice and vigilant efforts to use the evidence to close gaps (see, for example, Rosen, 1994, 2003). However, we argue in the next section that it is only in closed systems (e.g., laboratories) where variables can be experimentally controlled and manipulated and where gaps can be brought to near zero (i.e., where practice and theory are matched or nearly matched or outcomes can with some degree of certainty result from standardized interventions). Gaps, depending on the nature of the object of practice or study, can be large or small. In some cases, especially in closed systems of the physical world (i.e., laboratory, or experiment), they can often be reduced to zero; here, the theory (e.g., bacteriology) may provide nearly all the knowledge necessary to engage in practice, though not always effective in open systems, or to at least provide adequate accounts of the behavior of physical events.

At best, in the human sciences and practice, we strive for what the critical realist Andrew Sayer calls *practical adequacy*. Knowledge is practically adequate when "it generates expectations about the world and about results of our actions which are realized" (Sayer, 2000, p. 43). There will always be a gap in the practical adequacy of our knowledge, that is, it will vary in relation to where and to what it is applied (Sayer, 2000, p. 43). Yet another source of variation is to be found in the degree to which knowledge may be practically adequate with respect to some practices but may not be adequate with respect to others. For some, the quest is for an exacting fidelity (e.g. evidence-based practice) between the model and practice: success is measured by the distance between them (Freire, 2006). Factors potentially affecting the distance between knowledge and practice are either minimized by methodological maneuvers or are altogether ignored.

A gap may also occur when theory fails to account for some part or all of the experience or where practice is open to influence outside of theory. For example, where scientific racism used theory to engage in practice, it did so on the basis of manipulation of the gap. Science and its practitioners subscribed not only to the political ideology of fascism (Szollosi-Janzi, 2001). They also engaged in methodological debates. In short, the gap may be increased or diminished by forces (e.g. political, ideological, religious, cultural, and disciplinary) exogenous to theory itself or theory may be used to exploit the degree of gap that exists between any given theory and its practice. Or the gap may also be produced by real limitations placed on theory by certain material conditions of practice: policy environments, spatial constraints, funding sources, competing paradigms, and so on.

In some cases, competing paradigms may capture some but not all of practice reality. And this may go unrecognized or misrecognized (i.e., it may be seen by those adhering to a particular theory or paradigm as though they are in competition but may in fact only be accounting for one aspect of the practice situation).

METHOD OR METHODOLOGY?: MINDING THE PHENOMENOLOGICAL PRACTICE GAP

Methods, on the one hand, are techniques that must be skillfully deployed to collect and analyze data. A *methodology*, on the other hand, includes specific claims about what exists (ontology) and the criteria for making causal explanations (epistemology). Engaged scholarship shifts the debate away from method toward methodology, recognizing the potential incommensurability of ontological and epistemological claims among theories. For example, what behaviorists take to be real and knowable will in most cases be incommensurable with what psychoanalysts expect to be knowable. This was not true, however, for Piaget or for the contemporary cognitive scientist and only Nobel Prize-winning psychiatrist, Eric Kandel. They both recognize commensurability between cognitive and psychoanalytic understandings of the mind (Kandel, 2005, pp. 72–75). Real incommensurabilities, moreover, may yield quite productive differences (i.e., different understandings of the same object) that should not be glossed over by debates about proper technique: quantitative versus qualitative.[23] These differences may be used to advance understanding of objects, to see the same object from distinct perspectives, or to account for different causal mechanisms (or countervailing forces) at work. Too often researchers engage in all-consuming debates about methods (i.e., technique) and fail altogether to make clear their methodological assumptions or offer a clear rationale for why certain choices have been made. At other times, when we gloss over important methodological differences, we may fail to achieve more complex understandings of our objects of study or, even worse, altogether ignore them.

Think of it this way. Methods refer to *how* we conduct research. *Methods* refer to our research *techniques* (i.e., experiments, surveys, interviews, observation, participant observation, ethnography). And the objects we study (i.e., bacteria or viruses, schools or hospitals, minds or brains, families or neighborhoods, violence and wars, ethnic conflict) should always govern the choices we make about techniques. Yet again and again we choose methods before we know anything about their relevance to the objects of study. Or we train graduate students in research methods before we give careful consideration (i.e., philosophical) to what it is they propose or wish to study. Just as often we propose methods for research that are fundamentally divorced from what matters most to people. And it is in this way that we divorce what we value from what we research. We would not, for example, choose to study the bacteria that cause ear infections with methods devised by anthropologists to study schools or prisons. And if we want to understand the lived experience of life in urban public schools, we're not likely to succeed with surveys.

Methodology, unlike method, refers to the rationale or logic of these choices. Methodology, in short, refers to *why* we choose one method over another. And it includes assumptions we make about what exists and what causes what exists. Methodology requires that we look into how we come to know what we know. We often see research papers, mistakenly, with section subtitles, methodology, or with the language, "we use survey methodology." These terms, *method* and *methodology*, refer to very different kinds of activities: technique and the rationale for the use of a particular technique with a particular theory under particular circumstances. Why, for example, do we choose ethnography[24] or ethnographic methods to study everyday experience in an urban school or hospital? Why not use a survey or an experiment? These are methodological questions. Or why not use an experiment to study a social revolution? Because revolutions happen in time, in open systems, where variables cannot be closely monitored or manipulated. We cannot make revolutions happen under measured conditions anymore than we can make a family behave as we do bacteria in a petri dish (i.e., controlled temperature, humidity, etc.). Revolutions and family dynamics unfold in open systems. In short, for clinical social work, methods comprise tools to gather and analyze data.

LOOKING BENEATH THE SURFACE: EMPIRICISM AND BEHAVIORAL OUTCOMES

In our professional and personal lives we are continuously involved in offering to ourselves and to others—to varying degrees and with differing measures of awareness—explanatory or causal accounts of our mental states, our intentions, our moods and feelings, our actions (or lack of action), violence, child abuse, risk of exposure to illness and disease, fear of crime, conflicts in our personal and professional relationships, economic recessions, and so on (Clarke & Hoggett, 2009; Hollway & Jefferson, 2000; Brakel, 2009). Some use *common sense* to explain the world, that is, they use sensory inputs and offer simple explanations based upon what they see or hear. Think of the commonsense explanation: the earth looks flat (with our eyes) therefore it must be flat. In our commonsense world we don't seek to understand the underlying meanings or causes of things, the things beyond our sensory grasp or experience. We don't look at what the critical realists call causal mechanisms or structures (i.e., the intransitive dimensions). Others, especially in the physical and natural sciences (though not limited to science) look for the causes of things. They look beyond the surface of events to seek deeper and sometimes hidden (i.e., things we cannot see) causes or meanings: gravity or strings in physics, molecules in biology or chemistry, theories of mind or unconscious motivations in psychology and psychoanalysis (Clarke, 2006; Clarke & Hoggett, 2009). Still others simply accept explanatory accounts (theories) based upon authority: someone tells us *it is so* and we accept their explanatory accounts; the church, for example, at one time insisted that the earth was the center of the universe.[25] Some who trust only their senses would be called *empiricists*: seeing is believing, the proof of the pudding is in the eating, show me the data.

Empiricism is an *ontology*[26] that gives priority to immediate sensory experience: what is "real" is equated with sense impressions of it. Put differently, reality is reduced to how we know it: what we know (ontology) to how we know it (epistemology). Roy Bhaskar (2008, p. 5), among the most important of the critical realists, calls this the *epistemic fallacy*: statements about *being* are interpreted as statements about *knowledge*.[27] *Behaviorism* is a good example of empiricism (Fischer, 1973, 1981; Thyer, 1995, 1988). For behaviorists, observable behavior and events (i.e., human actions) are emphasized at the expense of unobserved (i.e., unobservable mental states, schemas, drives, unconscious states, dreams, etc.).[28] Accordingly, mental terms or concepts (i.e., unobservable terms) are replaced with behavioral concepts or terms (i.e., observable terms). Social work (see Houston, 2005), according to this epistemology, should focus not on the mind, the self, or other internal states but on perceptible behaviors (Mattaini & Moore, 2004, pp. 55–67). Indeed, for the radical behaviorist in social work (Houston, 2005, p. 8) the sources or explanations of behavior (Frogget, 2002, pp. 31–48) are entirely external (i.e., environmental).[29] And because of this, approaches to treatment, not surprisingly, followed a *behavioral outcomes* model. The model, also followed in education, has many troubling features, all related to the emphasis given to empiricism and *measurable or verifiable objectives* or *outcomes*. According to the behavioral outcomes approach, behaviors should be observable. And by confining treatment objectives to observable or empirically verifiable outcomes, it was assumed that these criteria could be met. But in clinical social work and most of mental health practice several problems resulted.[30] First, it assumed that the language used to formulate objectives could be made sufficiently precise as to eliminate need for *interpretation*. Some have called this manualization.[31] Second, it presumed that clinical practice (i.e., are you meeting your treatment objectives?) could be evaluated by objective outside observers (i.e., other therapists, researchers, evaluators, insurance companies, quality assurance) and by referring solely to the stated objectives (i.e., measurable, observable treatment goals) and without reference to the context of treatment, the modes of therapeutic action, the clinical process, the working alliance, or the treatment relationship (i.e., transference and countertransference). Third, it assumed that stated objectives contained what was essential to the treatment and that by knowing (or by simply postulating) what was essential in this way (i.e., outcomes) one could expect to replicate the treatment (i.e., in terms of behavioral outcomes). Fourth, it assumed that once the practitioner knew the objectives, then with equal precision modes of therapeutic intervention could be applied across (i.e., generalized) cases. In short, one should be able to read the therapeutic action backward from the stated objectives. Fifth, it assumed that by focusing exclusively on posttherapy outcomes, one could altogether avoid what in the treatment was actually contributing to the outcomes (Shedler, 2010). And by not looking at the therapeutic process (i.e., using qualitative methods, in particular, the case study), it was made to appear that the therapist and the client each relate to objective, external standards (i.e., behavioral goals). This altogether elides the complex ways in which the therapeutic situation is saturated with psychic and social tensions—each with unique forces of desire, attraction, repulsion. Moreover, these tensions are not always evident or worked out with awareness (Clarke & Hoggett, 2009; Hollway & Jefferson, 2000). Indeed, many have argued that much of what makes the expert practitioner is not the rigid adherence to the manual or rulebook (Dreyfus, 1986). They describe forms of knowledge (more will be said about this in the final chapter of this book) rooted in intuition, judgment, tacit knowledge, unconscious processes, and values.

Variables-based research (i.e., positivist methodology) defines causation as a statistical or regular association among events. Here's how the logic works. I want to show how child abuse is related to subsequent psychological difficulties. Where I find child abuse, X, I then find subsequent and lowered school performance, Y: Y must follow X in time. Or where I find child abuse I find subsequent drug abuse, mental illness, or homelessness. Or where I find cigarette smoking, X, I subsequently find lung cancer, Y, oat cell carcinoma. These are statistical associations; often they are very strong associations. However, there are many questions and problems with this approach (i.e., positivism or variables-based research) to explanation and understanding of causality. First, the number of times that something happens cannot account for the cause of its happening; and it is only in *closed systems* where there is ever a consistent, regular, predictable relationship among events or variables. Let us take lung cancer for example. Not everyone who smokes (x) gets lung cancer (y). Why is that? Because other complex mechanisms (i.e., genetics, cellular dynamics, other environmental exposures, immunology, nutrition, etc.) and dynamics act together or separately to produce effects; and sometimes in various combinations they work as countervailing forces (i.e., as mechanisms to keep cancer cells from forming). In short, no strength of association (i.e., smoking and cancer) among variables (i.e., statistical significance) offers a causal account of them (Keat & Urry, 2011, pp. 7–18; Smith, 2010). Second, predicting the likelihood of an event's occurring in association with another event (e.g., pain in the ear associated with bacteria) does not explain the association. It says one thing only: one event happens, which is followed by subsequent events. In order to explain the association between Tyshawn's infection and the associated pain, one would have to move beyond statistical association to molecular chemistry and biology and to the structure of cells involved in toxigenesis, and to the many and complex psychological and social dynamic mechanisms in his life (i.e., attachment and loss, grief, class and poverty).

The variables approach to causation has dominated the social sciences, policy science, and social work (Fay, 1975, 1976, 1987; Steinmetz, 2005b) since World War II. Especially since the 1970s, social work, like other human sciences (i.e., economics, psychology, sociology, political science), has made a strong epistemological commitment[32] to understanding causality as the regularity of empirical events (Fischer, 1973; Breen & Darlaston-Jones, 2010).[33] For example, Meinert, Pardeck, and Kreuger (2000) write in their book, *Social Work: Seeking Relevancy in the Twenty-First Century*, that only two interventions offer social workers a solid, scientific basis for intervention: behavioral and cognitive therapies. About humans as natural objects not unlike rats or amoeba or bacteria, they write:

> From a behavioral perspective, individuals are viewed as biological entities that respond to the events which happen to them. People are seen as largely products of their environment. In other words, individuals are responders to their environments, and these environments shape both functional and dysfunctional behavior. . . . Clients are seen as

entities [our emphasis] that respond in a predictable fashion to any given stimulus . . . [and] react in essentially the same fashion as infrahumans (2000, pp. 112–113).

And although social work has allied with other human sciences in defense of empiricist ontology (Fischer, 1973, 1978; 1981; Kirk & Fischer, 1976; McNeece & Thyer, 2004; Thyer, 2001), it has not done so without debate (see, for example, Heineman, 1981; Saleeby, 1993) and departures from the normal practice of variables research (e.g., psychodynamic theory in clinical social work or more recently, constructivism, feminist theory, mindfulness, and some who use rational choice theory).[34] For example, in social work, unlike sociology, psychoanalysis has always been an influential force and continues to offer an alternative to social work's prevailing empiricist and behaviorist modes (Borden, 2000; Brandell, 2004; Kanter, 1989). At the same time, although there have clearly been many dissident voices, the overwhelming trend in social work has been toward variables-based research.[35]

From a critical realist perspective, causation is not established through the observation of empirical regularities among sequences of events. What causes something to happen has nothing to do with the number of times it has been observed. Instead, explanation results from identifying causal mechanisms, how they work, discovering if they have been activated, and under what conditions in *open systems*. Furthermore, it involves discovering the nature of the structure or object possessing the causal power(s) under investigation. Critical realism disarticulates causation from the establishment of empirical regularities. And by so doing it enables us to see how unique events (and repeated ones) can be caused by the same structures or mechanisms (Houston, 2005). Second, it allows us to consider *necessity* without a preoccupation with establishing regular statistical associations among events (2005). Third, explanatory accounts can be offered without the requirement of making repeated observations: what causes an event, an emotion, a thought, or behavior, has nothing to do with the number of times it has been observed (or not observed). Fourth, social work has long been plagued with tired old debates about idiographic and nomothetic approaches, that is, the notion that idiographic raw data, "is waiting to be processed by 'nomothetic' theory machines" (Steinmetz, 2004, pp. 383–384). The first is thought to be unscientific and a way of understanding the "unique" and particular and the second is considered a more reliable way of establishing law-like and scientific pictures of the general. The uniqueness of social work objects of study (e.g., minds, families, individuals, emotions, patterns of interaction and communication) should not be seen as a barrier to rigorous and relevant explanation or understanding. Fifth, the quest for generalizable knowledge is different from establishing how cause works (Danermark et al., 2002, pp. 73–78). Generalizations (Manicus, 2006, pp. 97–102) offer accounts of the common presence of phenomena, not how they are produced; in short, generalizations are to be distinguished from the explanation of how a cause works. Much of the literature in the human sciences and social work confuse these.

Finally, a critical realist methodology accounts for the open system component of all social work practice. Contexts, by definition, have many layers of causal mechanisms; therefore to study practice, researchers need critical realism to account for complex causal explanations that unfold in open and continuously dynamic practice settings. Quantitative methods can be used when engaged scholarship researchers decide that some practice components can be defined (i.e., relatively fixed) and their regularity confidently established. Often, however, as we have argued in this chapter, this is not possible. In particular, meanings in social work settings are constantly developing and changing. Thus, qualitative methods are ideally suited for collecting data for engaged scholarship projects that focus on the moment-to-moment experience in the real worlds of practice. In the next three chapters, we provide a quick-start guide for deploying several qualitative methods to study practice. We use critical realist ideas and engaged scholarship as methodological guides for how to use qualitative methods to study phenomenological practice gaps.

2

Quick-Start to Qualitative Research for Practice

In this chapter we illustrate the book's key concepts—open system, phenomenological practice gap, brute and institutional facts, and engaged scholarship—by applying them to qualitative research methods. It is a jargon-free, how-to discussion aimed at demonstrating the utility of qualitative methods for conceptualizing and initiating research focused on practice. Research starts with identifying aims and questions, all of which require three activities: data collection and management tools, an analytic strategy, and interpretation. Although these activities are typical of all research projects, what makes for successful achievement is integration. Our learn-by-doing strategy in this chapter will prepare the student and practitioner to initiate engaged scholarship research that is informed by critical realist assumptions.

We introduce, with step-by-step instructions, three established qualitative methods (i.e., thematic, grounded theory, and narrative) and software to manage and analyze data. Our instruction is informed by one practical idea: regardless of skill level, research will be conducted, and not just imagined, when data are actually collected and analyzed. Indeed, for more in-depth discussions there are numerous qualitative textbooks and articles that offer comprehensive treatments of specific perspectives and approaches. In brief, rather than comparing yourself with experienced researchers and feeling inadequate about what you don't know, which often leads to deferring to a research "expert," our learn-by-doing strategy encourages the practitioner to use qualitative research to initiate engaged scholarship projects: a central aim of this book. And finally, we use an example from our research on psychiatric medication to illustrate all the chapter objectives.

AIMS AND QUESTIONS

In doing practice research, the aim is to understand some type of event, circumstance, interaction, or intervention. No practitioner or researcher has an omnipotent eye that "sees" practice directly. Practice requires "theory" to see, understand, and explain. And theory assumes a philosophy of social science. In research, aims and questions depend on methodology (i.e., philosophical assumptions) and methods (i.e., research techniques) for "seeing" the object of study: the practice event or interaction in question. This is true regardless of quantitative or qualitative methodology. Thus, in general, the results of a research project are always *symbolic representations* of aims and questions. A numerical symbolic system is used in quantitative research. In other words, research findings or results stand in or (re)present the object of study: the actual practice reality (i.e., lack of engagement, termination, assessment, policy changes, etc.). Qualitative research uses written narratives (i.e., narrative representation) to present findings. Moreover, all research findings are value laden. The latter is never more present than in the decision to study a specific aim and question; in choosing what to study, we inevitably make a value judgment.

What is the difference between an aim and a question? An aim, on the one hand, points to the most abstract conceptualization of a project. Questions, on the other hand, make concrete or empirical connections to the abstract. An aim draws a boundary around the numerous practice realities and identifies a specific target. A question aims at the target and hits exact points where data are found; data are the lifeblood of research. In other words, an aim is a view from 30,000 feet above ground and a question is a view from ground level.

Let's use a travel analogy as an example. One makes general plans to travel 500 miles from point A to point B: the aim is to go to a specific city and return. Is airfare expensive? Does the city have mass transit? Questions identify the data needed to achieve a specific travel objective; answers to queries reveal the tangible and practical aspects of an actual as opposed to imaginary trip. Queries, therefore, do the work of moving beyond the abstract. Research questions reveal the *concrete and empirical* (i.e., data) pathways to general research aims.

For example, one might wonder how children living in various child protective settings—children whose parents have relinquished parental rights through legal action—are treated with psychiatric medication. This aim is motivated by a value that medications are powerful drugs and should be carefully administered, especially with children; in the United States, for example, an eight-year-old boy in foster care committed suicide while on numerous psychiatric medications (see, http://www.dcf. state.fl.us/initiatives/GMWorkgroup) and this contradicts a social work value that children in protective custody should be "protected." Broadly, the aim focuses attention upon foster children prescribed psychiatric medication. Questions, however, spotlight particular targets that are connected to data: Are foster children prescribed the same number of psychiatric medications as their non-foster counterparts? Are group home settings, in contrast to kinship or foster home settings, more likely to use medication treatment? And how do foster children make sense of how medication works? These questions examine environment or context effects (foster care vs. non-foster). In short, questions point to data that will satisfy curiosity about (i.e., an aim is foremost what you are *generally curious* about) foster children and medication treatment; in doing so, some questions point to qualitative methods (these are discussed later in this chapter) and others point to quantitative ones.

Identifying Practice Aims and Questions for Qualitative Research

Start with practice when identifying aims and questions for an engaged scholarship project. Pay attention and listen to clients, colleagues, and yourself. Wonder about how a practice theory, treatment, or intervention is supposed to work in the open system of a work setting. When policy or organizational issues constrain how theory should be practiced, wonder about its potential as a research aim. What are you facing in practice every day that the evidence-based manual or prescribed theory does not account for? Drill into particular practice experiences. They are full of phenomenological practice gaps and, therefore, research aims.

Box 2.1 Identifying Research Partners

1. Read the literature connected to the research aim and identify potential partners.
2. University department websites list biographies and vita of potential partners.
3. Search the Internet for nonprofit policy institutes that identify publications and researchers similar to the research aim.
4. Study government websites (local, state, and national) and identify potential research partners.

Social workers have often been asked to monitor clients for compliance to social welfare policies and treatment protocols, for example. How does one resolve the gap between coercive policies and empowerment theory? Social work will never be without knowledge/practice gaps. Indeed, the lifeblood or energy of the profession is its jurisdictional claim over finding solutions to everyday problems. And wherever a gap between theory and practice exists, a clinical engaged scholarship aim is somewhere nearby. Once you have identified a knowledge/practice gap and begin to formulate research questions, then engage potential research partners. Box 2.1 lists suggestions for locating a research partner.

For example, social work has a long history of conceptualizing the person-in-environment as a bio-psycho-social ontology: we are body-brain-mind-selves living in historically specific societies and cultures (Froggett, 2002). Biological theories themselves are not new to social work. Treatment of severe mental illness has included an array of body treatments: electroshock therapy, lobotomies, and insulin shock therapy (Braslow, 1997). And in the last fifty years, we have been confronted with the most pervasive of all biological interventions: psychiatric medications. Medications are very portable, which is one practical reason they are used around the world and across the life span. For-profit pharmaceutical industries have accomplished global distribution, in part, by using the random controlled trial (RCT) as the exemplar of evidence-based medicine (Healy, 2009). When applied to mental illness, medication (i.e., psychotropic treatment) is often considered a first-line treatment. Yet what does medication do for the end-user: the medicated? Neurotransmitter and chemical theories of the brain, when practiced as psychotropic treatment, do not tell the medicated what medications do for them. A drug is a *brute* fact; they work on neurotransmitters according to specific biochemical laws. However, drugs are also *institutional* facts; their administration and meanings are mediated by social conventions. Drugs do not have intrinsic chemical power to produce and reproduce the medication meanings that circulate among prescriber, patient, family, peers, and teachers; meanings are constructed by everyday social interaction. In sum, by examining a routine mental health experience, a research aim is drawn around an institutional fact: the meaning making potential and liabilities of psychotropic treatment.

Next, identify questions. Let us continue with the example from psychotropic treatment. Imagine that a sixteen-year-old female and her mother are referred to a practice setting. The daughter has been expelled from school, has a history of cutting (i.e., self-injury behaviors), stays up all night, and is often irritable and verbally abusive. The mother turned to a pediatrician who referred to a child psychiatrist. Interviews resulted in a bipolar disorder diagnosis and a prescription for medication. The mother pondered. Her husband opposed medication: "she will grow out of it like I did." There are side effects to be considered. The mother weighed the costs and benefits and eventually agreed. The daughter was not altogether reluctant. She felt guilty about the pain she believed she had caused the family. The psychiatrist did not believe that medicine alone would solve the problem and he referred to you, a social worker. Your training and experience has been with psychosocial interventions, including cognitive-behavioral and psychodynamic. You are skeptical about the use of psychiatric medication with children and adolescents. However, increasingly your referrals include adolescents who have been taking psychiatric medication for months, even years. In some cases, they are taking multiple medications. You could ignore the medication and say to yourself, client, and parent: "The doctor is the expert on medication. Take your questions about medication to her." Then you learn that the parents repeatedly ask the psychiatrist for medication changes whenever new behavioral or emotional problems arise, and this seems counterproductive to psychosocial interventions.

Split treatment—prescription treatment and psychosocial therapy conducted by different practitioners—is common today because the vast majority of psychiatrists and doctors prescribe, leaving psychosocial therapy to the psychologist or social worker. In other words, policy, theory, and practice split and then fragment the client's bio-psycho-social reality into seemingly inseparable parts: brain, mind, and sociality. Although splitting biological and psychosocial treatments is consistent with the dominant social division of labor in mental health, it leaves us with a serious question: *How does split treatment affect overall client outcomes?* Thus, a question narrows the aim and points to data. Another question might focus on how families differently make meaning of a child's medication and how these might differentially influence mental health outcomes.

Next, thinking with an open system perspective, ask questions from multiple points of view: client, therapist, parent, psychiatrist, teacher, or sibling. Write as many permutations that the specific practice example serves up. What effect does splitting the treatment produce? Or, rewrite as a statement: splitting the treatment requires that I constantly remind the mother and the adolescent to take their medication questions to the doctor. Ask the question from the adolescent's point of view: "I wonder why my doctor does not talk about therapy and my therapist does not talk about my medication." Or, take up the doctor's perspective: "If the mother made sure the daughter took the medication, I could be more confident about the type of medication and dosage." Each perspective leads to different questions, thus data. Framing an aim and a question from multiple perspectives is critical because it identifies the open system parameters and a pool of potential engaged scholarship participants: parents, doctors, researchers, medicated patients, teachers, and social workers.

QUALITATIVE METHODS

Recruitment

With an aim and question in hand, it's the research design that delivers answers. A crucial part of the design is sampling and recruitment. Who do we recruit? How do we recruit? Where do we recruit? How do we consent? Just because you have identified the perfect research question does not mean "they" (i.e., the research participants) will participate. Engaged scholarship projects increase recruitment success because involving participant stakeholders in designing the research decreases the chance that recruitment efforts will be met with an unenthusiastic response.

Few would agree to take a trip without knowing the destination, how they are getting there, expectations of the plans upon arrival, and how long they will be there. The same is true for research participants. A study may require collecting data in client homes, or what researchers call naturalistic settings. Before committing oneself to such a study, it is advisable to inquire about the likelihood that clients would consent; a preliminary investigation should identify individuals willing to invite researchers into their home. Often, institutions or organizations have institutional review boards (IRBs) that mediate access to research participants. If your relationship with the IRB is not established beforehand, recruitment is likely to fail. Box 2.2 describes the functions of IRB and lists three websites for further details. An engaged scholarship strategy means that principal investigators do not assume that recruitment will be easy; *they build relationships that anticipate recruitment strategies and success.* This is not true for secondary data: data already produced, fixed,

---

Box 2.2 Institutional Review Boards

Institutional Review Boards (IRB) are used in the fields of health and the social sciences. IRB reviews assure, throughout all research phases, that guidelines are followed to protect the rights and welfare of research participants. All universities and colleges have IRBs. Numerous social service and mental health agencies have IRB equivalents. In short, *all* research that involves humans requires objective (by individuals not directly associated with the research) review to assure participant rights and welfare. Individuals appointed to IRBs review research protocols, including informed consent documents, recruitment strategies, and participant compensation. IRB reviews examine the ethics of the research and its methods, and carefully scrutinize informed consent procedures so that potential participants are fully informed and voluntary. IRBs have continual review procedures to protect the safety of participants once they are enrolled and throughout the project. The following are three websites that provide national and international guidelines:

   http://ohsr.od.nih.gov/index.html (National Institute of Health, Office of Human Subjects)

   http://www.who.int/rpc/research_ethics/en/index.html (The World Health Organization)

   http://www.fda.gov/ScienceResearch/SpecialTopics/RunningClinicalTrials/GuidancesInformationSheetsandNotices/ucm113709.htm (United States Department of Health and Human Services)

or formed (memos, case progress notes, and organizational outcome data). With the latter, one consents for access to private data that has been stored somehow and somewhere. In contrast, collecting primary data, which is produced firsthand during the project, requires recruitment and consent of the individuals who serve up the data.

A research aim specifies who is to be included in the research. It does not identify where, when, or how often. It does not specify the inclusion (i.e., characteristics that respondents must have to be included) and exclusion (i.e., characteristics that place respondents outside the scope of the study) criteria. Indeed, sampling is both practical and philosophical. The former has to do with the mechanics of recruiting a sample and can flex with context; the latter is shaped by the ontological assumptions embedded in the aim and question and is, therefore, relatively inflexible.

Return to the travel analogy. Once in an automobile, you can make practical shifts related to driving speeds and routes, but you are now constrained by that mode of transportation. In research, *early decisions always influence later ones*. Sampling is one of the earliest decisions. In research, recruitment appears to be the last step. To the contrary, success at recruitment is made when deciding on aims and questions. And this is another reason why engaged scholarship is productive; research partners (e.g., academics, practitioners, administrators, policymakers, and clients) build strategies for assessing the potential and limitations of accessing specific research populations. One must answer a simple question: How large is the pool of research participants and what steps are necessary to access the numbers required by the study? One does not know actual recruitment numbers until the project begins consenting, but having research-practice partners that work closely with potential participants increases the likelihood of recruitment success. Box 2.3 provides resources for exploring sampling techniques and philosophies.

Data, Data Collection, and Data Management

What is qualitative data? Broadly, qualitative refers to data that describes an object's qualities or meaningful properties. When standing before Edvard Munch's painting *The Scream* (see Wikipedia website for an image, http://en.wikipedia.org/wiki/The_Scream), ask yourself: What feeling, thought, or action does the painting evoke? Your answer is

Box 2.3 Sampling

It is not possible to collect data from everyone, thus researchers must sample (unless, of course, it is an in-depth case study where the N = 1). A sample represents a selection of participants from a larger pool. In general, qualitative researchers utilize four methods: theoretical, purposive, convenience, and snowball. The following is a general resource list that will help you think about a sampling strategy; it is not meant to be comprehensive but rather a place to begin.

Internet

http://www.qualres.org/HomeSamp-3702.html (Robert Wood Johnson Foundation)

Articles & Books

Bryman, A. (2008). *Social research methods.* 3rd edition. Oxford University Press.

Corbin, J. M., & Strauss, A. (2008). *Basics in qualitative research: Techniques and procedures for developing grounded theory.* Sage publications.

Curtis, S., Gesler, W., Smith, G., & Washburn, S. (2000). Approaches to sampling and case selection in qualitative research: examples in the geography of health. *Social Science & Medicine*, 50(7), 1001–1014.

a narrative (oral or written). On the other hand, while looking at the same painting, were you asked to rate the painting on a scale from 1 to 5 (1 = neutral, 3 = frightened, and 5 = horrified), then your answer has been transformed into quantitative data. And as long as the scale content was determined to be valid by standard measurement techniques and it reliably worked for various respondent groups (i.e., it was normed properly), then the instrument could be used on large populations to determine the *most common* response to *The Scream*. Where questions do not seek the most common and fixed response, but rather the experience-near in the open system of life contexts (see Box 2.4 for a definition of phenomenology and experience-near), then qualitative data are sought. Critical realists argue that common response inquiries are bound to closed system assumptions. An inquiry assuming open systems would investigate how a particular meaning becomes fixed or free-floating. And for practitioners, it's not the common but the particular meaning a client gives to a life experience—past, present, or anticipated—that is most relevant. A common response focuses a practitioner's attention but until the particular is investigated, knowing the most common cannot predict in open systems how specific clients might respond.

If qualitative data are to be collected and analyzed, researchers need to make a record of the experience; process recording, audio recording, or video recording are typical. In short, what starts out as a live experience, in the moment, or in-vivo, has now been fixed by some method of recording that transforms a response into textual data. The text can be your written case notes or audio or video recordings; whichever, now you are working with *narrated text* (i.e., qualitative data). So, how are data collected?

Qualitative data are collected by following two distinct methods and by a third that is sandwiched between them. Each method is designed to collect *experience-near, phenomenological* data (see Box 2.4). It could be argued that data collection methods are distinguished by how near in time the researcher is to the respondent's experience. One method, ethnography, participant observation, or the clinical encounter, is a form of data collection that is often called naturalistic or in-vivo—in the client's real-life situation. And of all collection methods, it is the closest to real-time. For example, a researcher could be a museum visitor and

---

Box 2.4 Phenomenology and Experience-Near

"Phenomenology studies structures of conscious experience as experienced from the first-person point of view, along with relevant conditions of experience. The central structure of an experience is its intentionality, the way it is directed through its content or meaning toward a certain object in the world. We all experience various types of experience, including perception, imagination, thought, emotion, desire, volition, and action. Thus, the domain of phenomenology is the range of experiences including these types (among others). Experience includes not only relatively passive experience as in vision or hearing, but also active experience as in walking or hammering a nail or kicking a ball. Conscious experiences have a unique feature: we experience them, we live through them or perform them. Other things in the world we may observe and engage. But we do not experience them, in the sense of living through or performing them. This experiential or first-person feature—that of being experienced—is an essential part of the nature or structure of conscious experience: as we say, 'I see / think / desire / do . . . ' This feature is both a phenomenological and an ontological feature of each experience: it is part of what it is for the experience to be experienced (phenomenological) and part of what it is for the experience to be (ontological)."

Source: http://plato.stanford.edu/entries/phenomenology/ (September 9, 2011)

along with all other visitors view *The Scream*; one would observe and record how individuals respond to the painting. In addition to your unobtrusive observations (with IRB permission), you could ask visitors to answer questions about their experience. Adding the latter component depends on your aim and question; if you want data free from researcher influence, then quietly observing visitor response might be enough. However, if you desire to test a hypothesis about how prior experience with trauma, for example, affects the viewing experience, open-ended questions might be necessary. And as long as you are asking questions onsite while respondents are actually viewing the painting, then you are ethnographically—observing and or being part of a social interaction—collecting data.

The second data collection method is called *retrospective*—looking back at events or experiences that have already taken place—because collection is removed in time and space from the experience. Compared to ethnography, data are collected after the experience; it could be several hours, a day, a month, a year, or ten years, depending on your aim and question. For example, 9/11 in the United States has had remarkable effects, even ten years post event. Ask yourself an open-ended question about 9/11. What did you feel when you first heard that airplanes had crashed into the World Trade Center? This type of question evokes an experience (i.e., emotion, thought, or action) that is removed from present time. Asking this kind of open-ended question is the most common type of *primary data collection*: data directly observed or collected by the researcher. Other data include respondent written documents (e.g., journals or diaries) that describe relations, experiences, and events. Let's return to the exhibit of the Munch painting. From the curators you learn that there was an exhibit twenty years ago. Visitors were asked to record responses. We no longer know the circumstances of the exhibit but we do have *secondary data:* data collected in the past by someone other than the researcher. In general, retrospective data are of two types: (1) open-ended questions, asked by the researcher, of here-and-now respondents, and, (2) data that were recorded in some representational form. Here, the intention of using the information as research data were not known or even expected at the time they were produced. Examples of the latter might include organizational memos, social work progress notes, clinical assessments, termination summaries, and in general, any type of data (written or audio/video recorded) created by practitioners or clients.

Box 2.5 Video in Qualitative Research

Bergman, H. F., Preisler, G., & Werbart, A. (2006). Communicating with patients with schizophrenia: Characteristics of well functioning and poorly functioning communication. *Qualitative Research in Psychology*, 3: 121–146.

Buchbinder, M. H., Detzer, M. J., Welsch, R. L., Christiano, A. S., Patashnik, J. L., & Rich, M. (2005). Assessing adolescents with insulin-dependent diabetes mellitus: A multiple perspective pilot study using visual illness narratives and interviews. *Journal of Adolescent Health*, 36(1): 71.e9–71.e13.

Buchwald, D., Schantz-Laursen, B., & Delmar, C. (2009). Video diary data collection in research with children: An alternative method. *International Journal of Qualitative Methods*, 8(1): 12–20.

Heath, C., Hindmarsh, J., & Luff, P. (2010). *Video in qualitative research*. London: Sage.

Miles, Bart W.(2006) "Moving out of the dark ages: An argument for the use of digital video in social work research." *Journal of Technology in Human Services*, 24(2/3): 181–196.

A third data collection method blends present-time (in-vivo) and after-the-fact (retrospective) strategies. These are data available through Internet blogs and websites, which blur distinctions between in-vivo and retrospective because the immediacy and online presence of the data gives it an in-vivo quality. For example, one could compare early childhood intervention services by identifying websites and visiting a specified number on a given day. Program websites and blogs are viewed in real time and represent respondent reactions or organizational priorities that may relate to a specific research aim and question. Another practice is the use of respondent generated audio and video recordings or written diaries (Box 2.5 offers examples of video research). Video and Internet research strategies remove the influence of researcher presence and collect data by asking respondents to make in-vivo, real-time recordings. The researcher analyzes data after-the-fact but the respondent captured experience as it was occurring, again blending in-vivo and retrospective methods.

To Use Or Not to Use Software Technology?

If the research project is small in scope, a few responses from a handful of respondents, then the use of technology to organize and manage data is not helpful. However, if data are collected over time and if audio recordings and transcriptions are numerous, data management is not to be underestimated. It is an overwhelming feeling to collect data and see hundreds upon hundreds of typed pages accumulating on your desktop. Imagine managing a five-year project studying adolescent attitudes and experiences of psychiatric medication; the research aim is to compare the attention-deficit, hyperactivity deficit (ADHD) psychostimulant experiences among different ethnic groups of adolescent males and females. Moreover, the project utilizes a questionnaire with twenty-five, open-ended questions; enrolls 200 youth (100 males and 100 females from four ethnic groups); and interviews respondents four times annually for five years. In short, 100,000 responses are available for data management and analysis. Software technology is available to store, manage, and analyze thousands of open-ended, recorded responses.

There are two related technology and data management decisions. The first is related to how respondent answers have been recorded and how those recordings are accessed for listening or transcription. The latter answers the question: What methods will be used to record data? Answering this question and at the same time planning your analytic strategy is a necessary integrative action. If handwritten field or case notes, for example, were not read into an audio recorder and then transcribed, then analysis would be limited to reading and re-reading the original, handwritten or typed notes. Moreover, respondents in an ethnographic study (or clients in therapy) do not present their stories in a simple linear fashion that corresponds to the researcher aims and questions. Therefore, the ethnographer's hand-written notes would be limited to using a cut and paste (i.e., by hand) method for organizing and linking one note on page 5, for example, with another co-related note on page 86. However, ethnographic research often assumes that narratives should be analyzed in the context of the experience that generated them; thus, handwritten data are necessary and useful. Recording data by hand, or reading and re-reading handwritten notes, is a technology-free strategy for linking data collection, management, and analysis.

Thus, choosing recording methods and strategies is a practical and philosophical matter that depends on the amount of text the research project will accumulate and on how data recordings are conceptually linked to specific research aims. Hundreds and thousands of ethnographic hand-written entries may be too much to manage. Reading written field notes (or case notes) into a recorder and then transcribing the notes would create a text file (i.e., Microsoft Word or Apple Pages), and this file retains the original context of the written narratives, but now the transcriptions could be used by software for data linking and organizing. The latter strategy gives the researcher more management flexibility in reading and analyzing data, so it is a strategy we highly recommend. Indeed, a novel way of managing audio recordings by using iTunes software is described in Box 2.6.

Box 2.6 Audio Recording and Management

Turn your laptop computer into a digital audio recorder and efficiently manage research data. First, search online for audio recording software; we have used NCH Swift Sound (RecordPad Sound Recorder v. 3.03, http://www.nch.com) because of its record, pause, and stop features, which are simple to use. Load and set up the software, e.g., RecordPad; for device, choose sound in, choose wav format, and then define the pathway where the software will store the audio files (i.e., hard drive). Connect an external microphone to the laptop microphone in-jack. For practice, with software open, click record and answer a simulated research question; when finished, click stop and mark done. Next, go to the file folder where you instructed the software to store the audio files. You will find the audio wav file and it will be named "Untitled" with a number after it. Click on the file name and choose rename; if this were an actual research respondent, rename the file with the ID number and the question number of your semistructured questionnaire (for example, 001001, would represent the first respondent (001) and the first question asked of that respondent (001).

Data management software is needed next. Apple iTunes software is free and can easily be tricked into managing your research files (http://www.apple.com/itunes/download). *Important!* Dedicate a laptop as an iTunes research (i.e., in iTunes known as music library) library and don't mix personal music files or podcasts with your research files. A dedicated research iTunes library has a single folder where all research audio files are stored and this can be password protected (or stored on removable disk) to meet IRB confidentiality and security demands. To load the practice audio file you created, open iTunes, click on File and click on add file to library. Find the folder you stored the practice audio file, highlight the file, and click open. The file is now in your iTunes "music" library, though think of it as an audio research library.

Imagine that you have several hundred (or thousands) respondent recordings representing different respondent characteristics: male, female, age, ethnicity, and various other research demographic characteristics.

Because your files are in iTunes, use the technology to sort by any respondent characteristic. Sorting produces efficiencies. Sort all respondent answers to a specific question; for example, save as a smart playlist (from file menu, choose smart playlist), then transcribe only that question. Sort and create a smart playlist of just female answers to a specific question; moreover, dock an iPod (or other mp3 player) and download just those files for quick listening. The sorting capabilities of iTunes are enormous. Use it to efficiently manage hundreds of audio files. Never face the overwhelming task of trying to locate one track on a two-hour interview; instead use iTunes to find the file immediately.

The second decision involves the use of software specifically designed for managing and analyzing qualitative data. However, before we introduce qualitative software, it is helpful to think about different strategies for analyzing collected data. Different strategies make different demands on the software.

DATA ANALYTIC STRATEGY

Once collected and efficiently managed, how do you analyze data? A comprehensive discussion of qualitative data analysis is not our aim. Instead we provide an introduction to three related methods that are useful and commonly used in research. Box 2.7 gives a list of exemplar books and articles describing thematic, grounded theory, and narrative. Qualitative data analysis is foremost a means of data reduction, that is, reducing large amounts of text to manageable bits or representations. There are various methods for reducing qualitative data. In other words, although during analysis one constantly engages the entirety of the collected text, it is not practical for findings to be presented in original form. Reproduction of hundreds of pages of transcripts, written notes, case records, and hours of audio and video recordings to a research audience is not practical, nor does it recognize that research requires *interpretation*. Research serves up data but for what purpose? The aim and question is a means to a higher end of understanding a phenomenological practice gap. In other words, a critical realist approach to research assumes that facts do not speak for themselves; if they did then data reduction would not be necessary: simply reproduce the collected

---

Box 2.7   Thematic, Grounded Theory and Narrative Resources

Boyatzis, R. (1998). *Transforming qualitative information: Thematic analysis and code development.* Thousand Oaks, CA: Sage.

Braun, V., & Clark, V. (2006). Using thematic analysis in psychology. *Qualitative Research in Psychology* 3: 77–101.

Charmaz. K. (2006). *Constructing grounded theory: A practical guide through qualitative analysis.* London: Sage.

Corbin, J., & Straus, A. (2008). *Basics of qualitative research: techniques and procedures for developing grounded theory.* Thousand Oaks, CA: Sage.

Denzin, N. K., & Lincoln, Y. S. (2011). *The Sage handbook of qualitative research.* Thousand Oaks, CA: Sage.

Fraser, H. (2004). Doing narrative research: Analysing personal stories line by line. *Qualitative Social Work* 3(2): 179–201.

Herman, D. (2007). *The Cambridge companion to narrative.* Cambridge: Cambridge University Press.

Mattingly, C. (1998). *Healing dramas and clinical Plots: The narrative structure of experience.* Cambridge: Cambridge University Press.

Padgett, D. (2008). *Qualitative methods in social work research.* Thousand Oaks, CA: Sage.

Shaw, I. (2011). *Evaluating in Practice.* Burlington, VT.: Ashgate Publishing Company.

Shaw, I., and Gould, N. (2001). *Qualitative social work research.* Thousand Oaks CA: Sage.

Oktay, J. (2012). *Grounded theory.* New York: Oxford University Press.

Wells, K. (2011). *Narrative inquiry.* New York: Oxford University Press.

---

narratives in their entirety and make them available for others to read. Data reduction should be transparent so others can recognize your assumptions and follow your techniques. Thus, data management is an integral part of analyzing because data are not reduced without constantly working (i.e., constant reading and listening to) or managing the original respondent narratives. How?

Data reduction techniques integrate with other research phases; one cannot analyze what has not been collected. And one can't collect what the aim and questions have not focused on. Still, all the original data can't be published. Thus, analytic strategies describe the data reduction method and provide a list of instructions describing the analytic steps that lead to findings. Were others (the research audience) to follow your data reduction instructions, there is a reasonable chance they would identify similar findings. The latter is sometimes called a reliability check.

In short, data reduction methods and implementation add up to an analytic strategy. Standard analytic strategies are used independently or in an interdependent fashion. Choosing a strategy is always dependent on the research aim and question. We have chosen to review three qualitative methods— thematic, grounded theory, and narrative; it has been our experience that with an introductory understanding of these, analysis of qualitative data can begin. Moreover, hundreds of examples are available to learn from and we have provided in Box 2.8 a short list of the journals where such studies can be found; we encourage the reader to browse the journals and read studies that use one or more of the three strategies summarized.

Box 2.8 Short List of Qualitative Research Journals

Action Research International
Cardiff Papers in Qualitative Research
Culture, Medicine and Psychiatry: An International Journal of Comparative Cross-Cultural Research
Discourse Analysis Online
Discourse Processes
Discourse Studies: An Interdisciplinary Journal for the Study of Text and Talk
Ethnography
The Grounded Theory Review: An International Journal
International Journal of Qualitative Methods
International Journal of Qualitative Studies in Education
International Journal of Social Research Methodology
Journal of Advanced Nursing
Journal of Contemporary Ethnography
Journal of Family Psychotherapy
Narrative Inquiry
Qualitative Health Research
Qualitative Inquiry
Qualitative Research
Qualitative Research in Psychology
Qualitative Research Journal
Qualitative Social Work
Qualitative Sociology
Quality & Quantity: International Journal of Methodology
Social Science & Medicine
Sociology of Health & Illness: A Journal of Medical Sociology
Symbolic Interaction

Thematic Analytic Strategy

Thematic analysis is a commonly used qualitative method to identify, report, and analyze data for the meanings produced in open systems by social workers and clients (Boyatzis, 1998; Braun & Clark, 2006; Patton, 2002; Riessman, 2008). A theme is a ". . . patterned response or meaning within the dataset" (Braun & Clark, 2006: 82). And because thematic analysis has great flexibility, it has been applied to the social sciences (Braun & Clark, 2006) and medicine (Gabriel et al., 2000). The significance of a theme is its "substantive significance," not its frequency (Patton, 2002: 467). Substantive significance refers to the consistency of a theme across and within study participants. It is also significant when findings deepen understanding of current knowledge about clinical social work. Consistency, on the other hand, requires systematic coding procedures to produce reliability. If, for example, other researchers used the same dataset and followed the same procedures, one should find consonance in the assignment of the same or similar themes to respondent answers. And because thematic techniques do not provide statistical tests of significance, themes are significant by virtue of (1) skillful identification of new themes and confirmation of themes identified in the clinical literature; and (2) confidence in the systematic nature of the coding procedure.

The first step in a thematic analysis is aimed at the discovery of descriptive patterns. What themes could be derived from an investigation of adolescent experience of psychiatric medication, for example? An identification of a patterned response would satisfy an overall curiosity (or research aim) about the use of medication with adolescents. And a thematic analysis could reveal specific answers to a clinical question that addresses a phenomenological practice gap (e.g., adherence or nonadherence). Although drugs are manufactured and tested using theory drawn from pharmaceutical science, this theory does not compel someone to take medicine. Nor does it tell them what it does in their bodies. In large part, identifying a patterned response is a basic unit of analysis. Patterned behavior, emotions, thoughts, and beliefs provide the building blocks for situating the research aim inside a larger, stratified, practice reality. How does a desire to take medication get constituted (see Longhofer & Floersch, 2010)? Studies using thematic analysis often report detailed descriptive data about a practice question. Indeed, the first step in a critical realist approach to research is to identify the empirical level (i.e., what is actually experienced) data in your clinical practice.

How are patterns recognized? What is a pattern? Researchers compare units of text and sort them into categories of umbrella and subthemes, which are assumed to represent some aspect of the phenomenon. By comparing discovered themes with prior experience, patterns are identified. And, of course, a hoped-for outcome is that a theme emerges that is not found in the literature or prior experience of the researcher.

The first step is to code the data, meaning reducing large chunks of data (i.e., quotations) into smaller chunks. When you code you are essentially reducing a chunk of data to a few words. We will use the word "cat" as an illustration. Wikipedia describes cats as,

> . . . strong, flexible bodies, quick reflexes, sharp retractable claws, and teeth adapted to killing small prey . . . their acute hearing and ability to see in near darkness to locate prey . . . they hear sounds too faint for human ears, they can also hear sounds higher in frequency than humans can perceive . . . they rely more on smell than taste, and have a vastly better sense of smell than humans. Despite being solitary hunters, they are a social species and use a variety of vocalizations, pheromones and types of body language for communication. These include meowing, purring, trilling, hissing, growling, and grunting. (http://en.wikipedia.org/wiki/Cat, November 1, 2010)

Wikipedia's numerous descriptors are reduced to one word—cat. In a like manner, qualitative coding is the process of labeling respondent quotations with a few words (i.e., codes) that evoke a meaning that represents the larger quotation (stands in for "cat") the code is attached to. Skill is involved in completing the latter task without *misrepresenting the respondent*. Making a list of coding instructions provides coders a consistent guide for data reduction. A typical list includes: (1) read the entire textual transcript (or listen to the entire recording); (2) in a second reading, identify all quotations that refer to the research aim and question(s); (3) code each identified quotation by attaching a code name; in most instances create a code name from some of the respondent's actual words—called in-vivo, initial, or open coding; (4) compare quotations attached to a specific in-vivo code and determine which ones match the code you created (and with those that do not fit, either create a new code or attach it to another code that better fits the quotation); and finally; (5) compare and sort the in-vivo codes into higher level or umbrella codes—sometimes called axial coding. In sum, think of coding like you would of Russian nesting dolls, a set of dolls of decreasing sizes placed one inside the other. Likewise, thematic coding is the process of building a set of codes of larger sizes (i.e., units of meaning) placed one inside the other. The smallest are called in-vivo and they fit inside larger codes until no other code can be imagined as containing the smaller ones.

Because thematic data analytic techniques reveal patterns by constantly comparing codes with themselves and among codes, it is not surprising that thematic work has been compared to content and grounded theory methods (Bryman, 2008; Riessman, 2008). While content analysis consists of comparing and sorting themes or patterns, its aim is to quantify (according to predetermined categories) content in a systematic and reliable manner (Bryman, 2008). It differs from thematic analysis because content analysis, in large part, establishes significance by frequency of themes. Grounded theory (GT) methods assist in using identified themes and investigating how they relate conceptually to one another. GT is especially useful for any research aim that seeks to *build a conceptual framework for understanding a given practice gap reality.*

Grounded Theory Analytic Strategy

Kathy Charmaz has aptly noted "grounded theory has evolved into a constellation of methods rather than an orthodox unitary approach" (Charmaz, 2008: 161). Glaser and Strauss (1965) pioneered the method to study hospital staff, patient, and family communications. Derived from sociological fieldwork, GT was built upon observation of social interactions and interviews with dying patients. The aim of GT is to generate hypotheses using theoretical constructs generated from bottom-up data. In addition to coding the data for a list of themes, the purpose of GT is to construct grounded theories that theoretically describe a process "of unfolding temporal sequences that may have identifiable markers with clear beginnings and endings and benchmarks in between. The temporal sequences are linked in a process and lead to change. Thus, single events become linked as part of a larger whole" (Charmaz, 2006: 10). Charmaz's emphasis on temporality and sequencing makes GT different from thematic work. Yet in spite of differences, there are coding techniques that overlap and go beyond thematic analysis. These include

- In-vivo/line-by-line coding—assigning codes to particular quotations.
- Focused coding—sorting similar in-vivo codes into broader categories of similar concepts.
- Axial coding—connecting larger categories of codes with their individual subcategories, specifying how they relate to one another.
- Memo-writing—elaborating relationships between codes and categories in an early attempt to organize the data into an emergent theoretical network of relationships.
- Constant comparison—comparing all levels of codes and identifying which generate consequences or under which certain events follow.
- Theoretical sampling—interviewing a variety of respondents to delineate the boundaries of one's theory. This differs from sampling until no new "themes" emerge (Charmaz, 2008), but instead relates to creating a full description of the conditions under which one's theory operates.

The ultimate outcome of a GT study is a theory or set of propositions that describes the mechanics of the phenomenon under study and from which further study hypotheses can be generated (Hallberg, 2006).

In the original conceptualization of GT, coding, data collection, and analysis were iteratively linked; initial coding, for example, generated nascent hypotheses to direct ongoing data collection. Researchers looked for confirming and disconfirming examples of hypotheses. And data collection was complete with a full theoretical description of the phenomenon. Theoretical description, then, served as a foundation for generating further hypotheses. Strauss and Corbin (1994) argued against equating thematic analysis with GT because thematic can consist of conceptual coding as an end itself, whereas with GT, the aim is to articulate relationships among identified themes or constructs (Strauss & Corbin, 1994, p. 277). Carolyn Oliver has combined critical realist philosophy with grounded theory because she argues, "it is this kind of research that offers the best chance to emotionally engage practitioners and build relationships between researchers, policy makers and service providers to reinforce theory-practice connection in a profession in which research has often struggled to impact the front line" (Oliver, 2011, p. 13).

Narrative Analytic Strategy

Among the three methods reviewed, narrative is the most difficult to define; across many disciplines, no common understanding exists (Herman, 2007, Riessman, 2008; Wells, 2011). Thus, when it comes to defining narrative and narrative method, it is best to avoid oversimplified understandings and equally important to clearly specify the uses of method and diversity of strategies (Fraser, 2004, p. 196). There is one very important difference between thematic, GT, and narrative technique: narrative does not typically discuss line-by-line or in-vivo coding strategies, but focuses instead on the temporality and sequencing of storied experiences or the linguistic structure and use of language.

The material of narrative analysis is the multiple modes of representation used to reference and make sense of human experience. Of course, the central mode *is language* and therefore in the human sciences and social work, researchers collect oral and written narratives and related speech acts (Floersch, 2000; Summerson-Carr, 2010). For Riessman and Quinney narrative is a window into "human interaction in relationships—the daily stuff of social work" (Riessman & Quinney, 2005, p. 392). Marie-Laure Ryan's understanding of narrative is especially relevant to social work practice and research. She writes that "narrative is about problem solving; narrative is about conflict; narrative is about interpersonal relations; narrative is about human experience; and narrative is about the temporality of existence" (Ryan, 2007, p. 24). Moreover, it is when a text or "story" contains these elements that they are considered narrative, not just a chronology of events.

Many have argued that narratives are the central mechanism for meaning making. In literary theory, for example, plot refers to narrative events that move the story toward achievement of artistic or emotional effect. The plot's work in a narrative is rooted in the tension between the beginning, middle, and end; this dynamic produces forward movement, anticipatory feeling, and suspense. Paul Ricoeur argued that narrative functions to give our daily experience a sequential and temporal meaning; indeed, if individuals lack the capacity to narrativize, Ricoeur argued they would not be able to comprehend time (Pellauer, 2007, pp. 71–73).[1] Others, like Ricoeur, make similar and sometimes more far reaching claims about the power of narrative to produce effects (Vollmer, 2005; Dennett, 1992, 1993; Neisser, 1994).

Andrew Sayer (2000) offers a critical realist discussion of narratives, noting especially that some narratives have the power to produce effects and others do not. A chemist's narrative highlights a drug's chemical properties. A pharmaceutical salesman, speaking to a psychiatrist, pronounces the latest clinical trial findings. Teachers report problematic student behavior and its effect on parents can be powerful. Doctors construct narratives about chemical imbalances, hoping to persuade patients to take medication like diabetics take insulin shots. Parents speak of complications at home. And so on. These narratives speak to different levels of the patient's (e.g., adolescent) psychotropic treatment reality: the drug has chemical properties; school environments, to be effective, desire attentive students; and adolescents, often desperately, want to feel "normal." A critical realist analysis peels away each narrative layer and investigates psychotropic interventions from multiple perspectives.

DATA ANALYTIC SOFTWARE

Introduction

Before starting our quick-start to ATLAS.ti software, it is important to note that there are other programs to choose from. We are illustrating ATLAS.ti because we have experience with it. And like most skill-based software programs, the more you use it, the harder it is to switch (if you are devoted and passionate about Microsoft/PC or Apple/MAC, then you know what switching means). Equally robust is the qualitative software, NVivo (http://www.qsrinternational.com/products_nvivo.aspx). If you are not financially or experientially committed to particular software, then try demos of each product and choose the software that works for you. The latter is important.

The goal here is to describe a quick-start approach to using software for data analysis. ATLAS.ti supports two types of qualitative work: data management and analysis. Figure 2.1 is a screen shot of a sample project that is described next.

From its home page, download a free demo copy of ATLAS.ti (see, http://www.atlasti.com/demo.html). It is not a time limited download, meaning it would require you to buy it after ten days, for example. The demo gives you access to all of its functions; the free demo *does limit* the

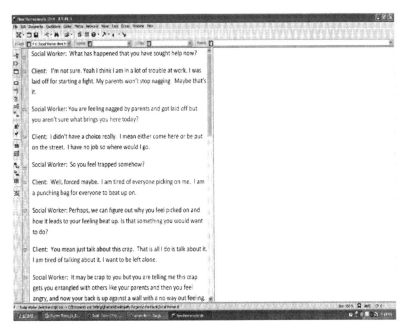

Figure 2.1 ATLAS.ti Software.

number of documents you can analyze, so it is a good idea to check the website for current information about demo limitations. Nevertheless, in learning a quick-start approach and for deciding whether the software is right for you, using the free demo software is a practical way to get started. You could try this with NVivo as well. We assume you can download software from a website, or that you can find someone to help download the software to your computer; usually the download automatically creates a file called "scientific software" and places the ATLAS.ti software in the main program file folder.

Begin by going to the scientific software folder and clicking on the ATLAS.ti icon (an image of the planet earth). When opening the first time, it may ask you: Open a New Hermeneutic Unit? The answer is yes. (Practice opening and closing the software.) An open screen will look similar to Figure 2.1, although the left of your screen will be a blank page (i.e., no assigned data yet). In the upper left hand corner of the screen, click "File," and then click "Save." When the save menu opens, you have two tasks. *The first is to notice the folder you are about to save the file to.* The default will send the file to the scientific software folder, but it is wiser to save the new project to a file folder where its location is easy to recall and find. Create a folder in the "my documents" folder (on desktop) called "research projects" and then give the project you are saving the following file name: "practice project." In the instructions below you will continue to use the "practice project" file name. Now, click the save button. You will be prompted as to where you want to save the file. Save it to the "research projects" folder. The HU "practice project" is now saved to a folder called "research projects." Notice, the only change to any new or freshly opened ATLAS.ti screen *is the file name* in the uppermost left hand corner of the screen; the file name identifies it as a unique project that can be reloaded.

It's that simple! You have created a shell for a research project. What is a hermeneutic unit (HU)? A detailed discussion of hermeneutics can be read online at http://plato.stanford.edu/entries/hermeneutics/. Here, think of a hermeneutic unit as a research project and its *aim is to interpret the meaning* of an oral or written text. We are forever engaged in interpreting meaning. And so it is with research respondents. ATLAS.ti was conceived and created by authors heavily influenced by the interpretive research tradition.[2] Thus, program code was written into the software that automatically names a research project a Hermeneutic Unit. The HU just created was called "practice project." In general, when you face the ATLAS.ti screen (see Figure 2.2), the upper left-hand corner is the space for the file name (the name you gave your research project), the second line from the top is the main menu bar, the third line contains icons for shortcuts like "save," and the fourth contains the HU managers: primary documents, quotations, codes, and memos.

Imagine that the HU unit is a bucket. Inside the bucket you will have four types of research objects: (1) primary documents, (2) quotations, (3) codes, (4) comments and memos, and (5) relations among 1, 2, 3, and 4. The first object to drop in your HU bucket is a primary document (PD). PDs are derived from your data collection efforts. Some kind of written text, audio, or video material was collected. (Because audio and video require advanced operations that are beyond a quick-start introduction and most researchers use transcribed text, we are not illustrating how to use ATLAS.ti for analyzing audio or video.)

In Figure 2.1, the text on the left side of the screen is the content of a primary document. Now you may be wondering: How are documents attached or assigned to a particular HU? There are several routes but we describe one foolproof technique. Think about it this way. You have textual transcripts (or audio, video, and other images) collected for the

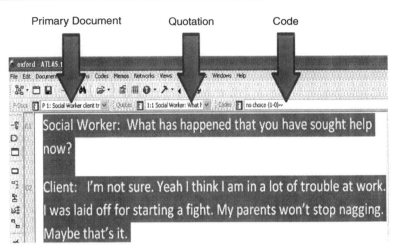

Figure 2.2   ATLAS.ti Three Key Program Functions.

purpose of answering your research questions; these transcripts become PDs in ATLAS.ti. Indeed, as data, transcripts need to be connected to your software.

Let's assign primary documents to the open "practice project" HU. *First*, copy, move, or save some type of primary (i.e., your written texts or transcripts) document to the same folder where you saved your HU (recall, this was the "research project" folder). *Important!* Primary documents *always* need to be in the same folder that your HU unit is saved to. The "practice project" folder is the location that primary documents must reside and remain for the duration of analysis. Why? Because this is how ATLAS.ti finds the primary document(s). Indeed, in ATLAS.ti, when coding a primary document, you are never directly working on or affecting the actual document. Think of the HU unit (the ATLAS.ti screen you are looking at) as a transparent sheet of paper laid over your primary document. The coding and analytic work is stored on the transparent-like paper of the HU file, *not on the actual primary document file*. Thus, each time the HU is opened for work, the software goes to the HU file folder ("practice project") and grabs the associated PDs. When reopening the HU project, the PDs and the HU are *automatically joined* and you are ready to work. This feature of ATLAS.ti is one of the most important for you to understand, so take a few minutes to practice and integrate this.

Second, the next step in assigning PDs to the HU is to highlight the PDs in your "practice project" folder and one at a time (or all at once) drag and drop them into the PD manager (not the icon, but the empty rectangular box to its right—the arrow in Figure 2.3 is pointing to the box). Practice steps one and two by dragging and dropping primary documents into your saved HU project called "practice project." When finished, your HU will appear similar to Figure 2.3. The first document you assign is automatically given an ATLAS.ti number P1, and the second P2, and so on. The unique identification number (0001 or parentfocusgroup, etc.) that the primary document was originally named will be to the right of the primary document number. In Figure 2.3, it is *P1: Social Worker Client Treatment* (treatment is truncated); as part of an IRB approved research project, we had given the file name "Social Worker Client Treatment" to the transcript of a specific social worker/client interaction.

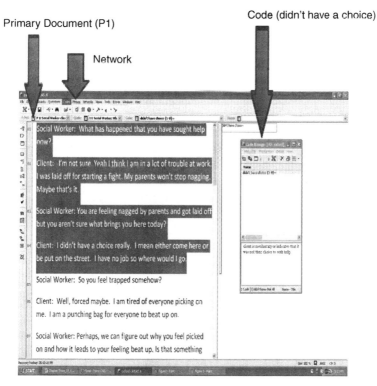

Figure 2.3 Illustration of HU.

Caution! Once a PD has been assigned to an HU and you have started coding the PD, *do not change* the contents of the PD because ATLAS.ti expects every word and line to be in the same position when it freshly opens the project. There is one exception to this rule; if you did not change the text, but added new text below the line or word you last coded, technically you could add new text without affecting how ATLAS.ti reads the document. But, play it safe! Have the written transcript (the data) in the final format (font size, spacing, and data content) before assigning to the HU.

Before advancing to the next section, practice the above several times. Open and close your HU unit, for example. Navigate back and forth from the "research project" and "practice project" folders to integrate where the HU file and primary documents reside. Memorize how ATLAS. ti grabs the primary documents when opening. Now, you are ready to learn basic coding.

Selecting Text and Coding

Selecting a quotation, making a code, and navigating among text, quotation, code, and code manager is described next. Except for the content of the primary document, your HU looks similar to Figure 2.3. Go to the primary document manager and highlight any assigned document and it will open to view, as depicted in Figure 2.3. Place the cursor in the open document and left click on the mouse and highlight a portion of text. (In Figure 2.3, the grey highlighted text is an example.) Next, move the cursor to the menu bar and click on "codes." A drop down menu will appear. Click on the first choice: "create free code" (see Figure 2.4). At the same time, a menu box opens called "free code(s)."

Inside the "free code" pop-up menu type the word "code1" and click OK. Next, move the cursor to the code menu bar again. When the code pop-up menu opens, move down and click on "code manager." A code manager menu will open (see Figure 2.3). Drag the open code manager with the mouse and move it to the right of your primary document text (as it is depicted in Figure 2.3). Your screen view will now look similar to Figure 2.3. For practice, highlight text in the primary document. Next, with the code manager open to the right, highlight "code1" and with the mouse, drag and drop the code on top of the highlighted text. In the margin to the left of your text, notice how the code is linked to the quotation by brackets.

Free Code popup Menu

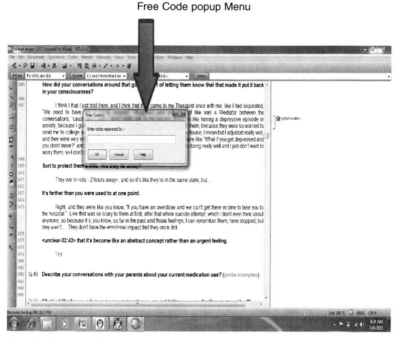

Figure 2.4 Making a Code Name.

Two ways to code text have been described: (1) typing a new code from inside the free code menu and, (2) by dragging and dropping a code already used. Great! Practice by making several new codes: code2, code3, and code4. Notice that these codes are accumulating alphabetically in your code manager. Next, navigate from text to code manager and back again. Highlight and drag code2 over a new quotation. Fantastic.

Next, write a comment on "code1." Inside the code manager, highlight "code1" and right click the mouse: a pop-up menu will appear and one choice among others is "edit comment." Click on edit comment. When the edit comment menu opens (see Figure 2.5), type one or two sentences that describe what you think the code means, represents, or refers to; then, click "save."

For example, the highlighted quotation in Figure 2.3 has a code in the right margin: "didn't have choice." The "didn't have choice" code appears in the code manager (open and to the right on the screen). And when the code is highlighted, its attached comment is displayed at the bottom of

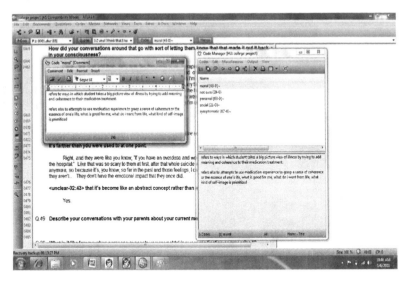

Figure 2.5 Making a Comment.

the code manager: "client is involuntary or indicates that it was not their choice to seek help." In Figure 2.5, the "moral" code is highlighted, so the comment defining that code is shown. Attaching comments to codes defines the code and assists in reliably using the code. For example, when attaching an existing code to a new quotation, read the comment description before attaching the code. This step assists the coder in creating new codes *only* when an existing one does not adequately represent the quotation (i.e., the code doesn't fit the quotation).

You have learned basic coding using ATLAS.ti. Practice the preceding steps and integrate these new skills before advancing to the next section.

Descriptive and Conceptual Coding

In the previous section, coding was described in a technical manner. However, coding is data reduction; therefore, it is also conceptual work. Deriving code names from respondent words reduces a larger block of quotations to short code names and is called descriptive or in-vivo coding. Indeed, returning to the preceding discussion about themes, a descriptive code is an emerging theme. Descriptive coding is the closest to the actual data, and because the code name is derived from actual respondent voices (transcribed text), a type of validity is established. In other words, a descriptive code should evoke in the coder (or outside reviewer) a thought that requires little effort in "seeing" the data. Descriptive codes should register in the reader's mind a direct link to the actual quotation; in the earlier example (Figure 2.3), the "didn't have choice" is a descriptive code. The client sought help, in part, out of a sense that he had no choice of his own. The "didn't have choice" descriptive code can now be attached to any quotation, within and across primary documents, that evokes a similar thought. The "didn't have choice" code is now a bucket that the coder is filling with as many examples as the entire dataset serves up. In sum, the first step in conceptual coding is descriptive coding. This work will produce numerous codes and a type of glossary or index to your data; the index is the starting place for the next level of coding (Figure 2.5 has five codes, for example).

The next strategic step, conceptual coding (in grounded theory called axial coding), is largely dependent on the aim and research question. Imagine an investigation of client motivation for seeking help. Through descriptive coding of clinical process notes, or recordings of initial client meetings (recall, in ATLAS.ti, these transcribed interviews are now called primary documents), a help-seeking index is created. In Figure 2.3, we attached a "didn't have choice" code to all quotations that referenced those clients who felt they were pressured or forced into treatment. Yet are all examples of "didn't have choice" equivalent? The latter question challenges researchers to think more abstractly and conceptually about their descriptive codes. Indeed, "didn't have choice" may represent several types of help-seeking categories. And knowing the difference might promote better and more efficient clinical engagement, our research aim. Thus, conceptual coding is the work of looking inside the "didn't have choice" descriptive bucket, for example, and developing a strategy for separating examples into more abstract, umbrella categories.

For illustration, let's use an everyday food example. A table stacked with food items is prepared, and you are asked to identify (i.e., research aim) a fast food category that would meaningfully represent the food items. Descriptive coding sorts the items into similar categories: pickle, lettuce, tomato, ketchup, mustard, beef patty, and bread—toasted light brown and two halves the shape of a full moon. No single food item (pickle, lettuce, etc.) could represent the whole, but when "seeing" the separate items as a group, the items evoke in your mind: "hamburger." In sum, comparing each food item and sorting similar food into a unique bucket (i.e., codes) is descriptive coding. By comparing the contents within each bucket and conceptualizing these as related (or not related, which means remove that quotation from the bucket), conceptual coding assigns a higher level, or abstract code (e.g., hamburger), to the lower level codes (e.g., pickle, lettuce, etc.). Of course, you won't be coding food. However, you would code the numerous descriptive parts of social worker/client engagement (i.e., initial call, setting an appointment, making the initial appointment, identifying what brings them in now, etc.) and assign higher-level codes (i.e., transference or countertransference) to particular descriptive interactions.

In ATLAS.ti, the network tool assists with conceptual coding. Return (Figure 2.3) to the descriptive example "didn't have a choice"; imagine the possible reasons a client might feel that they didn't have a choice; one could be a condition of probation or outpatient commitment. Another might be parental threat to stop financial support. Still, there may be no other counseling center in the region that has a sliding-fee scale. Each of these examples represents a different involuntary dimension for why a client might initiate treatment. Moreover, in trying to fulfill your research aim of understanding engagement, each of these examples may require slightly different engagement approaches.

The network bucket collects related descriptive codes so they can be sorted into higher-level conceptual or dimensional codes. To start, navigate (see Figure 2.3) to the second line at the top of the screen and there you will see a "network" button; click on it and then click on "new network view." A pop-up menu will open and ask for a name of the network. For now, give it the name: "involuntary." A network view is created (see Figure 2.6). When conceptual coding, you are essentially sorting descriptive codes into buckets of related codes. Thus, think of the network tool as a bucket that is filled with descriptive codes that can be sorted into relationships (for a refresher, review paragraphs above on descriptive and conceptual coding).

With your mouse, drag the "involuntary" network view and position it to the left of your open code manager; if both are open you will see them side-by-side on the screen (see Figure 2.6). Next, grab and drag descriptive codes (e.g., code1 and code2) into the network view and drop

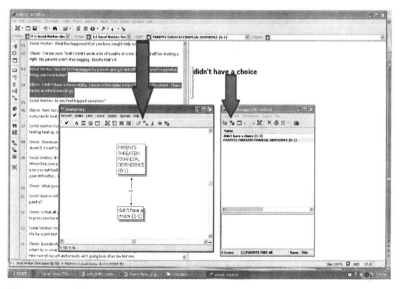

Figure 2.6 Making a Network.

them; notice they now appear in your network view. In our illustration, we dropped "didn't have a choice" into the network view.

At the top of the open code manager (see Figure 2.6), click on "codes" and then click on "create a free code." When the free code pop-up menu appears, type—PARENTS THREATEN FINANCIAL DEPENDENCE—and then click "OK." Notice the code appears in your code manager just as you typed it (you have just learned another technique for creating a code name). With your mouse, grab, drag, and drop the conceptual code into the "involuntary" network view. The code "didn't have a choice" refers to a quotation in which the client felt he would be on the street if he did not initiate counseling.

Inside the network view, left click once on one of the codes you placed there—code1 or code2. Next, at the top of the open network view on the third line, to the left of the scissor icon, there is another icon with two rectangular boxes connected by a line (see Figure 2.6). Left click on this icon (i.e., it is called the link or relations tool) and a cross appears with a red line. Position the cross over the conceptual code "PARENTS THREATEN FINANICAL DEPENDENCE," left click and a pop-up menu appears. Choose the option: "is associated with." A line creating a relation between the descriptive and conceptual code is created. You now have a "didn't have a choice" example connected to a higher-level concept: parents who threaten to cut off financial assistance if their son does not seek help. Now any time you have another quotation (from the same or different clients) referring to a parental threat to reduce financial assistance if counseling is not initiated or adhered to, then drag and drop the descriptive code over the new quotation; by doing so, this step will automatically accumulate these quotations in the "involuntary" network view (or bucket); it will also automatically link it to the code: "PARENTS THREATEN FINANICAL DEPENDENCE."

You have learned the basics and can begin a quick-start application of ATLAS.ti. We provided the least amount of software complexity so that you could start a project with the least amount of "software" intimidation. There is much more to learn. ATLAS.ti has many powerful tools, as so does NVivo. You have two choices for further training: (1) learn-by-doing, just click and learn; or (2) find a workshop or consultant who can provide additional training.

CASE ILLUSTRATION: YOUTH EXPERIENCE OF PSYCHOTROPIC TREATMENT

In this illustration we integrate critical realism and engaged scholarship with our methods. We use an everyday practice concern, psychopharmacological treatment, as the example and demonstrate how a clinical research aim and question can be generated from first identifying a specific *phenomenological practice gap*. Next, we design data collection methods and analytic strategies. Throughout, we return to ATLAS.ti and discuss how it can be used to manage and analyze data.

No matter how fine-tuned psychiatric drugs (i.e., brute facts) become—even with the additional billions that will no doubt be spent toward their refinement—we will always need to interpret their effects. Why? Drugs are *brute facts* (see chapter 1) operating according to neuro-anatomical and neurotransmitter determinants. Laboratory studies of chemical properties, clinical trials of newly developed drugs, and neuro-science experimental studies strive to establish scientific laws; that is, they seek to identify a brute fact, an unchanging neuroanatomical and chemical substrate that determines behavior. A critical realist perspective does not deny neuroanatomical and chemical substrates. Instead these entities have powers and liabilities to produce physical and biological effects, given certain controlled assumptions. However, critical realism does not subscribe to a flat ontology of brain, body, and mind. It rejects a simple linear, stimulus-response, or reflexive theory of brain-body-mind-behavior. Sensory inputs and motor outputs have a stratified ontology with multiple layers of biology, chemistry, neuroanatomy, mind, and environment, each influencing emotional, cognitive, and behavioral outcomes. Some of these processes are not transparent. They do not appear in a Petri dish. Drugs do not produce in everyone identical emotional, cognitive, and behavioral effects; even within an individual, the same effects may vary moment to moment. Drugs influence behavior in multiple ways and there are many reasons for why individuals choose them. The latter concerns are the result of "institutional facts." With medication, it is an institutional fact that a gap between the "desired" and the "actual" effects will be present. How often does a drug deliver exactly what is promised and what is hoped for? Sometimes drugs do and sometimes not. Even the smallest gap requires the medicated to make meaning of how drugs are experienced in and communicated through bodies. How we make meaning is always a part of our social and institutional experience (i.e., institutional fact). The distance between the actual and perceived experience of medication treatment shapes the meaning making process. And while neurotransmitters do not have the power to assign meaning, the properties of social and psychological entities do possess these emergent powers (Sayer, 2000); only the person (and those in their social surround) consuming a medication can make it a meaningful experience. These critical realist assumptions about psychotropic treatment underscore the need to organize engaged scholarship projects to investigate the "subjective experience" of psychotropic treatment.

Medication policy and practice are realized in the social worker/client interaction. Although not always sought, and often underappreciated by bench scientists and policymakers, identifying the institutional facts—how medication becomes a meaningful treatment—is a fundamental engaged scholarship *aim*. Theorists and policymakers are not held accountable if practitioners do not identify and write about the many gaps that exist when biological theory is put into practice. And we make researchers accountable when forming engaged scholarship projects. Bench scientist, psychiatrist, Food and Drug Administration official, pharmaceutical salesman, social worker, and the medicated all have *different yet interdependent points of view or knowledge claims* about medication treatment and effectiveness. Each group makes meaning (though in different ways, some according to scientific rules, others by experience) about what medications do and what they are for. Social workers, in particular, value "starting where the client is" because it supports client empowerment. At the very least, to act upon empowerment values, social workers must ask the medicated about their experience of taking medication. What does it do for you? What problem does it solve? What is your future on medication? Moreover, the values of a social worker influence the questions an engaged scholarship project would seek to answer. A bench scientist is typically not concerned about the end user; a pharmaceutical salesman has a unique motivation. Thus, each stakeholder has a different point of view and therefore values about psychopharmacological treatment. Yet stakeholders are not independent of each other and their knowledge claims lead to value claims: "medication treatment is good for all people." When an individual consumes medication, all stakeholders are implicated in the effects. Therefore, all stakeholders should be at the research table to design aims and questions that would bind together their different but interdependent medication interests. Engaged scholarship research would specify how different levels of medication reality produce different effects. Drugs affect the body, which affect the brain. Most have side effects. With children, a lot is at stake because their brains are still developing. Parents want stability at home. Teachers want quiet in the classroom. The psychiatrist wants compliance. Each of these stakeholders have different knowledge interests, values, and power; therefore, they have unique powers to affect the child's medication experience.

Illustration: Research Aim and Questions for Medicating Adolescents

How do adolescents make meaning of their psychotropic experience? What is known about their experience and, if known, how would it contribute to psychopharmacological knowledge? Over the past twenty years, adolescent use of psychiatric medication has grown substantially, causing concern among researchers, families, and practitioner groups (Cooper et al., 2006; Olfson, Marcus & Weissman, 2002; Thomas, Conrad, Casler, & Goodman, 2006; Wong, Murray, Camilleri-Novak, & Stephens, 2004). Researchers have therefore called for studies of safety and efficacy because, it is argued, children and adolescents metabolize medication differently from adults. Yet despite increasing scientific investigation into the effectiveness and tolerability of psychotropic agents in young people, there is a paucity of data on how adolescents subjectively experience treatment. We concluded from our review of the literature that we should not assume that youth and adults make meaning of illness and medication treatment in the same manner. Indeed, social scientists have emphasized the many ways, active and passive, in which adults understand mental illness, diagnosis, medication treatment, and adherence (Charmaz, 1990; Conrad, 1985; Karp, 1996; Kleinman, 1988). Among adults with major depression, for example, David Karp (1996, p. 102) concluded that "the experience of taking antidepressant medications involves a complex and emotionally charged interpretive process in which nothing less than one's view of self is at stake." Thus, while the knowledge gap about the safety and efficacy of youth psychotropic treatment is gradually being addressed, we turned our attention to the gap between desired and actual treatment experiences. Research on safety and efficacy addresses how youths' bodies and brains metabolize drugs. Drug metabolism, however, is just one level of determination, one level of a stratified body-brain-mind-society ontology.

Parents and teachers worry about falling grades. Adolescents worry about weight gain or drowsiness, both common side effects of antipsychotics. Medication treatment and its effects produce different meanings depending upon power, perspective, and knowledge. Engaged scholarship can make visible what the pharmaceutical industry has taken for granted. For the industry, blood circulates drugs to neurotransmitters (i.e., brute facts) and produces, one hopes, a knowable effect. This is not true for patients, doctors, families, teachers, and friends, however, for whom meanings continuously circulate in maximally open systems (i.e., institutional facts) and where questions are raised about what medications are for, what they do, and how long will they be taken. Specific *research questions* must point to data. Thus, we asked (1) How do adolescents experience and talk about psychotropic treatment? (2) What do they think the medications do for them? (3) How do they know medications are working?

Given the critical realist assumptions about psychotropic treatment, qualitative methods can address a specific phenomenological medication practice gap, a level of medication reality that bench scientist and clinical drug trials have not studied. Engaged scholarship should involve the adolescent and offer findings for the larger community (e.g., psychiatrists, pharmaceutical companies, bench scientists) to discuss. Such findings would widen the scope of bio-psychopharmacological treatment to include meaning making. In the next section, we describe a project that involved adolescents medicated with psychiatric drugs. We first describe our data collection and analytic strategies. We conclude by relating the findings to critical realism and social work practice in the open system of psychopharmacological intervention.

Data Collection

The qualitative data were gathered by using a semi-structured interview instrument (TeenSEMI), an adaptation of an adult version, Subjective Experience of Medication Interview (Jenkins et al., 2005; 1997). The TeenSEMI was produced by eliminating or modifying questions for adults (e.g., questions about work, marriage, and recovery) and developing age-relevant questions (e.g., questions about school, peer, and family interactions). The final interview schedule, approximately 150 questions, taking approximately two hours, included nine categories related to illness, treatment, and medication: (1) treatment, illness, and medication history; (2) perceptions of medication; (3) managing, monitoring, and reporting of medication experience; (4) parent and adolescent interaction regarding medication management; (5) illness and medication stigma; (6) medication management and school interactions; (7) peer interactions and medication management; (8) access to mental health services and medication experience; and (9) ethnicity, gender, and religious influences on the medication experience.

Open-ended questions were constructed to minimize the effects of asking respondents leading questions. Instead of asking, "What is your diagnosis?" which would presuppose illness as "a diagnosis," subjects were asked, "You see Dr. X, would you describe in your own words what you see him/her for?" The follow-up was, "Were you concerned enough about what you just mentioned that you yourself wanted to seek help from Dr. X?" Only after nine open-ended questions did interviewers ask, "Have you ever been given a diagnosis or name for the concerns we have been talking about?" The TeenSEMI was also constructed to elicit positive and negative feelings about illness, treatment, and medication. For example, "What do you like about the medication?" had a companion question, "What don't you like about the medication?" Interviewers were instructed to follow the direction taken by respondents; however, the semi-structured schedule provided guidelines for assuring that most would talk about some aspect of the nine categories listed above.

Two researchers pilot-tested the TeenSEMI by observing one another's first interviews, listening to the recordings, and then modifying questions to make them developmentally appropriate, less leading, and more conversational. To minimize inter-interviewer variability, additional interviewers (four total) were trained by observing interviews conducted by the principal researcher.

Sample and Recruitment

A convenience sampling technique was used by recruiting adolescents through discussions with professional staff and by posting flyers at a university hospital adolescent mental health, outpatient clinic; community mental health outpatient setting; and an alternative high school for adolescents with emotional and behavioral problems. Without the assistance of administrators and staff, we would not have been able to efficiently recruit respondents; the sampling was successful because of our engaged scholarship approach to recruitment. Adolescents, ages twelve to seventeen, meeting DSM-IV criteria for a psychiatric illness and currently prescribed a psychotropic medication were eligible. Participants were excluded when parents reported that the adolescent had not taken psychiatric medication at least once in the past thirty days. Moreover, adolescents with developmental disability (i.e., IQ lower than 70), a pervasive developmental disorder, seizure disorder, or an organic brain disorder, were not enrolled. The latter sampling strategy sought to reduce cognitive differences in the sample.

In addition to data produced with the semi-structured instrument, we collected adolescent and family demographics and psychiatric/medication treatment history. The Kiddie Schedule for Affective Disorders for School-Age Children Present and Lifetime Version (K-SADS-PL) (Kaufman et al., 1997) was used to determine participant diagnoses and the Child Global Assessment Scale (Shaffer et al., 1983) was used to assess overall functioning at home, with peers, and in school. The K-SADS-PL, a semistructured research interview, has been used as a standard to assign diagnostic categories in clinical drug trials or psychosocial intervention studies. It assesses symptom constellations according to DSM-IV psychiatric diagnoses in pediatric patients based on information provided by youth and parents or caregivers. The K-SADS-PL diagnostic interviews were conducted by a researcher trained as a "rater" to administer the instrument. The use of the K-SADS-PL does not resolve the many issues related to diagnostic validity because symptom-based diagnostic systems are known to be culturally and historically sensitive (Horwitz & Wakefield, 2007; Kirk & Kutchins, 1992). For example, controversy exists over whether or not bipolar illnesses are accurately applied to youth (Moreno et al., 2007; Smith, 2007). In our research, the use of the K-SADS-PL meant that the researcher/rater followed the protocols for symptom-based diagnosis, and when the outcome was bipolar, for example, trained raters (with a kappa ≥ 85) would have agreed with the diagnosis 85% of the time.

The research protocol was reviewed and approved by the university hospital institutional review board for human investigation. The parents/guardians of the research participants provided written informed consent, and all adolescents provided written informed assent prior to study participation. The interviews conducted under the auspices of this study took approximately six hours. Parents received $50 and adolescents $65, respectively, as honoraria.

The protocol led to the following sample profile. The average age was 14.3; 66% of the sample started medications at ten or younger (the youngest was five). At the time of the study, many were prescribed two or more, and among the comorbid conditions, mood and attention deficit disorders were the most common. Table 2.1 provides a demographic and clinical profile of our final participant pool.

Data Analytic Strategy

Responses to the TeenSEMI were transcribed. The sample yielded nearly 8,500 pages of transcripts and nearly 200 hours of audio recordings. We had nearly 4500 (30 x 150) audio-recorded responses, some ten seconds in length and some five minutes. In short, the data for this project were large enough to warrant using software, including Apple's iTunes (see Box 2.6).

In the first analytic step, coders identified themes in the medication experience. First, we read each of the thirty transcripts—sometimes

Table 2.1 Sample Demographics

Age	
12	5 (17%)
13	8 (27%)
14	4 (13%)
15	3 (10%)
16	6 (20%)
17	4 (13%)
Mean 14.3 (1.74)	

Gender	
Male	11 (36%)
Female	19 (64%)

Ethnicity	
African American	11 (36%)
Caucasian	15 (50%)
Hispanic	2 (7%)
Other	2 (7%)

Age started medications	
2.5	1 (3%)
3.5	1 (3%)
4	1 (3%)
5	1 (3%)
6	2 (7%)
7	0 (0%)
8	1 (3%)
9	7 (23%)
10	5 (17%)
11	3 (10%)
12	1 (3%)

(*Continued*)

Table 2.1 Sample Demographics (*Cont'd*)

13	2 (7%)
14	1 (3%)
15	1 (3%)
16	2 (7%)
Mean 9.66 (3.47)	1 (3%)
Number of prescribed medications	
1	11 (36%)
2	8 (27%)
3	8 (27%)
4	2 (7%)
5	0 (0%)
6	1 (3%)
Mean 2.17 (1.21)	
Diagnosis	
Bipolar spectrum/mood disorder	15 (50%)
Major depressive disorder	8 (27%)
ADHD	6 (20%)
Schizophrenia	1 (3%)

several times. Second, we identified (and highlighted with ATLAS.ti) all quotations that referred to how adolescents described what they thought medications were for; what they thought medications did for them; and how they conceptualized medication working. Third, we created codes and using ATLAS.ti linked them to quotations; in most instances we created a code name from some of the respondent's actual words: in-vivo coding. Fourth, quotations attached to a specific in-vivo code were compared to determine those that did not fit; we created new codes for mismatched quotations. Finally, we compared and sorted the in-vivo codes into higher-level or conceptual codes. A reliability and validity assessment of the final codes was produced by (1) double-checking to assure the codes referring to quotations were consistently applied across all interviews; (2) double-checking to assure codes were appropriately grouped under the thematic categories; and, (3) double-checking to assure themes were appropriately grouped under conceptual codes. The above coding strategy resulted in the identification of six salient themes: (1) emotional; (2) behavioral; (3) diagnosis; (4) cognitive; (5) body, and (6) intersubjective. This analytic work (see Box 2.9) provided a *descriptive* view of medication experience. In the second stage of the analysis, using the network tool (see Figure 2.6), quotations attached to

---

Box 2.9 Thematic Illustrations

Emotional (N − 275 quotations assigned to this theme)
  I don't remember none of the outbursts. I remember like last outburst that I had, I went. I just wanted to get out of the house, and I remember just wanting to get out of the house. I couldn't stand being in the house. So all that I remember is walking out of the house and starting walking, and I walked up to the mall, and next thing I knew, I was perfectly fine. (ID 0007)
  Behavioral (N = 326 quotations assigned to this theme)
  Yeah, because I'm hyper and I eat too much sugar and I'll stay up all night sometimes, and my mom says, "Take your pills." (0042)
  Diagnosis (N = 148 quotations assigned to this theme)
  Depression, mostly depression, multiple other things, anxiety that go along with . . . Anxiety and depression, like those are the main. (0024)
  Cognitive (N = 167 quotations assigned to this theme)
  Cause I usually don't pay attention before I was on it, and now that I'm on it, I get good grades. (0025)
  Body (N = 224 quotations assigned to this theme)
  I visualize it going in my brain and make some reactor go off in my brain and some chemical process comes through. I don't know, like some shock of chemical. They make it sound like . . . From the commercial they make it seem like those little neurons hit each other or something and they stop missing, 'cause they say I have a chemical imbalance too, that along with my depression. (0015)
  Intersubjective (N = 58 quotations assigned to this theme)
  My parents' happiness. They think I'm happier. The fact that I'm not outraged at everything and that I'm a little nicer to people most of the time. (0023)

the six themes were compared and grouped under dimensional catego-ries. In short, we re-read the quotations attached to each of the six themes and asked: What conceptual categories could subsume the six themes? In other words, with grounded theory technique, we showed how the six themes could be related and used to develop a conceptual framework for understanding the dimensional aspects of medication experience. Table 2.2 lists the three dimensions that our strategy discovered, along with illustrations of the related themes and in-vivo codes.

In the next analytic stage, we used narrative theory—temporality and plot—to look at the storied nature of medication treatment. We won-dered, for example, if the interview data could be reconstructed to exam-ine (Ryan, 2007) what adolescents thought about the need for medication and what problem the medication was solving (narrative as problem solving). Second, we wondered how the reconstructed narratives were intertwined with those constructed by parents, teachers, and providers, especially when it came to seeking and engaging the mental health system; thus controversy and conflict were always possible (narrative as conflict and interpersonal). Mothers and fathers, for example, often disagreed over medication treatment. Third, from the adolescent perspective, medication was inextricably tied to their everyday—in the now—experi-ence of moods, actions, and thoughts (narrative as human experience).

Table 2.2 Higher-Level, Umbrella, or Dimensional Categories

	Dimension	*Dimension*	*Dimension*
	Beliefs about need for medication	Beliefs about medication effects, including side-effects	Belief about hoped-for effects
Themes	Cognitive—in-vivo *code*: "I can't concentrate"	Cognitive—in-vivo *code*: "it clears up my thinking"	Cognitive—in-vivo *code*: "stay focused"
Themes	Emotional—in-vivo *code*: "I am too moody"	Emotional—in-vivo *code*: "makes me anxious"	Emotional—in-vivo *code*: "keep me stable"
Themes	Behavioral—in-vivo *code*: "I can't make friends"	Behavioral—in-vivo *code*: "I get better grades"	Behavioral—in-vivo *code*: "graduate from high school"

And finally, subsequent to swallowing the first pill, adolescents were engaged in making sense of life before medication, on medication, and making sense of their future life with medication (narrative as temporality and plot). In short, we wondered about the underlying mechanisms responsible for moving a particular medication story forward. How was time accounted for?

Peter Brooks (1992) writes about the activity of plotting or shaping a story. Others, in analyzing clinical narratives, have identified "therapeutic plots" (Mattingly, 1998, p. 72). "Therapists work to create significant experiences for their patients because if therapy is to be effective, therapists must find a way to make the therapeutic process matter to patients" (1998, p. 82). For Brooks, plotting is "that which makes a plot 'move forward,' and makes us read forward, seeking in the unfolding of the narrative a line of intention and portent of design that hold the promise of progress toward meaning" (Brooks, 1992, p. xiii).

We studied each transcript again and reduced the entirety to several related paragraphs that summarized the respondent story. Thematic and GT coding techniques fragment stories because coding reduces large chunks of data to several words. Narrative techniques avoid fragmentation by identifying larger chunks and linking them to form a storied experience.[3]

The narrative technique of identifying a medication plot is illustrated in Box 2.10. In the experience of a thirteen-year-old, African-American male diagnosed with bipolar spectrum disorder and prescribed four medications, you will see in Box 2.10 the subtle ways he compared life on medication with life before or without medication. This respondent compared "life before medication" as full of emotional breakdowns, anger, lack of sleep, and stealing. In his interpretation of the effect of medication, his present orientation, he said that it helped him think before acting. And in his particular medication plot, that is, what compelled him to go forward with medication, he compared life before medication, life on medication, and a future life with medication; he hoped, in projecting his life forward, that "everything will be under control" and that he would not "steal" from others. This narrative technique resulted in identifying the medication plot for each respondent in the study. Daily comparisons among the medicated and numerous others in their social networks, comparisons of life before and on medication (illustrated in Box 2.10), was identified as the motor that pushed the medication plot

Box 2.10 Medication Plot

First, he organizes perceptions about why he needs medications:
Interviewer: Could you tell me in your own words what was the reason, from your point of view, why you saw her [psychiatrist who prescribes the medication] or why you see her?

I see her because I had angry outbursts and 'cause I had like emotional breakdowns. I go to her to talk out solutions and ways you could handle it and like a tool to help. Like when I get angry, I just go off sometimes, then I'm just like, "Leave me alone. Just leave me alone, just leave me alone." Can't nobody talk to me.

Interviewer: You didn't mention a sleeping problem. This is the first time you've said that. So you always had a sleeping problem or just recently?

My mom said when she used to lay me down, I used to turn blue, so I couldn't really sleep on my back, and now my nose is kind of like broken. They said I can't really sleep on my back. I can't really breathe, so I have bad dreams or something and can't really go to sleep like other people go straight to sleep. It'll just take me a good three or four hours to go to sleep.

Interviewer: And how long have you had trouble falling asleep?

Ever since fourth grade.

Interviewer: And so when did you start taking a medication so you could fall asleep?

Like last year.

Next, the adolescent interprets medication effects:
Interviewer: What do you think medications actually do for your concerns?

That I can be able to think clearer.

Interviewer: What do you mean by think clearer?

Like instead of feeling I was always in a bad mood, I can like think, but it makes me make better choices, like when I'm mad at somebody, I want to punish them, then I think, "No, I don't want to do it." I just leave it alone for right now. . . . Like I used to be mad for an hour, and now it only takes me like a couple of seconds to get myself back together.

Interviewer: Can you give examples of times when you decided not to take your medications?

When some of the kids found out, or sometimes I forgot my meds and my mom bring them, and some of the other kids see me, they'll start making fun of me like, "Why you got to take your meds and stuff?" Then, in the summer I stopped taking meds. I started to steal and things, doing stuff that wasn't me.

Interviewer: How does medication help you stay healthy?

Helps me like to think clearer, take care of myself, like my hygiene, and to do things, like to keep my grades up and things.

Third, the adolescent describes hoped for effects and future outlook:
Interviewer: Some people believe that we should not take medication and fix ourselves. What do you think about that?
It depends on how really people see it. If you see it in your own way, like, "I need it," like if you want to make yourself do better, like if you want to do it on your own, that's OK, but you might have some problems on the way. But if you were to take meds or something, it'll help you get into groups that can help you when you get off the meds, like they can help you, and the medicine makes you think clearer, like "If I do this, I might go to. . . . If I rob I store or something, I might go to jail, but if I don't, I'll be good."
Interviewer: What are your thoughts about how things will change with your concerns/diagnosis as you grow older?
Everything will be under control, like my breathing, my anger.

toward the promise that doctors, teachers, parents, and even pharmaceutical companies made about how medications treat mental problems. In fact, it is argued in the next section that this meaning-making work is an institutional fact as powerful as the chemical's action on brain and body.

Engaged Scholarship Findings for Practice

Research findings require interpretation *for practice*. In this final section, we interpret our medication findings and describe how the next research iteration would test and refine the proposed conceptual framework. Our research aim speculated that meaning was essential to psychotropic treatment and that medication experience was more than a brute fact.

The "need" for medication does not originate in the nervous system as an automatic response (Moerman, 2002). Adolescent "need" for medication was an institutional fact, constructed through the social relations of medication treatment and management: family, school, mental health, social work, illness, and biopsychiatry discourses. Psychiatrists made flat ontological assumptions about brain dysfunction and chemical imbalances and saw, therefore, medication as a necessity. For parents, however, medication led to harmonious family relations, adolescent compliance, and school achievement. The school discourse centered on focus, concentration, and hyperactivity. Finally, because these discursive practices were socially constructed, specific, and context-dependent, adolescent "need" for medication, or the problem it hoped to solve, could not be generalized from one adolescent to another. The need for medication is not a brute fact. It is and remains an institutional fact and in practice should be treated as such. Thus, in each case of adolescent psychotropic treatment, participants should be queried about the problem medication is thought to solve.

Once a medication regimen has been connected to a problem in the mind of the adolescent, then all parties engage in interpretive work.[4] And interpretations are often premised on a comparison: life before medication with life on medication. This comparison, we speculated, produced a medication plot connecting the medication themes and dimensions about need and daily effects with the promise of a better life. Findings showed that adolescents compare need and effects daily. And they tended to report those that they and others perceived as beneficial; usually these had clear empirical referents: better school performance, less quarreling with parents, less moody, less fidgety, and fewer fights. Comparing school performance before and after medication was a common plot. Because the "actual" effects of medication were quite complicated for most (i.e., medications rarely, if ever, produce the same effects for everyone), there was often a "wait and see" attitude, where by comparing before and after experience, one *imagined* the effects of medication. This interpretive and imaginative work was further complicated by competing and contradictory interpretations among providers, parents, teachers, and adolescents.

Moreover, the unintended side effects, or adverse events, were also perceived and identified; these include present-oriented bodily, emotional, cognitive, or behavioral referents: tremors, giddiness, zombie feelings, weight gain, and hyperactivity. And because individual side effect profiles were unique and always changing, they required constant "comparative" monitoring by the adolescent, parent, and prescriber.

Expectation and promise was produced in an interpersonal tension between what the adolescent hoped for and what significant others (i.e., parents, peers, teachers, and clinicians) hoped for. This expectation was produced at multiple sites where adolescents engaged in relationships: school, home, mental health clinics or offices, and peer groups. There was, for example, a hope on behalf of the adolescent that their parents, peers, teachers, and clinicians recognized the "medicated" self as normal, not defective, and symptom free.

These findings have practice implications. Social workers have an obligation to help youth understand their medication narrative. Youth may need assistance in developing a narrative specific to their medication experience. In doing so, social workers are not treating medication as brute facts, but as institutional facts. The open system of medication meaning making does not assume a single, biological narrative. Instead, social workers should assist youth and their parents in closing the gap between diagnosis and medication treatment, between hoped-for and actual effects, by assisting all participants in the development of a medication narrative. Sometimes the narrative may include the decision to terminate medication treatment. In short, there is no way to predict the adherence outcome of a narrative; what is predictable is that some form of narrative generates *the meaning* that contributes to adherence or not.

Medication treatment complicates the monitoring of and adherence to medication, thus creating potential gaps between psychopharmacological knowledge and its application in open systems (i.e., schools, neighborhoods, residential treatment centers, foster families). Gaps exist when there is divergence between the academic/research field, especially clinical trials, which typically valorize controlled studies that seek overarching trends, and the open and fluid practice fields in the day to day lives and routines of youth and families. It is here that we used findings to conceptualize a medication grid. The grid can be used to map the myriad ways others engage patients in five elements of medication experience: (1) diagnosis, (2) prescription, (3) access to medication, (4) monitoring, and (5) reporting. In completing the everyday actions that the five elements require, grid participants (including the medicated) co-construct meanings of medication influence upon daily living; these dynamic interactions are various and sometimes overlapping, competing, or contradictory prescriber, parent, and youth *narrative constructions* of the medication treatment experience.

These narratives convey information based upon "processes of attention, interpretation, labeling, and social presentation" (Kirmayer, 2005, p. 833). Practitioners, patients, and family members may use different narratives in their labeling of the disorder; in their understandings of the cause, seriousness, and course of illness and medication treatment effects in/on the body and mind; anxieties about the illness and medication; and different expectations about preferred or ideal treatments and hoped for outcomes. Narratives refer to specific symptoms, syndromes, disorders, or to broader categories. Practitioner, family and social network, and patient narratives deploy varying theories of the body, brain, mind, self, and identity. What we called medication narratives referred to three illness and treatment questions (Floersch, Longhofer, Kranke, & Townsend, 2010; Floersch et al., 2009): (1) What problem (i.e., behavioral, emotional, and cognitive) does medication solve? (2) What are the actual effects (moment to moment), including side effects? (3) What is the future outlook on medication? Moreover, the central process of co-constructing narratives is associated with how various participants identify the emotional, behavioral, and cognitive effects of medication and construct meaningful narratives around them (Garro, 2000). Together the medication grid and the resulting narratives point to the significance of invested adults co-constructing with adolescents meaningful understandings that give shape to the attitudes toward and beliefs about medication treatment and adherence (Longhofer & Floersch, 2010).

And finally, to address gaps (Arnd-Caddigan & Pozzuto, 2008; Aram & Salipante, 2003; Longhofer & Floersch, 2004) among researcher, prescriber, and patient narratives, we propose the use of arbitrage (Van De Ven & Johnson, 2006), a conceptual framework and process for the integration of competing and sometimes incommensurable knowledge and practice claims (Boyer, 1990; Huff, 2000; Pettigrew, 2001; Starkey & Madan, 2001; Tranfield & Starkey, 1998). Arbitrage serves not to reconcile but to recognize differences. The production of knowledge about medication events, we argue, must occur through arbitrage, that is, through the use of comparison of different medication narratives (Bellefeuille & Ricks, 2010). And it is by identifying those features of medication events and experience (i.e., client, family, and practitioner) that appear invariant, or convergent (Azevedo, 1997), across the narratives that we can learn something about the true complexities of medicating events among youth. As with all parties to medicating children (Longhofer & Floersch, 2010), there are often inconsistent and contradictory perspectives about the causes of illness, rival narrative constructions of medication events (Floersch et al., 2010; Groleau, Kirmayer, & Young, 2006; Stern, & Kirmayer, 2004), and wide-ranging understandings of both the intended and unintended effects (biological, social, and psychological) of medication and the desired outcomes (Longhofer &

Floersch, 2010). Multiple and sometimes competing narratives, or "pluralistic perspectives should not be dismissed as noise, error, or outliers" (Van de Ven, 2007, p. 15), and that knowledge produced through arbitrage can be used to integrate the realities of direct practice with adolescents and the many and complex players in their medication grids (Longhofer et al., 2003). It is through this type of engagement, in collaboration and negotiation with the medicated and their myriad caregivers, that researchers and practitioners can jointly engage in practice-relevant research and research-relevant practice.

In the next chapter we illustrate how institutional ethnography was used to conduct an engaged scholarship investigation of a phenomenological practice gap (PPG) that was produced in a mental health system. Institutional ethnography (IE) is a qualitative research method that is particularly suited to explore PPGs produced by institutional facts. As with other approaches to qualitative research, IE begins with identifying aims and questions, data collection, and analytic strategies. We show how methods discussed in chapter 2 can be used within the framework of IE.

3

Institutional Ethnography

The central aim of this chapter is to illustrate how an engaged scholarship investigation discovered policy (and related constraints) effects on the everyday experience of case managers and clients. Specifically, we introduce the fundamentals of institutional ethnography (IE), and then we illustrate its potential for examining a policy-mandated, standardized practice.

Social workers are increasingly asked—or required by organizational and/or policy mandates—to deliver evidence-based interventions and to utilize standardized measures to evaluate practice. Standardization requires outcome measures that have been reliably and validly tested. Standardized interventions are like baking recipes; in using a recipe, one measures particular ingredients to create, for example, an apple as opposed to cherry pie. A standardized, "evidence-based" intervention is a group of specified practice means/ends actions that have been variables-based tested and found to be associated with desired client outcomes. "Fidelity" to an evidence-based practice means its implementation is in strict accordance with the "recipe."

The emphasis on standardized practices is driven by value commitments (Sayer, 2011, pp. 60–64). Imagine a child diagnosed with a serious illness. As a parent you would want the best "state of the art" treatment; that is, treatment that has been tested and offers the best chance of a positive outcome. In social work practice and research, moreover, we make value commitments: not every end is a desirable end. If our intervention produced racism it would not be a desirable outcome. Workers thus utilize interventions that help clients achieve the best (i.e., most valued) and desired outcome. However, in service environments where practitioners are fiscally challenged to do more with less, ends are often *specified* as the cost-effective best practice. For example, a standardized, time-limited cognitive-behavioral therapy for depression, which utilizes a standardized pretest and posttest of depression, is often considered a more fiscally responsible choice than a nonstandardized, interpersonal intervention. While *variables-based* (see chapter 1) empirical research supporting specific interventions (i.e., evidence-based practice) is the norm for standardized or manualized (i.e., producing a manual) practice, social work is practiced in open, complex policy and regulatory environments; the latter affect both the type of practice and the modes of implementation. In countries where health insurance companies or governmental agencies "manage" payment allocations (i.e., managed care), practitioner/agency reimbursement is typically tied to time-limited, treatments. Often decisions to reimburse are based on standardized interventions.

Qualitative research reveals gaps between the closed-system assumptions of standardized practice and the open system of actual practice (Shaw & Gould, 2001). The study of how standardized mandates are implemented or practiced in actual settings is critical where practice standardization is sought. And because institutional ethnography is an established method for studying the social processes of organizational life, it is particularly well suited for studying the effects of policy implementation.

OVERVIEW OF INSTITUTIONAL ETHNOGRAPHY

As stated in chapter 2, the aim of doing practice research or evaluation is to understand a social work event, circumstance, interaction, or intervention as it unfolds in open systems. Implementation of a specific policy inevitably affects local practice. Practitioners produce policy implementation by conducting activities that interconnect over time and space. For example, imagine that a college has instituted a new parking policy meant to redesignate parking lots by fields of study or discipline. The policy goal is to increase convenience by matching parking lots to student and faculty fields of study. To "implement" such a policy, a number of interrelated tasks must be completed. New parking tags have to be created, ordered, and mass-produced. Someone must match areas of study with particular parking tags, and particular tags with lots. Others need to distribute information about the new policy to students, faculty, and staff. Once the policy is implemented, numerous individuals must monitor the policy to assure that it is being implemented according to plan, including enforcing consequences—such as ticketing and towing. Although the people implementing this parking policy may never actually have contact with one another, and their perspectives and roles in managing the processes of parking may vastly differ, their work nonetheless is highly interrelated. The policy goal is to increase parking convenience for students, faculty, and staff; however, in an open system, institutional facts—including planned and unexpected—influence the actual implementation.

Using IE, the implementation of a policy can be studied; to do so, begin by drawing a flow chart of various interrelated actions, *beginning with one particular perspective among all participants.* Such interrelated tasks and activities work in concert to structure and coordinate the experience of "getting a legal parking spot." It is a *brute* fact that the car itself becomes gravitationally aligned (i.e., gravity exists whether we like it or have any conception about it or not) to a particular parking spot on earth; but "getting a legal parking spot" is an *institutional* fact (see chapter 1). Parking policymakers and targeted drivers socially construct, through their actions and interpretations, the lived experience of "getting a legal parking spot."

Let's develop the parking example further. Start thinking about IE by identifying all the related tasks that result in parking a car. Imagine driving to campus. You are trying to find a parking spot; you consult a map (created by someone) to locate an appropriate lot; you make sure that the new parking pass is clearly and appropriately displayed. You locate an open spot, park the car, and walk to class. Several minutes later, an attendant drives by to confirm that the parking tag matches the new policy for that lot. Although the administrators implementing the policy, the parking attendant monitoring the policy, and the driver are likely never to meet, social processes have created "textually mediated" (Campbell & Gregor, 2002) relations; drivers use maps and attendants read parking passes. Like parking, social work unfolds in environments where intertextual interactions structure the particular ways of doing social work. These organizational activities produce *institutional* facts and are indicators of "social organization" (Campbell & Gregor, 2002). Thus "getting a parking spot on campus," which may seem routine and just "the way things are," is actually produced by *institutional* facts structured by people and actions before and after the actual parking event. These activities also involve values. We value cars. And because we value cars we must give considerable emphasis to parking them.

So what does parking a car have in common with social work practice? Simply put, practices are tied to policies and procedures that structure activities such as "completing an assessment with a client" or "filling out an outcome measure with a client." Just as the implementation of a campus parking policy is essentially a series of means/ends actions and processes occurring over space and time, *implementation of social policies entail interrelated activities of social workers in real time across locations and dates, which organize what we can and cannot do with our clients.*

To understand all the potential constraints and influences of a particular practice experience, such as "filling out an outcome measure with a client," one needs to ask *how* the social organization structures practice; for example, who are the people involved, and what activities must be organized in order to properly "fill out an outcome measure." Ethnography, which may combine both in vivo and retrospective approaches (see chapter 2), is the research method of choice in seeking to understand *how* something occurs in real time and space (Mosse, 2003; Schultze & Boland, 2000; David, 2003; Werner, 2004; Pettigrew, 1997). In studying how practice activities and related policies interrelate, Wedel et al. (2005) and Smith (1987, 2005) specifically advocate an ethnographic approach that expands the ethnographic field (traditionally defined according to geographic boundaries) to encompass extended, interrelated social processes among people who may never meet face-to-face but whose work tasks nonetheless affect each other. According to Wedel et al. (2005), "today, 'the field' often consists of loosely connected actors with varying degrees of institutional leverage located in multiple sites that are not always geographically fixed" (p. 39).

Although the name "institutional ethnography" (IE) suggests investigative processes similar to those of traditional (cultural) ethnographic methods (with localized fields defined by geographic boundaries), IE is

---

Box 3.1 Different Kinds of Ethnographies

Introduction/overview of ethnography:

- Agar, M. (1996). *Professional stranger: An informal introduction to ethnography*, 2nd ed., Academic Press.
- Fetterman, D. M. (1998). *Ethnography*, 2nd ed., Thousand Oaks, CA: Sage.
- Hammersley, M. (1990). *Reading ethnographic research: A critical guide*. London: Longman.
- Harris, M., & Johnson, O. (2000). *Cultural anthropology*, 5th ed., Needham Heights, MA: Allyn and Bacon.

Using ethnography to understand social work practice:

- DeMontigny, G. (2005). *Social working: An ethnography of front-line practice*. Toronto: University of Toronto Press.
- Floersch, J. (2004). A method for investigating practitioner use of theory in practice. *Qualitative Social Work*, 3(2), 161–177.

Using ethnography to understand social work policy:

- Campbell, M., & Gregor, F. (2002). *Mapping social relations: A primer in doing institutional ethnography*. Garamond Press: Aurora.
- Mosse, D. (2003). Good policy is unimplementable? Reflections on the ethnography of aid policy and practice. Paper presented at the EIDOS Workshop on "Order and Disjuncture: the Organization of Aid and Development," London 26–28.
- Shore, C., & Wright, S. (1997). *Anthropology of public policy: Critical perspectives on governance and power*. London: Routledge.

---

not primarily focused upon a rich detailed account of cultural effects—the usual end-result of traditional ethnographies. Rather, the IE approach introduced in this chapter and developed by sociologist Dorothy Smith (1987) describes a detailed account of the *interconnected social processes* that structure and organize everyday experience. Smith (1987) uses the metaphor of the cube—emerging in perspective when points are connected—to illustrate how IE investigations strive to "see" the translocal, transtemporal relations (processes) coordinating people's activities in particular local sites. (See Figure 3.1.)

To generate an account of interconnected social relations (processes) across individuals, organizational practice, and policy areas, IE assumes (1) that aspects of individuals' material life experiences are socially organized

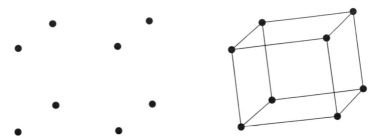

Figure 3.1 Cube Metaphor for Institutional Ethnography (IE).
Source: Smith, D. (1987) in Devault, M., Institutional Ethnography: Online Resources and Discussion. URL: http://faculty.maxwell.syr.edu/mdevault, accessed 2/15/08

through the interplay of institutionalized, extended social relations (i.e., processes) and (2) that tracking and explicating the embedded nature of these social relations (processes) is empowering and useful to the individuals whose everyday lives are being affected (Smith, 1987, pp.133–134).

Social relations (processes)—particularly the translocal, transtemporal processes—are realized, in part, through what Smith has called the "textually-mediated social organization." To tap into this dimension of social organization, IE employs fieldwork methods to study the dominant "texts-in-use," for example, the documents social workers use in practice (Smith, 1999). In social work, a text-in-use includes documents such as a progress note, a treatment or service plan, or an assessment form.

To reiterate, institutional ethnography (IE) is a qualitative method that treats the web of interrelated relationships of a given socially organized field of work (i.e., child welfare, mental health, juvenile justice, aging) as the ethnographic "field" or object of inquiry. In traditional cultural ethnography, the field is usually a geographic location such as a neighborhood or community, and the purpose of the investigation is to understand cultural dimensions. IE, in contrast, identifies and traces the web of relationships and activities that socially organize a given social phenomenon (e.g., "getting a parking spot"). The aim is to delineate *how* that social phenomenon is actually produced in real time in maximally open systems (see chapter 1 for discussion of open systems).

The basic premise of IE entails seeing a field through *particular standpoints*. This is in contrast to the researcher assuming the god's-eye point of view. For instance, in "getting a parking spot," the field includes the

---

Box 3.2 Standpoint Theory Resources

Standpoint theory, and the related idea of "partial perspective" (Collins, 1990; Haraway, 1988; Harding, 1991; Harstock, 1983), offers a way to begin to understand the complexities of interrelated and differing stakeholder perspectives in a given policy implementation effort. Depending on our role in a given endeavor, we all have a "partial perspective" of how things work as a whole. For instance, service users and frontline social workers implementing an agency-wide clinical practice change would be likely to have firsthand understandings (some shared, some differing), that an administrator would not be likely to have access to in the same way; however, the decision-making power regarding what is being implemented agency-wide is typically the responsibility of (and power held by) the administrator. Conversely, frontline clinicians conversely may likely not have thorough awareness of policy issues related to what they are attempting to implement.

- Collins, P.H. (1990). *Black feminist thought: Knowledge, consciousness, and the politics of empowerment.* New York: Routledge.
- Haraway, D. (1988). *Situated knowledges: The science question in feminism and the privilege of partial perspective.* Feminist Studies 14 (Fall): 575–599.
- Harding, S. (1991). *Whose science Whose knowledge? Thinking from women's lives.* Ithaca, NY: Cornell University Press.
- Hartsock, N. (1983): "The Feminist Standpoint: Developing the Ground for a Specifically Feminist Historical Materialism," In S. Harding & M.B. Hintikka (Eds.), *Discovering Reality. Feminist Perspectives on Epistemology, Metaphysics, Methodology, and Philosophy of Science.* Dordrecht: Reidel, pp. 283–310.

---

interrelated activities of people over time and space that create parking regulations, passes, monitoring, and enforcement. Each person in the field has a different vantage point. This is similar to the idea of touching, in a dark room, different parts of an elephant and describing the elephant as the one part touched; some would say the elephant is "a tail" whereas others would claim, "it's a trunk" or "a leg."

IE provides a systematic way to connect the elephant's body parts so that each part can be seen as a whole: an "elephant." The researcher takes up one standpoint within an *open system* and seeks to see how various standpoints are connected via social processes.

This focus on creating knowledge through a multiplicity of standpoints is highly congruent with the *engaged scholarship* approach.

As mentioned earlier in chapter 1, Van De Ven (2007) describes engaged scholarship as a

> form of research for obtaining the different perspectives of key stakeholders (researchers, users, clients, sponsors, and practitioners) in studying complex problems. By involving others and leveraging their different kinds of knowledge, engaged scholarship can produce knowledge that is more penetrating and insightful than when scholars or practitioners work on the problems alone (p. 9).

Instead of privileging a single standpoint (and knowledge base), IE assumes that each perspective offers a unique entry point for understanding social processes. Within any series of social processes, various standpoints are considered *different yet interdependent.*

Returning to the "getting a parking spot" example, one could enter the field from a college student standpoint. Each standpoint experiences unique tensions; these tensions are essentially manifestations of a PPG. For example, when a student drives to the new parking spot and discovers—despite the newly implemented parking policy which aimed to increase parking convenience—that parking is not available in a timely fashion and within a reasonable distance to class, the student experiences tension. For this student, the new parking policy has fallen short of its promise. Likewise, due to PPGs, standardized social work interventions implemented in an open system are likely fall short of their promise.

To study the gap or PPG between the promising new parking policy and the actual implementation, a student could use institutional ethnography. Difficulties in locating a parking spot could be related to numerous issues, including but not limited to poor mapping/instructions, misallocation of parking spaces by areas of study, class scheduling and related traffic flows, overuse of particular parking areas by those not authorized, lack of enforcement, and so forth. While each of these would be important to understand, the starting point or "entry" into these interconnected social processes is the students' lived experience (see chapter 1 for discussion of phenomenology) of "getting a parking spot." An institutional ethnographer identifies how the processes entailed in "getting a parking spot" fit together and where difficulties and *disjunctures* emerge (i.e., lack of fit between reality and expectations/needs, see

Townsend, 1998; Pence, 2001). Specifically, the institutional ethnographer would begin *from the standpoint of those* with the most knowledge of "getting a parking spot." Clearly, students who seek parking would have this sort of expertise; they repeatedly search for parking so their standpoint would be one from which to enter the field of social activities and processes that implement the policy. Through connecting the dots and understanding how parking processes interrelate in reality, the gap between policy promises and the actual experience of parking can be understood.

IE embraces and insists upon "going local"; the *standpoints* of specific individuals (whose everyday work and experiences are being focused upon) are considered to be *the* valid entry point into a given set of extended social processes (Smith, 1987, 2005). As explained by DeVault (1999), "the Institutional Ethnographer takes up a point of view in a marginal location; she 'looks' carefully and relatively unobtrusively, like any field worker, but she looks from the margins inward . . . searching to explicate the contingencies . . . that shape local contexts" (p. 47).

In sum, institutional ethnography is a qualitative method well suited for studying open systems and PPGs. When a one-shoe-fits-all mandate is applied to a specific practice environment, practitioners will observe that many clients don't fit the hoped-for outcome. The open system of practice serves up nuance, difference (Sayer, 2011, pp. 59–67), and above all the juxtaposition of practitioners' tacit, theoretical, and technical-rationale knowledge (i.e., knowledge prescribed in a manual). What to do? In the remaining sections of this chapter we illustrate how to conduct IE as engaged scholarship.

An administrator whose mental health agency was attempting to implement a standardized measure approached Janet Hoy. The administrator was seeking research assistance to understand the difficulties that agency staff and clients encountered while implementing the instrument; other agency administrators expressed similar concerns and interest in research, and an engaged scholarship project was born! In collaboration with various stakeholders—policymakers, local agency administrators, practitioners, and clients—participants agreed to use institutional ethnography; the aim of the research was to identify, among staff and clients, gaps between the mandated instrument and real-life application.

Box 3.3 Institutional Ethnography (IE) Resources

Example of IE study:

- Pence, E. (2001). Safety for battered women in a textually mediated legal system. *Studies in Cultures, Organizations and Societies,* 7(2), 199–229.

Guides for doing IE research :

- Campbell, M. (2006). Institutional ethnography and experience as data. In D. Smith (Ed.), *Institutional Ethnography as Practice* (pp. 91–108). Toronto: Altimira Press.
- Campbell, M., & Gregor, F. (2002). *Mapping social relations: A primer in doing institutional ethnography.* Garamond Press: Aurora.

IE data analysis:

- McCoy, L. (1995). Activating the photographic text. In M. Campbell & A. Manicom. (Eds.), *Knowledge, experience, and ruling relations: Studies in the social organization of knowledge.* Toronto: University of Toronto Press Incorporated.
- McCoy, L. (2006). Keeping the institution in view: Working with interview accounts of everyday experiences. In D. Smith (Ed.), *Institutional ethnography as practice* (pp. 109-128). Toronto: Altimira Press.

In-depth works on IE and social organization of knowledge:

- Smith, D. (2005). *Institutional ethnography: A sociology for people.* Toronto: AltaMira Press.
- Smith, D. (Ed.) (2006). *Institutional ethnography as practice.* Toronto: AltaMira Press.
- Smith, D. E. (1987). *The everyday world as problematic: A feminist sociology.* Boston: Northeastern University Press

---

The research was conducted in the state of Ohio (US) and was funded by the Ohio Department of Mental Health; because of IRB (institutional review board) confidentiality requirements, we will keep the exact locations anonymous. First, we introduce the mandated policy. We then talk about sampling and recruitment, data collection, management, and analysis. Finally, we interpret findings. We employ a user-friendly style so that you can easily see how to use institutional ethnography; in the boxes you will find more in-depth coverage of the method and related discussions.

APPLYING INSTITUTIONAL ETHNOGRAPHY:
STATE POLICY IMPLEMENTATION

The Ohio Department of Mental Health (ODMH) is a leader in the development and delivery of client-driven, mental health recovery-focused services and practices. There are numerous definitions of mental health recovery. The ODMH defines recovery as a "personal process of overcoming the negative impact of a psychiatric disability despite its continued presence" (see, http://www.mhrecovery.com/overview.htm). Through years of collaborative research with a diverse group of mental health clients, clinicians, family members, administrators and other stakeholders, the ODMH created a standardized measure of mental health recovery for use in the public mental health system (ODMH, 2002). The state then enacted a policy—referred to as the Ohio Consumer Outcomes Initiative—that required community mental health centers to complete and utilize a standardized measure, referred to as the Adult Consumer Form (see Appendix). This measure consisted of sixty-seven close-ended questions and Likert scale items that measured four primary constructs (Roth, 2005). The four constructs were

- Quality of life (12 items)
- Symptom distress (15 items)
- Empowerment (28 items)
- Community activism and autonomy (6 items)

A cross-section of policymakers, administrators, practitioners, family members, and clients had endorsed the principles of mental health recovery and the *value* of using measures to assess change (Hoy, 2008). However, among case managers the completion of the Adult Consumer Form was often referred to as "doing the outcomes," or "more paperwork we have to get done." Somewhere between the collaborative creation of the Adult Consumer Form and its implementation in the open system of mental health service delivery, outcome measurement was experienced as burdensome paperwork. And between intention, promise, and actual practice, a PPG was created. Yet in the field the experience of the gap was largely unrecognized. Engaged scholarship was employed to see and understand the gap.

Aim and Question: Identifying Tensions as Entry into a PPG

Case managers expressed tensions in attempting to incorporate the Adult Consumer Form into their everyday work. In open systems, noticing a tension is the first step in recognizing a PPG. Sources of tension are sometimes easily identifiable and can occur as a result of specific incidents, such as when a client makes a serious suicide attempt. Other times, however, the source of tension is more difficult to pin down and can be related to policy and administrative processes and constraints. And while such system processes *are not readily visible*, they routinely organize how social work practice occurs. Policy-related and system-related tensions occur when confluences of system processes, such as policy mandates, don't fit frontline reality; hence a policy-to-practice PPG is experienced. According to Townsend (1998):

> these tensions are not experienced as such; rather, professionals . . . tend to feel overwhelmed, inadequate, or not fitting into the system . . . herein lies the disjuncture: a fundamental contradiction between divergent ways of routinely organizing power . . . this contradictory organization of power is so embedded and invisible that it is experienced as taken for granted routines that seem natural and unquestionable. . . . (pp. 153–154)

A research aim helps draw a boundary around a particular practice reality and identify a potential target; in this instance, the use of the Adult Consumer Form. In this illustration, the research aim was to examine gaps between policy and practice that resulted from implementing a standardized measure of mental health recovery. As stated in the previous chapter, research questions reveal the *concrete and empirical pathways* (i.e., data) to general research aims. Thus, two research questions were asked: (1) How do case managers and clients understand and use the Adult Consumer Form? (2) What mental health system-related processes affect case managers' and clients' experiences of the Adult Consumer Form?

These questions point to data that will address the research aim and are framed so that institutional ethnography collects and links the empirical data—the understanding and experience of case managers and clients—with the social processes of "doing" the standardized outcome measure.

APPLYING INSTITUTIONAL ETHNOGRAPHY: SAMPLING AND RECRUITMENT

The "social field" was defined first as the social processes occurring within the institutional arrangements that comprised mental health provider agencies, county mental health boards, and the ODMH (the research remained open to discovery of other institutional entities). Janet Hoy entered these social processes through identifying and immersing herself in the everyday experiences of frontline clinicians and clients as they completed and attempted to utilize the standardized measure of mental health recovery.

The Provider Agencies Within the "Field"

The four participating provider agencies (a.k.a. community mental health centers) in this study were four of the largest providers of public, outpatient mental health services for adults in Ohio. Three were located within the same large, predominantly urban county and governed by the same county mental health board (within this county, addiction services were governed by a separate board). The fourth agency also served an urban population but was governed by a different board. While each agency context was unique, there were specific site similarities:

- Each had an annual operating budget of between 10 and 20 million dollars.
- Each employed between 60 and 80 case managers.
- Each served between 3000 to 5000 mental health clients.
- Each was headquartered in an urban setting in Ohio.
- Each had multiple satellite offices in both urban and suburban settings.
- Each served predominantly low-income individuals.
- Each relied heavily on Medicaid (federal and state) revenue.
- These sites differed in terms of ethnicity of the staff and clientele:
- Predominantly Caucasian staff and clients
- Predominantly African American staff and clients
- Approximately, 50:50 Caucasian/African American staff and clients
- Approximately 50:50 African American/Caucasian clients but predominantly Caucasian staff

The degree of site compliance—outcome survey completion and submission to ODMH—also varied. In order for an agency to be in compliance, 80% of the enrolled clients needed to complete the survey; by this definition, only one of the four was in compliance. And at the time of the study, as a contextual factor, three of the four were operating with budget deficits. Two of the four sites were multiservice centers (i.e., providing services in addition to mental health services). Yet at all sites the most common service was outpatient behavioral health. All four served predominantly low-income clients; the vast majority of these had either public health insurance (Medicaid or Medicare) or no health coverage. Each site offered community supportive treatment (formerly referred to as case management) and psychiatric services to individuals living with severe mental illness. These program services were part of a continuum of care designed to help individuals live as independently as possible in the community.

Recruitment Strategy

Through dialogue with administrators from each of the four sites, and in compliance with IRB, Janet Hoy developed a recruitment plan. She began by attending routine case management team meetings and presenting a ten-minute overview of the study questions and procedures, as explicated in the consent form. Flyers describing the study were given to all case managers at the meeting, and extra flyers were left for staff not in attendance; these were placed in the absent staff mailboxes and included contact information (Figure 3.2). When interested case managers contacted Janet by e-mail or phone, face-to-face appointments were arranged to review the consent form and answer all questions. Case managers signed the consent and were provided a copy of the form. Participating case managers then sent a mailing to individuals on their caseload. Janet relied on the case managers' clinical judgment to exclude any client (1) who was psychiatrically unstable to the extent that participation could pose a detriment or barrier to his or her ongoing care, or (2) whose participation would pose some other detriment to the client's mental health due to circumstances specific to that individual, or (3) who was unable to provide informed consent due to mental or other impairment. Janet next met with interested clients and their case managers at the managers' offices (per client request). She gave a brief overview of the study, as explicated in the client consent form, and answered questions. She met with a total of seventeen clients, and they all decided to participate.

Date:_____

Dear_____:

As your CPST (Community Psychiatric Treatment Support) worker, I am writing to let you know that a research study is being planned at our agency that may be of interest to you. As a client of our agency, you may be eligible to participate. Final eligibility is determined by the researchers from Case Western Reserve University doing the study.

Even if you are eligible, *your participation in this or any research study is completely voluntary.* There will be no consequences to you whatever if you choose not to participate, and your regular mental health care will not be affected in any way by your choice.

Compensation for your time in the amount of $30 in Visa gift cards would be paid (a $15 card after the researcher observes us for the first time, and a second $15 card after you complete an interview with the researcher which would happen about 2 months after we're observed for the first time). And, if you do choose to participate, you will be sharing important information which could ultimately help others dealing with mental illness.

If you are eligible and choose to participate, the study will involve:
- Having a researcher observe and take notes during our routine meetings for about two months, to see how we use the Consumer Outcomes Surveys (a mental health survey we ask people to fill out at this agency).
- Doing a tape-recorded interview with a researcher about the Consumer Outcomes Surveys
- Allowing your chart to be reviewed by the researcher, so she can see how those involved in your mental health care are writing about the Consumer Outcomes Surveys.
- To ensure confidentiality, all notes and tapes kept in a safe and locked office, and no names or means of identifying you (or others) will be used

If you are interested in participating, please contact me within the next two weeks at_____, and I will arrange a meeting with you, me, and a researcher, so that you can further explore whether you would like to participate.

Sincerely,

Figure 3.2 Sample Recruitment Letter.

Recruitment Results: Case Manager Participants

A total of nine case managers agreed to participate. Case managers' education ranged from a bachelor's degree in a non-license-eligible field to a master's degree with additional specialized training in chemical dependency; years of service ranged from three to thirty (Table 3.1). Case managers provided supportive services to mental health clients (see explanation of "client" below); ongoing service planning and coordination; linkages

Table 3.1 Case Manager Demographics

Education	License	Years in Field	Years at Agency	Gender	Race	Caseload Size
MSW	LISW/ CCDC III	30 years	over 20 years	F	African American	50
BA in Psychology; MA in Health	None	6 years	6 years	F	Caucasian	40
MSW	LISW	10 years	5 years	M	Caucasian	40
BA in Psychology	None	5 years	5 years	F	African American	40
BSW	LSW	6 years	7 months	F	African American	40
BA in Sociology	None	4 years	2 1/2 years	F	Caucasian	40
BSW	LSW	18 years	10 years	F	African American	18
BA in Psychology	None	3 years	1 year	F	Caucasian	65
BA in Sociology	None	20 years	5 years	F	Caucasian	40

to resources and other agencies; assistance in monitoring and management of psychiatric symptoms; crisis intervention; and advocacy. Case managers functioned in a social work capacity, although credentialing for case management work varied widely within and between agencies in Ohio.

Recruitment Results: Adult Mental Health Client Participants

Requirements for eligibility for client participation included age eighteen years or older, current use of case management and community support services at one of the four participating urban mental health centers, and ability to provide informed consent. A total of seventeen client

Table 3.2 Mental Health Client Demographics

Client	Age	Gender	Race	Education	Employment	Income	Diagnoses
1	26 yr	F	African American	Some college	None	SSI	Mood d/o w/out psychosis
2	27 yr	F	Caucasian	High school diploma	None/seeking	SSI	Mood d/o w/out psychosis; Anxiety d/o; Personality d/o
3	33 yr	F	African American	Enrolled in college	None	SSI	Mood d/o w/out psychosis; BPD
4	36 yr	M	Caucasian	High school diploma	None	SSI	Mood d/o w/out psychosis
5	38 yr	M	African American	Some high school	None/seeking	SSI	Psychotic d/o; CD
6	39 yr	F	Caucasian	Some high school	none	SSI	Mood d/o w/out psychosis; Personality d/or
7	41 yr	M	African American	Enrolled in GED	Part-time	Wages	Mood d/o w/out psychosis
8	41 yr	F	Caucasian	Some college	Part-time	SSDI & wages	Psychotic/Mood d/o; Anxiety d/o; Personality d/o
9	45 yr	M	Caucasian	High school diploma	None	SSI	Anxiety d/o
10	47 yr	M	Caucasian	High school diploma	None/seeking	Friends & family	Mood d/o w/out psychosis; Anxiety d/o; CD

(Continued)

Table 3.2 Mental Health Client Demographics (*Cont'd*)

Client	Age	Gender	Race	Education	Employment	Income	Diagnoses
11	48 yr	F	Caucasian	BS degree	None/seeking	SSDI	Mood d/o w/out psychosis; Anxiety d/o; Personality d/o
12	53 yr	F	Caucasian	High school diploma	None	SSI	Anxiety d/o; personality d/o
13	55 yr	F	African American	GED	None/seeking	SSDI	Mood d/o w/out psychosis; Anxiety d/o; Personality d/o
14	55 yr	M	African American	High school diploma	None	SSI & SSDI	Psychotic d/o; Anxiety d/o
15	57 yr	F	Caucasian	BA degree	None	SSI	Psychotic d/o
16	64 yr	M	Caucasian	High school diploma	None	SSI & SSDI	Psychotic d/o
17	73 yr	M	African American	Some high school	None	SSI & SSDI	Mood d/o w/out psychosis

d/o = disorder
SSI = Supplemental Security Income
SSDI = Social Security Disability Income
BPD = Borderline Personality Disorder
CD = chemical dependency

participants working with the nine case managers were recruited. Table 3.2 provides specific diagnostic and demographic details for each of the participating clients.

Administrative and Other Participants

Janet used an IE construct of "processing interchanges" (Pence, 2001) to trace the use of the Adult Consumer Form and to identify the work of "absent others" (i.e., individuals who were not immediately present but were part of the process of implementation). For Pence (2001), processing interchanges includes sequences in which a given text (i.e., Adult Consumer Form) enters a locality (i.e., a specific mental health center in Ohio), is processed (which may entail modifying, checking, or creating a new related text), and is then forwarded to its next destination. McCoy (1995) describes this social process as texts being "activated" (read or otherwise used).[1] The identification of "processing interchanges" allows for an exploration—anchored in the material conditions of case managers and client life—of the textually mediated social processes that connect, across time and space, the implementation of the Adult Consumer Form. Dorothy Smith (2005) elaborates on this:

> the text and its transformations coordinate people's action; each move initiates a new action on its arrival at someone's work site; the product is passed on, transformed or not, to the next site, where it again initiates an action. . . . Thus, not only do texts mediate the process of coordinating each stage of work with the next, but they also coordinate the whole work process. . . . (p. 173)

In order to recruit the "absent others," Janet conducted interviews with case managers. She asked them to identify all others "who have been significant in his/her use of the outcomes" measure; they were also asked for permission (all answered affirmative) to contact the potential interviewee. Here particular attention was paid to case manager and client identification of any document related to the use of the outcome measure. Janet distinguished administrative/others (supervisors, quality assurance staff, etc.) from frontline groups (clients and case managers) by the institutional roles the former played in mediating between the state policy mandate and frontline attempts to implement. This snowball sampling

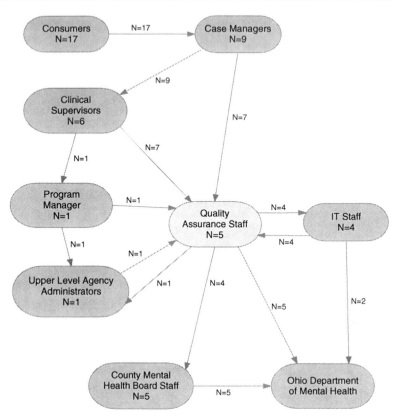

Figure 3.3 Snowball Sampling.

strategy[2] was continued until no new names or documents were generated (Figure 3.3). A total of twenty-five administrative/others were identified and twenty-two agreed to participate.

DATA COLLECTION, MANAGEMENT, AND ANALYSIS

Over a period of ten months, Janet used participant observation, interviews, and a review of charts to collect data to answer the question—*How do case managers and clients understand, experience, and use the measure?* The standpoints of managers and clients were points of entry into the extended social processes shaping the use of the outcome survey.

Participant observation included two and a half months at each of the four research sites. Following IE methods, Janet sought to

1. *Observe* supplementary uses of the Adult Outcome Form, such as planning and documenting services and related tasks
2. *Identify* the experiences and actual use of the Adult Outcome Form
3. *Map* an integrative account of understandings, experiences, and uses of the Adult Outcome Form and how these occur within the everyday work of case managers and clients

Janet conducted participation observation with case managers and clients; she essentially shadowed case-manager dyads as they went about their everyday activities, including, but not limited to, activities related to the policy mandate. She spent about two and a half months at each agency, observing the managers and clients during both routine case management activities (e.g. filling out an application for housing assistance, discussing interpersonal and medication concerns, completing treatment plans, etc.) and in the completion and discussion of the standardized recovery measure (i.e., Adult Outcome Form). During or after such observations, or both, and always with permission from the participants, Janet wrote systematic notes to organize observations. In ethnography, these are commonly called field notes. There are many resources that can help explicate the techniques of fieldwork; for examples see Van Maanen's (1988) *Tales of the Field* and Agar's (1996) *The Professional Stranger.* Janet used the following approach:

1. She wrote detailed, nonevaluative notes (e.g., avoiding generic, value-laden words such as "bad," "messy," "cluttered," etc.,) *describing* what was being observed, such as "a desk completely covered with stacks of charts and other paper piles."
2. She wrote detailed, nonevaluative notes (again avoiding words such as "angry") *describing* actual behaviors, such as "raised his voice and pounded on the table."
3. She wrote detailed notes about her *own* feelings (see chapter 5 for discussion of how all social work research is always and necessarily evaluative), reflections, and thoughts relating to 1 and 2 above.

To collect more data about case managers' and clients' perceptions, understandings, and self-described experiences of using the standardized measure, semistructured individual interviews were completed and digitally recorded. With interviews, the activities observed during participant observation could be clarified, expanded upon, and grounded in the standpoints of those closest to the experience of using the measure. Open-ended questions were constructed to elicit the participants' retrospective (see chapter 2) and current understanding and experience of using the Adult Outcome Form. [For resources on constructing semistructured interviews, see Seidman's (2006) *Interviewing as Qualitative Research* and Kvale and Brinkmann's (2008) *Learning the Craft of Qualitative Research Interviewing*]. Figure 3.4 lists the questions asked of clients and Figure 3.5 lists the questions asked of the case managers; to maximize comparison of responses both within and across client and manager subgroups, the interview questions were similarly constructed.

Interview data were transcribed and handwritten field notes were typed and transformed into Microsoft Word documents. The creation of

---

Semi-structured Consumer Interview: Understanding and Using the Consumer Outcomes

1. **How did you first you hear about the Outcomes.** Who was involved? What did they say and/or do? What did you think about the Outcomes at that time?

2. **Tell me about your current understanding of the Consumer Outcomes survey.** What do you think it is about? Why do you think it is being used?

3. **How did you complete the survey?** (Hard-copy or on a computer? At home or at the mental health center? By yourself or with your worker or someone else?) What was it like for you to complete the survey? How did you think and feel as you answered the questions?

4. **Who and/or what was helpful to you in doing the survey?** How were they helpful and/or important?

5. **Have you gotten a summary of your survey results? If yes, tell me about how they were shared with you, and what you thought about them.** What did you do with the results at that time? Have you thought about or done anything with them since? If yes, tell me about that.

6. **Any other thoughts about using the Outcomes survey that you'd like to share?**

Figure 3.4 Sample Semistructured Interview Questions: Consumer Version.

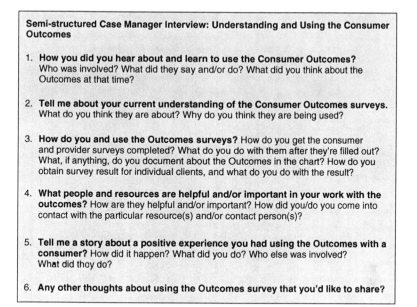

Semi-structured Case Manager Interview: Understanding and Using the Consumer Outcomes

1. **How you did you hear about and learn to use the Consumer Outcomes?** Who was involved? What did they say and/or do? What did you think about the Outcomes at that time?

2. **Tell me about your current understanding of the Consumer Outcomes surveys.** What do you think they are about? Why do you think they are being used?

3. **How do you and use the Outcomes surveys?** How do you get the consumer and provider surveys completed? What do you do with them after they're filled out? What, if anything, do you document about the Outcomes in the chart? How do you obtain survey result for individual clients, and what do you do with the result?

4. **What people and resources are helpful and/or important in your work with the outcomes?** How are they helpful and/or important? How did you/do you come into contact with the particular resource(s) and/or contact person(s)?

5. **Tell me a story about a positive experience you had using the Outcomes with a consumer?** How did it happen? What did you do? Who else was involved? What did thoy do?

6. **Any other thoughts about using the Outcomes survey that you'd like to share?**

Figure 3.5 Sample Semistructured Interview Questions: Case Manager Version.

four (data related to one site became one primary document) ATLAS.ti primary documents (see chapter 2) was a management decision that kept site data distinct, allowing for quick comparison within and across agencies.

Using thematic analytic techniques (see chapter 2), in-vivo codes were assigned to chunks of the collected data; for example, participants typically referred to the Adult Consumer Form as "the outcomes" or "the surveys." This was done to stay as grounded *in the participants' own descriptions* of their experience as possible. Next, all in-vivo codes and attached quotations were checked for proper fit with the code. Then, across the four sites, in-vivo codes were compared and an exhaustive list was generated that yielded a description of participant experience of implementing a mandated measure. Grounded theory was used in the next analytic step. Looking at how the themes were connected via umbrella concepts produced a conceptual framework for understanding the experience and use of the standardized recovery measure. To check for validity (Kuzel & Like, 1991), and in keeping with the engaged scholarship approach, feedback from case managers and clients was solicited to identify themes and the resulting framework; in other words,

---

Box 3.4 Practice Ethnography

- DeMontigny, G. (2005). *Social working: An ethnography of frontline practice.* Toronto: University of Toronto Press.
- Floersch, J. (2004). A method for investigating practitioner use of theory in practice. *Qualitative Social Work,* 3(2), 161–177.

Janet sought to compare her analysis with that of other engaged scholarship participants. Notes from participants' observation work were compared with the written progress notes of the same event to further confirm the meaning workers attributed to completion of the Adult Consumer Form (see Floersch, 2000).

The second research question–*the system-related processes that affect case manager and client experiences of the Adult Consumer Form*—was addressed using snowball sampling (i.e., by asking case managers "with whom do you talk or interact with about the standardized measure"). In collaboration with various stakeholders, Janet traced the actual social trajectories of "texts-in-use" across the service system; such social processes (i.e., written documentation) interconnected individuals who never actually met.

Written communication is a very significant and often overlooked social process that has temporal and geographical boundaries greater than immediate spoken communication (Smith, 2005; Wedel et al, 2005). Pence (2001) explains textual social processes as sequences in which a given text enters a locality, is processed, which may entail modifying, checking or creating a new related text, and then often forwarded to the next destination. McCoy (1995) describes this as textual activation. Thus Janet collected and reviewed all written communications that were connected to implementing the Consumer Outcomes Initiative. Examples included clinical records, e-mails, memos, tracking sheets, Ohio Administrative Codes, online manuals, and online websites of private certification agencies. These texts-in-use allowed exploration of the interconnected processes entailed in implementing the standardized measure of mental health recovery.

Next, in collaboration with stakeholders, Janet mapped the sequencing of the identified texts as they were processed throughout the system (see Figure 3.6). The result integrated data collection and created

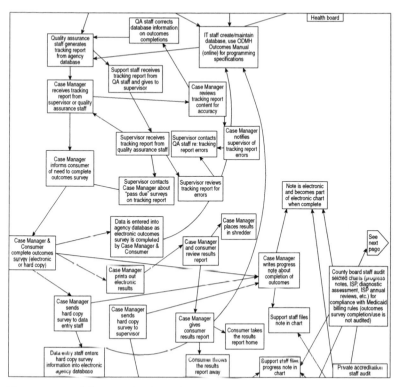

Figure 3.6   Partial Processing Interchange Map.

a narrative account of interrelated social processes embedded in and connected to frontline manager and client experience of the standardized measure. Figure 3.5 has a shaded box depicting the case manager (i.e., case manager/community psychiatric supportive treatment staff) and client completing the standardized measure. Once completed (see the subsequent boxes in Figure 3.5), the measure made its way through various agency and mental health system processing points. For example, once a hard copy of the measure was accomplished, the manager placed it in an envelope and sent it by inter-office mail to data-entry staff. The data-entry staff entered the measurement information into a computerized database—created and maintained by information technology staff—and quality assurance staff used the dataset to generate a tracking report. Because of a policy-driven requirement to "turn the form in" by particular dates, each agency created a monthly tracking report that tracked due and past due dates for each client on a manager's caseload. Such monthly reports were generated by a respective agency's quality assurance department and then sent to case manager supervisors, who in turn reviewed and forwarded them to case managers. Managers, in turn, reviewed the reports and made attempts to contact any client that had not yet completed a survey. In this way, such texts-in-use *socially organized and actualized* the policy implementation of measuring recovery outcomes within the open practice system.

FINDINGS

In collaboration with other engaged scholarship stakeholders, Janet identified tensions in cross-agency implementation and explored how her interpretations matched local understanding and experience (Kuzel & Like, 1991). Based on collaborative reworking, she generated the findings. Janet used a thematic and grounded theory data analytic strategy (see chapter 2) for two reasons: to reduce the risk of "deductive disclosure" (i.e., deducing specific agencies' and participants' names from the details of the data), and to maintain an analytic focus on *institutional* rather than *individual* processes. Devault and McCoy (2006) argue that linking quotes with identifying information risks individualizing the analysis. Dorothy Smith (2006), the founder of institutional ethnography methodology, likewise states:

> some institutional ethnographer writers suppress personal information about informants in order to keep the focus on the institutional processes they are describing; they identify quoted speakers only by their location in the institutional work process of which they speak (e.g. nurse, client, teacher, administrator). (p.41)

Thematic Analysis: Case Manager "Doing the Outcomes"

Among case managers, thematic analysis identified six themes related to the processes of "doing the outcomes":

1. Knowing the outcomes
2. Fitting the survey in
3. Tracking the survey

4. Filling out the survey
5. Getting and understanding the results
6. Documenting

"Knowing the outcomes" had two subthemes. Each of these illustrate the tension between manual instruction and application or doing; that is, knowing what the outcomes were for and knowing how to do the outcomes. All managers reported receiving written instruction on how to use the outcome measure; however, they also reported that they had not referred to instructions. *Doing* is more immediate than the manualized instruction for *how to do it*, and it speaks to managers who depend upon experiential learning. For example,

> I remember getting a folder they put together, but I never used it. Stuff like that is generally not helpful for me . . . usually if someone tells me and shows me [one on one], it is much easier for me to catch on than using one of those guidebooks. . . .

Doing was entangled in webs of client need and manager time constrains. For example:

> We got references or some information in the training, but it's more in my head, and it's not something I think gets prioritized very much in the course of doing a case management job. I mean a lot of it [case management] is fire fighting, you know, so I think that worrying that you're getting the Consumer Outcomes Survey, you know, making sure that you're applying it perfectly isn't something that case managers worry about. It's something that we try to get done and then move on to the agenda that's more pressing. . . .

Similarly, "fitting the survey in" encompassed two subthemes: completing the survey alongside emergent client need, which was typically referred to as "real client needs"; and fitting the nonsymptom survey content into treatment planning. A manager recounted an incident where they felt pressured to do a survey:

> she [client] came in very upset , and it was one of those things where I felt like I needed to get this done, had to get it in the chart, it was the time of year that they were really on us about these, you know, chart

reviews were coming up from the State or Mental Health Board, and I found myself pushing it and I'm glad she did stop and say 'look, I can't do this' because it sort of grounded me that I needed to, we needed to talk about what she needed to deal with, which was more important, in my eyes. I mean this is also someone I had worked with for roughly about three years. So I mean I was doing this more obligatory sort of perfunctory need and that it was due, and she really had something real to tend to. . . .

Case managers indicated that treatment plans needed to be "symptom-focused" in order to meet "medical necessity" criteria. They also stressed that they had difficulty making the outcome measure "fit" the treatment plan. One illustration succinctly stated the tension:

by 'medical necessity,' it is about the symptoms, what mental health symptom does the client have that makes the service or goal or whatever you're doing 'medically necessary' . . . if it's not 'medically necessary,' we're not supposed to be doing it, the agency doesn't get paid for it. . . .

It was not easy to integrate survey constructs (i.e., quality of life, symptom distress, empowerment, and community activism and autonomy) into practice:

feeling empowered, safe in your housing, liking your life, those are important things to know about a person you're working with, no question, in terms of helping that person. . . . I'm just not sure how they fit in [with 'medical necessity']; sometimes the housing fits because the housing can get disrupted by symptoms, but with the other stuff, it's harder to fit it together. . . .

More than others, "tracking the survey" was discussed at great length. Case managers routinely received due and past due dates for survey completion. These tracking reports served as reminders (from supervisors and quality assurance staff) to complete the survey: "the report kind of keeps the outcomes in my mind as something that needs to get done. . . ." "Using the tracking report" and "dealing with inaccuracies" were described as intertwined processes. Often reports erroneously showed "past due" when it had already been completed. This became so annoying to some that they created their own list and cross-referenced it with the "official" tracking report. Once during a participant-observation event, a manager pulled out of a drawer a tracking report and compared it with her list: "look here, all these people they have marked as 'past due,' they are done . . . it is scary that with so much riding on the outcomes, that the [tracking] information isn't accurate. . . ."

Others relied on their own recollections: "I'd see my client's name listed as past due, but could clearly remember us doing the survey say two months ago . . . this happens a lot. . . . " Once a tracking report discrepancy was identified, they typically took this information to supervisors to "show that I'd done them, so I didn't hear about it . . . eventually the tracking report would show it, sometimes there would be some glitch and I'd have to redo the outcomes, but usually it was just the tracking report not keeping up with who was done. . . . " Still,

> I highlight the people where it says "past due"; some of them are past due because they refuse to take it so it always shows up as past due; and then some of them I just forgot to do or the client hasn't been coming in, and I highlight those so I can remember to remind the client, and then when I schedule the appointment, I'll put it in the notes section of my schedule. That's how I usually try to keep up with them. . . .

Dealing with "ongoing pressure" to "get them done when they're due" was also conveyed as a subprocess under "tracking the survey." "Pressure" was typically experienced through e-mails, supervisory discussions, staff meetings, and memos.

"Filling out the survey" referenced the act of completion. Actual completion was something done "together" (i.e., the manager read the survey question and recorded the answer—called oral survey administration) or "by yourself/themselves" (i.e., the client read the question and recorded the answer); completion experiences also varied according to electronic verses paper and pencil. "Translating" the survey was a different type of work and it occurred most often during oral survey administration (all but three clients requested oral survey administrations). First, case managers often had to translate "confusing questions." For example, a manager translated a survey question for a client struggling to understand; she first encouraged the client's own understanding of the question; but quickly, when the client became frustrated and distressed, the manager redirected:

> Case Manager: "Are you in treatment because you want to be?" (Reading survey question aloud).
> Client: "Is that mental health treatment? Or drug treatment? I don't have a drug problem. Or is it some other kind of treatment? Or am I just not getting it?"
> Case Manager: "Just go with whatever you think 'treatment' means, and answer by that."
> Client: "But I don't know what it means, I'm confused, I guess I just don't get this stuff" (voice rising).
> Case Manager: "No, no, you're right, that could be a confusing question. I think they're referring to mental health treatment there."

Second, "translating" occurred when clients indirectly answered a standardized question by giving a specific life example; managers often had to translate or match the client's idiosyncratic answer to the form's preloaded response category. For example:

> Case Manager: "I am usually confident about the decisions I make." (Reading survey question)
> Client: "I don't know . . . I'm thinking about going back to work, my daughter has housekeeping work I could do, but the baker down the street said she needs some part-time cleaning help, too."
> (The case manager and client had a brief discussion about the pros and cons of each of these options and what social security reporting would entail; then they returned to the survey.)
> Client: "I think I'll work with my daughter. I feel sort of confident about that."
> Case Manager: "So that would be. . . . 'Agree'?" (Looking back at the survey question)
> Client: "Yes."

Across all research sites, "understanding results" was described as a struggle. Case managers identified a need for "fewer numbers, more words"; "pictures or graphs"; and to "have it tell us something, like a paragraph about the client." A graphical comparison of previous and current survey results was also desired. The numerical format was perceived as impeding clinical usefulness:

> it's all those numbers, and it doesn't explain what the results mean, it just regurgitates the questions and scores in a different way . . . it'd help if it actually talked about findings or described the client or something . . . and also if it showed how the client's answers changed from the last time . . . then we'd have something good to talk about. . . .

While the policy mandated that survey results should be used in goal setting and measuring achievement, this was not reflected in client progress notes. Progress notes simply indicated that the survey had been completed; no specific aspects or content of client responses were noted. Progress notes included: "did the outcomes with client" and "completed the outcomes survey." Thus, the case record focused on completion and not on how the survey content was actually utilized in treatment.

Thematic Analysis: Client "Doing the Outcomes"

Clients identified four themes related to the process of completing the Adult Consumer Form or "doing the outcomes":

1. Making sense of what the outcomes are for
2. Filling out the survey
3. Getting/understanding results
4. Understanding myself better

Three of these overlapped with case manager experience and reflected much of the same institutionalized processes. However, the experience of "understanding myself better" was unique to clients.

In making sense of the survey's purpose, clients expressed uncertainty about whether "doing the outcomes" would directly help them; or would it indirectly help them by "helping the agency to do a better job with what I need." All understood the survey as "doing the outcomes" and as something that was "done when it was due, because it needs to be done." One client referred to the process as "No Consumer Left Behind." This client had cleverly linked the survey to the US (2001) "No Child Left Behind" policy, which supported standards-based education reform through setting high standards and establishing measurable goals to improve educational outcomes in schools.

"Filling out the survey" overlapped with case manager themes but also encompassed processes unique to clients. When offered a choice, twelve requested "together" or oral administration of the survey; one referenced vision difficulties and the remaining cited other reasons. Clients cited two interrelated processes: translating abstract question categories into unique life situations; and in answering the questions, "being reminded" of something they wanted their respective case managers to know. "Being reminded," meant

> even though the question is more of a general 'Do you feel upset?' you're like 'Oh yeah, this and that happened and I was so upset and I meant to tell my case manager', and then you do it [tell the case manager] . . .
>
> it [the survey question] brought it to the surface, I had pushed it down, tried to bury that feeling, what was happening, I wasn't going to tell her [the case management staff], I don't know why not, but the one question triggered me back to it and I knew I needed to tell my worker, right there and then, and it poured out of me. . . .

When responding to a general survey question, clients often understood the question by translating into a specific life situation. For instance, in response to a question about "feeling afraid," one client described a recent bus ride and an associated panic attack; his case manager listened attentively and then prompted him to select a response (i.e., "strongly agree," "agree," "disagree," "strongly disagree") that most approximated the fear. In sum, for clients, "getting and understanding results" was a theme similar to case manager experience. They expressed a desire for narrative and graphic information, as opposed to numerical information:

> they should use words to tell you instead of numbers, like a personality profile or something that you can read easily that says you're this or that at the present time. . . .

it would help to have last year and this year's results pulled together so I could look at both of them and think on it better, maybe like a graph or something that you can look at and understand easy, whether you've improved or changed. . . .

The client theme "understanding myself better" referred to a sense of empowerment, conveyed when disputing survey results. Case managers explored and supported their client critical evaluations of the reports. Clients identified difficulties with wording and fixed-response categories as a major source of inaccuracy:

> I didn't understand some of the questions as worded, I guess, so the answer I gave wasn't really what I meant and the results don't fit me. . . . when the questions didn't have a middle response I was forced to choose when my real answer was neutral. . . . so the scoring didn't reflect what I was really thinking when I took the test and I don't like my responses. . . .
> I kind of felt like some of the question wording was off, so that my answer didn't show how I was thinking and feeling. . . .
> I don't think it [the results] reflected me very well, so 'cause like some of the questions I answered, didn't have the right response, a neutral response. . . .

In sum, by identifying how the survey results didn't accurately reflect their "thinking and feeling," clients indicated that the survey evoked self-reflection: "figuring out why I disagreed helped me to think more about what was going on with me. . . ." Increased self-awareness was not the intent of the survey. Instead, it was an unintended consequence that was produced in an open system; *in the gap between the survey's intent and its actual implementation*, a phenomenological practice gap (PPG) was produced. In everyday case management, the implementation of the Adult Consumer Form became a site for the production of a unique PPG. The mandate was to measure recovery outcomes. Implementation required two key partners: case managers and clients. Each had to bring the survey—in IE terms a subordinate text—into the routine of "case management." Thus, survey implementation mediated the worker and client *relational experience* and created a PPG tension. As they implemented the measure, managers and clients, in action, constructed meaning. A gap between the hoped-for policy implementation goals and their realization in "doing the outcomes" was inevitable.

Analysis: Conceptualizing "Doing the Outcomes"

In comparing the themes derived from the thematic analysis (see above), two umbrella or higher-level dimensions (see chapter 2, grounded theory) were identified. The two dimensions were

1. A compliance-driven organization of time that displaced a direct-practice focus
2. A paradigm conflict between the medical model (understood by case managers as "medical necessity" and "focusing on the symptoms of the mental illness") and mental health recovery, which encompassed the medical model, but also other non-medical model constructs such as empowerment

Experienced as tensions, these dimensions show how implementation in an open system produced a unique PPG. First, IE illuminated how the extended social processes—administrative, supervisory, quality assurance activities, and board activities—were compliance-focused (i.e., compliance with one or more regulatory bodies). When asked who was essential in implementing the Adult Consumer Form, no case manager referenced their client and no client referenced anyone but their case manager. Policy implementation had bound two partners together and they alone experienced the tension. However, data collected during participant observation confirmed that case managers remained client-centered in their work: treatment planning; attending to client need, linking to resources, and other routine management activities. Thus, completing the survey was something to get done, a nuisance that was unavoidable. And this "have-to" attitude trickled down to the client. Implementation became a compliance-focused activity. This was compellingly illustrated in client language that referenced externally imposed compliance requirements, as opposed to outcomes that would assist their recovery. For example:

> my case manager said my treatment plan is due, so I came in to do it. . . .
> it's time to do the outcomes survey again. . . .
> she [the client's case manager] said it was due again, so I'm doing it [Adult Consumer Form] again. . . .
> it's something we have to do, so we do it [Adult Consumer Form]. . . .

Second, complying with regulations was related to yet another dimension: divergence between medical and recovery paradigms. This gap (in IE terms a disjuncture or tension) was exemplified when managers retrofit "nonsymptom" aspects of client recovery into a medical necessity paradigm. Specifically, across all settings, case managers voiced a sense that the "nonsymptom" questions of the Adult Consumer Form were "not fitting with medical necessity." Thus, in treatment planning, under everyday practice conditions, the intention of the survey was undermined by the confluence of textually mediated, divergent aims: (1) a symptom-focused medical model, and (2) a recovery philosophy that included nonsymptom constructs, such as empowerment. The latter was most visible during oral administration of the survey.

Case managers read survey questions and waited for client response; recall, oral administration was the expressed preference of twelve clients. To illustrate, a client was asked an abstract survey question, and she responded by sharing a specific scenario in her life, a situation the case manager was unaware of:

> Case manager: (reads the following survey question with the expectation that the client will choose a Likert-scale response) "I feel powerless most of the time." (see Adult Consumer Form, Appendix, Question #55)
> Client: "I am bogged down, I'm not helping my daughter . . . my daughter's school isn't responding to my calls, I've met with her teachers over and over, I don't think they're giving her medicine but they say they are and she just looks worse and worse to me . . . she sits in her room, doesn't talk with me, let alone tell me if she's getting her medicine at school . . . and my daughter's counselor here isn't calling me back . . . I don't know what else to do. . . ." (Client is now crying—from participation observation field notes.)

Meanwhile, the case manager ceased reading the survey questions and stayed near the client's experience by obtaining the counselor's name and asking if she would want us (the center) to contact them. The client replied: "yes, please." Next, the manager recorded the information on a piece of notebook paper and clipped the paper to a "release of information" form, which they filled out together after the survey was completed. The case manager continued.

Case manager: "Back to the question, 'I feel powerless most of the time."

Client: "Every day, because of my daughter's situation."

Case manager: "So, 'Agree', or 'Strongly Agree'?"

Client: "There are times I feel like I can do something about it, though."

Case manager: "So. . . .?"

Client: "Agree."

In the twelve case manager-client dyads that completed the survey orally (i.e., together), all diverted specific survey questions away from the Likert-scale responses and toward a specific life situation. Case managers responded by exploring the concern and making informal notes on notebook paper or Post-it Notes. Most would then revisit the scenarios after the survey was completed. When questioned about their experience of such situations, managers repeatedly voiced a tension between "wanting to explore the concern raised" and "needing to get the survey done." Completing the survey generated clinical concerns beyond measuring recovery; the emergent clinical concerns meant that additional time was needed to address them. The latter created tension for already overburdened managers. In short, compliance meant more work. Thus, compliance-driven tensions, a PPG, subordinated here-and-now client "needs" to survey completion. This was ironic, given that the survey was to measure recovery from the disabling symptoms of severe mental illness.

Moreover, while the policy to complete a survey was mandated it was not, according to Medicaid regulations, a fundable activity. Medicaid created more tension when oral survey administration occurred. Honoring client choice and preference were key elements of a "recovery" philosophy. Yet in the here-and-now, case managers were confronted with a tension between completing the Adult Consumer Form in a client-centered fashion (i.e., oral survey) and completing it according to "medical necessity" contingencies (there were no participant observations of clients sharing specific life concerns when they filled out surveys by themselves). The disjuncture between recovery and "medical necessity" meant that the survey questions evoked feelings and thoughts that were recovery oriented, yet to address them, the activity did not fit the "medical necessity" funding requirement. Although numerous examples of clinical material surfaced as a consequence of the client's making unique meaning of specific survey questions, such interactions were not clinically documented (i.e., confirmed in a progress note). Rather, the compliance/completion imperative dominated the content of progress notes. The mandate, in practice, produced contradictory demands. Thus, in the open system of practice, workers and clients had to negotiate the gap between a standardized measure and the fluid meanings (e.g., clinical, compliance, and medical necessity) that implementation had served up.

Medical model and recovery ideas were easily traced (i.e., through the mapping of explicit implementation processes pertaining to the outcomes) to specific "regulatory texts." The narrower medical model ("medical necessity") was contained in Medicaid rules. Managers and clients did not read federal Medicaid rules; instead rules entered local practice through documents (created to demonstrate Medicaid compliance) such as diagnostic assessments and treatment plans that focused on "medical" symptoms. Figure 3.7 illustrates the documentation of medical necessity. In contrast, the Ohio Administrative Codes contained a detailed description of the Adult Consumer Form that contained explicit references to recovery: nonsymptom constructs. Figure 3.8 illustrates the textually mediated manner recovery entered manager practice vernacular.

These contrasting paradigms were present in case manager and client experience through what Dorothy Smith (2006) has called "subordinate texts"; here, the subordinate texts (e.g., symptom-focused treatment plan) were those that created compliance and related to specific "regulatory texts" (e.g., Medicaid rules pertaining to "medical necessity"). Across all research sites, a group of subordinate texts, connected to regulatory texts such as Medicaid rules, private accreditation standards, and state certification standards, were collectively referred to as "the chart." Most notably referenced were the diagnostic assessment, individualized service plan (ISP), annual review, and progress notes.

Dorothy Smith (2005) differentiates in a hierarchical sense between "regulatory texts" (e.g., rules, policies, procedures, etc.) and "subordinate texts" (e.g., assessment and treatment plan forms, which are produced as a result of specific regulatory texts and are capable of being interpreted as "proof" of compliance with the specific regulatory texts);

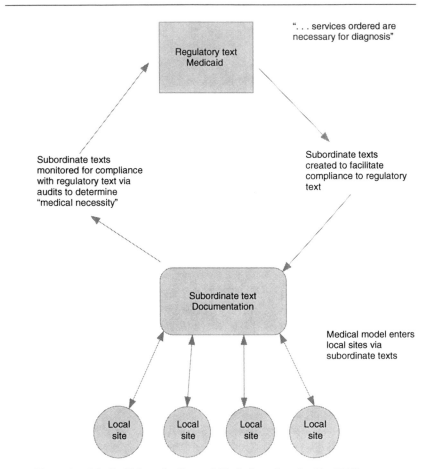

Figure 3.7 Medical Necessity Textual Circle (based on Smith, 2005).

she articulates "inter-textual circles" related to the inter-textual hierarchies between regulatory (policies) and subordinate (clinical documents such as assessment and treatment plan forms) texts as follows:

> from activating/reading the regulatory text, the question arises of what to do that can be fitted to the framework of that text; the work that is done to produce the appropriate [subordinate] text . . . must be readable as a text that fulfills the function ascribed to it in the regulatory text. . . . (p. 85)

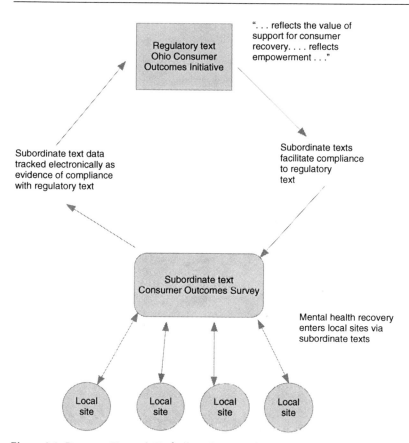

Figure 3.8 Recovery Textual Circle (based on Smith, 2005).

Case managers were not aware of the policies and regulations that affected their activities but typically they were aware of *documentation requirements*; they were responsible for writing client assessments, treatment plans, and case notes. While documentation was perceived to be a clinical function, in actual practice, it inevitably related to policies and regulations. In sum, case management activities in general, *and the documentation of such activities in particular*, were inextricably tied to texts. And, in the implementation of the state policy mandate to use a standardized measure of mental health recovery, case managers and clients produced a unique PPG, which is vividly illustrated in Figure 3.9.

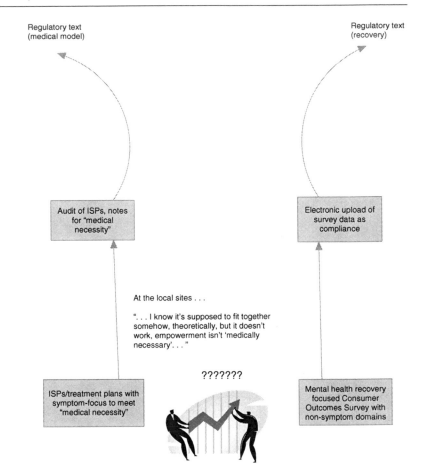

Figure 3.9 Paradigm Disjuncture as Lived Experience.

INTERPRETATION

A standardized, evidence-based measure created a phenomenological practice gap by fixing the meaning that in-vivo, open system practice produced. The Adult Outcome Survey did not adjust to practitioner and client unexpected actions and interpretations because it privileged completion over the clinical meanings the survey generated (i.e., in this instance by predetermined survey questions and response categories). This foreclosure created a specific gap at a specific time and place of implementation: public mental health outpatient sites. Moreover, PPGs like this are common in practice settings where national and local policies *regulate*, through mandates, what can be done, when, for how long, with whom, and by whom. Mandating survey completion meant workers had to manage the gap between the paperwork proving completion and the actual experience that "doing the outcomes" served up. Indeed, evidence-based interventions require internal and external audits of treatment plans and case notes because documentation (i.e., fidelity tracking) creates part of the empirical evidence that the EBP works. In short, manual-specific practices are made "real" through *documentation*. Today, numerous social service agencies have departments, referred to as quality improvement or quality assurance, that are devoted to ensuring that practice documents (e.g., assessment forms, case note forms, treatment plan forms, etc.) meet policy and regulatory requirements. In sum, standardized practices are implemented across open system settings; however, because standardization itself assumes a closed system, PPGs are inevitably produced.

The good intentions of the survey were overruled (Townsend, 1998) by the unintended consequences of its implementation. Clients wondered: what does this question mean? Practitioners interpreted. Clients responded. Implementation sank into a swampy (Schön, 1983) ground between what the survey promised to measure (i.e., recovery) and its practice, compliance. Its intent was undermined by *institutional facts*. Some case managers, acting reflexively (see chapter 5), adjusted the survey to meet the circumstance; they paused, listened, took notes, completed the survey, and then returned at a later date to work with client concerns. Reflexive practice, then, had the potential to open what the institutional facts had closed.

Clients, case managers, administrators, state officials, and other stakeholder groups had endorsed the principles of mental health recovery statewide. Yet when the principles were translated into practice, case managers and clients responded to myriad factors that went far beyond a simple interaction. These factors created a PPG that led an agency administrator to engage Janet; this resulted in an engaged scholarship project.

Using IE and an engaged scholarship approach, manager and client knowledge—about how the standardized measure was used—were revealed. Smith (2006) has referred to "buried dialogues" as the hidden conversations of organizational participants. The tension between the philosophy of recovery and the medical model was experienced as a buried dialogue: completing the survey allowed clients to voice buried mental health concerns.

With an engaged scholarship approach and an IE research design, knowledge of a PPG was coproduced. Using the findings of this research to reduce frontline "tensions" between recovery policy expectations and practice realities, one could

- Alter the format of the results to incorporate more narrative and graphic depictions
- Bring client-centered practices to the forefront in documentation (currently driven primarily by compliance)
- Promote oral survey administration as a clinical intervention

With an engaged scholarship approach, stakeholders discuss findings and suggest changes. In the case illustrated in this chapter, the gap between compliance and medical necessity should be addressed. And the next survey iteration should be studied in the same manner. Iterations would strive to close discovered PPGs by respecting how institutional facts and open systems require adjustments to time, space, and practice. In the next chapter, we explore how iteratively organized engaged scholarship projects can calibrate standardized interventions to open-system realities.

4

Engaged Scholarship
Qualitative Methods and Adapting
Evidence-Based Practice

INTRODUCTION

In this chapter we discuss how engaged scholarship and qualitative methods can be used to adapt or modify an evidence-based practice (EBP). Implementation of a standardized measure or intervention must consider factors (e.g., organization, cultural, and client) that affect, in unanticipated ways, the *relevance* of a standardized intervention. We argue that unintended or unanticipated implementation consequences refer to a phenomenological practice gap (PPG), a gap between the proposed model and its implementation. Specifically, methods discussed in chapter 2 are used to illustrate how an EBP can be adapted to fit the particularities of open systems and their unique PPGs.

Social workers are increasingly asked (or required) to deliver evidence-based interventions and to utilize standardized measures to evaluate practice. Let's return to the recipe analogy used in chapter 3. Imagine that a baker mixes ingredients to create a particular cookie: a chocolate chip, as opposed to a sugar cookie. If we eliminate the chips we still have a "cookie." For some, however, the chipless cookie might not be as highly valued, especially by those who crave chocolate. Similarly, while a standardized intervention includes stipulated practice actions—tested by variables analysis—some activities, depending on context, will be *more essential* than others. The literature on EBP often describes the essential activities as "core components" (Backer, 2001; Solomon, Card, & Malo, 2006). While a sugar-to-salt ratio is a core component of most cookie recipes, at some point, were the ratio to tip in favor of salt, the product would no longer taste like or be a "cookie." Think about this for a moment. What does *fidelity* to an evidence-based practice mean? This occurs when we implement a practice in accordance with the *recipe* for that practice. In chapter 1, we learned about the nature and quality of open systems. It is reasonable to assume that in open systems not all practice activities are equally valuable, easily implemented (if at all), appropriate, or even relevant to particular settings. Core components of EBP are not unlike the sugar-to-salt ratio in our cookie recipe. How much can one alter practice activities (i.e., the prescribed recipe and ingredients) and remain in conformity with the EBP? Modifying the cookie recipe is obviously much simpler (expert cooks, however, will always take into consideration variations in ovens, temperature, humidity and qualities of the flour, sugar, and other ingredients). The implementation of an EBP is not so easy. In open systems, knowing how, when, and why to modify is less clear. For example, can the core components include additional concepts and related practices (e.g., transference and countertransference) and still conform to the recipe?

We have discussed how qualitative methods can be used to identify institutional facts that structure client experience in open systems. In this chapter we consider how methods can be used to identify and address tensions between the internal characteristics (e.g., the structure, content, etc.) of EBPs and the practice contexts or settings.

ILLUSTRATION: IDENTIFYING AN IMPLEMENTATION RESEARCH AIM

According to the United States Department of Justice (Minton & Sabol, 2009), over two million people are incarcerated in prisons and jails. Moreover, 14% to 24% have a history of mental illness (James & Glaze, 2006). Imagine that a regional corrections administrator, concerned about the increasing numbers of adult inmates with serious mental illness, has approached a community mental health agency for assistance in identifying and implementing a brief psychosocial group intervention. Unlike prisons, jail settings involve two transient populations: those awaiting trial and others found guilty but not yet sentenced. This might be described as a revolving-door, a setting where it is difficult to implement treatment other than crisis services (Bauer, Morgan & Mandracchia, 2011).

With this context in mind, a mental health supervisor engages a researcher to identify an appropriate EBP. The researcher suggests an approach developed by Leonard Gibbs in *Evidence-Based Practice for the Helping Professions: A Practical Guide*. After conducting a COPES inquiry (Client Oriented Practical Evidence Search) and following Gibb's detailed instructions (http://www.evidence.brookscole.com/copse.html), including reviewing research databases and online resources, an Illness Management and Recovery (IMR) model is identified (see the Substance Abuse and Mental Health Administration, http://store.samhsa.gov/product/SMA09-4463). While research shows (Mueser, Meyer, Penn, Clancy, Clancy, & Salyers, 2006; Hasson-Ohayon, Roe, & Kravetz, 2007) the effectiveness of IMR groups (i.e., positive client outcomes), you discover no applications of IMR for incarcerated populations. However, you find a Wellness Management and Recovery (WMR) model, a variation of IMR, which is widely used in the region where the jails are located. Indeed, a WMR technical assistance website exists with resources for implementation (see, http://www.wmrohio.org/overview.html). WMR has a curriculum that combines psychoeducation, motivational interviewing, and cognitive-behavioral strategies in a group-based intervention (Bullock et al, 2005; Bullock et al., 2007; Mueser et al., 2002). A review of the WMR literature (Bullock et al, 2005; Bullock et al, 2007) suggests that

- Group sessions are provided weekly for ten weeks, with two hours for each session, with a break in the middle
- Groups are cofacilitated by an agency staff person *and* a peer provider (an adult who is living with a serious mental illness)
- Ten (manual specified) sessions cover the following topics:
  - Mental health recovery
  - Wellness
  - An understanding of mental health
  - The role of medication in recovery and wellness
  - Learning to manage symptoms and side effects
  - Effective communication
  - Communicating with your providers

- Coordinating your care
- Developing relationships and building social supports
- Planning for wellness

Based on your practice experience with adults, the supervisor knows that these topics are relevant for most inpatient and outpatient settings. But in further research we establish that no curriculum exists for promoting mental health recovery among incarcerated adults. With the results of the literature review in hand, the regional corrections administrator, the supervisor, and the researcher design an engaged project to adapt an EBP to jail settings.

The supervisor is familiar with WMR and thinks it might be a good fit with a few "tweaks." To begin, although the curriculum spans ten weeks (the group meets once per week for two hours), the average length-of-stay is only three. Some will be released to the community after sentencing, while others will be sentenced to prison and transferred. The *structure* of the WMR group (i.e., frequency and length of meetings) must be adjusted. As the curriculum is further scrutinized, you conclude that some topics (i.e., "Communicating with Providers" and "Coordinating Your Care") may not be relevant for those temporarily held in jails. While communication and coordination services are relevant for community living, the jail administrator wants the service provided *during incarceration;* moreover, incarceration constrains client choice. You ask: What are the barriers and facilitators to mental health recovery for incarcerated individuals? Your return to the research literature yields no results.

In the meantime, a social worker who works in jails reviews the WMR material and casually remarks, "that WMR stuff is so social work, good luck trying to get the corrections staff to take that seriously." You inquire: which parts and why? She responds:

> there's a lot of emphasis on empowerment and mental health recovery . . . they [corrections staff] are not necessarily concerned about inmate empowerment; but they do want less altercations and decreased recidivism, so you have to make sure you put it in language they care about if you want them to buy in.

Now what? While the WMR appears to fit in some respects, it has limits. The length and structure (once a week, two hours per group for ten weeks) are potential problems. You have discovered that some content needs adjustment and jail staff may not be willing partners. You have also learned that although knowledge about psychosocial group interventions for those living with a serious mental illness is robust and there is a known and proven curriculum, the evidence falls short of what is needed in a jail setting. We realize that starting from scratch and creating a new group is not the best use of resources. And lacking insight, participation, and knowledge from those familiar with jail culture, it would be nearly impossible to adapt the WMR. In short, in the open system of jail policy and practice, we must identify the unique and institutionally specific incarceration and staff experiences that are outside the original target WMR population and context. If WMR is to be successfully implemented in a jail setting, we must consider context-specific knowledge. How, then, are we to adapt the EBP to a jail setting? How do we adapt WMR and thereby anticipate phenomenological practice gaps?

Fortunately, we discover that adapting an existing EBP to new populations or contexts is not new. Moreover, we learn that numerous modifications of existing evidence-based interventions have been published and there are even approaches that implicitly use engaged scholarship (Bradbury & Reason, 2003; Senge & Scharmer, 2001). And because incarceration settings are unique (Rotter, McQuistion, Broner, & Steinbacher, 2005) and crowded disproportionately with persons of color and other oppressed groups (Kulkarni, Baldwin, Lightsone, Gelberg, & Diamant, 2010), we must account for the sociohistorical structures (e.g., causal mechanisms) that likely affect the mental health and illness experience (Kulkarni et al., 2010). Failure to account for them may add to existing service disparity (Alegria & McGuire, 2003). We know that evidence-based interventions that maintain fidelity to core components yet incorporate adaptations potentially increase relevance (Solomon, Card & Malow, 2006; Kelly, et al., 2000). Intentional structural and content deviations, incorporating contextual and population-related strengths and needs, have been called "positive variance." This occurs when deviations result in outcomes more relevant than promised by the original EBP (Litaker et al., 2006). The literature contains examples of health and human service adaptations that anticipated the need for positive variance:

- **Adapt-ITT model** (Wingood & DiClemente, 2008)—created to adapt HIV interventions

- **Formative Method for Adapting Psychotherapy/FMAP approach** (Hwang, 2009)—created to adapt individual therapies to new populations (populations different than those the therapies were originally developed with/for)
- **EBP Modification process** (Samules, Schundrich, & Altschul, 2009)—created to increase cultural competence and relevance
- **Ecological Validity model** (Bernal, Bonilla, & Bellido, 1995)—created to specifically modify psychosocial interventions for use with Hispanic populations
- **Cultural Adaptation Process model** (Domench-Rodriguez & Weiling, 2004)—created to modify a parent training curriculum for use with people of color
- **Guide to Fidelity and Adaptation** (Backer, 2001)—created for adapting substance abuse and prevention interventions
- **Consensual-Sequential Design** (Groleau, Zelkowitz, & Cabral, 2009)—created to adapt best practice guidelines for breast-feeding

Although there are differences across these approaches, we discover four key assumptions and methods:

- **An iterative/multi-stage process** that promotes cycles of knowledge coproduction (gathering knowledge, analyzing and integrating it, and testing the newly integrated and co-produced knowledge) among stakeholders that have different perspectives (Bradbury & Reason, 2003; Senge & Scharmer, 2001)
- **Focus groups or work groups** as a data collection method for gathering information and incorporating perspectives and knowledge from different stakeholder groups (Natasi et al., 2000; Allen et al., 1994)
- **Expert consultation** in integrating stakeholder recommended changes into the original EBP model to maintain "core components" (Solomon, Card, & Malow, 2006)
- **Pilot testing** the adapted EBP by obtaining input on feasibility, usability, and acceptability from stakeholders

Indeed, like positive variance and the methods described above, engaged scholarship partners anticipate a gap between a model and practice and therefore design a project that anticipates iterative adaptations. When engaged collaboratively, stakeholders coproduce an intervention that maintains fidelity to mutually identified "core components" while tailoring the intervention to better fit a particular client population and/or service setting context.

ILLUSTRATION: MODIFYING WELLNESS MANAGEMENT AND RECOVERY FOR JAIL INMATES LIVING WITH MENTAL ILLNESS

It is time to implement the jail adaptation. You are aware that administrators are a bit skeptical and uniformed about "positive variance" and "cross-adaptation principles." They ask: What has this to do with jails and how would you proceed? We suggest the following research design. First, conduct focus groups with incarcerated individuals and prison staff. Ask specific questions about the current content and structure of the WMR curriculum. Second, transcribe the focus group audio recordings. Using ATLAS.ti (described in chapter 2) and thematic analytic techniques to identify potential *adaptation themes* (e.g., suggested content changes, structure and intensity of the WMR curriculum). Third, with thematic findings in hand, consult with a Wellness Management and Recovery Coordinating Center of Excellence (http://www.wmrohio.org/overview.html)—a technical assistance center that trains and supports WMR users— or a known individual with WMR expertise to integrate recommended themes or changes into an *adapted* WMR. Fourth, pilot test the modified group; and after completion, conduct a focus group with participants to get feedback on usability and acceptability. And finally, use the post-pilot findings to make focused changes and then iteratively test the practice in the jail setting.

You learn that the supervisor and administrator are impressed but still skeptical; in particular, they question the feasibility of conducting focus groups with incarcerated individuals. However, you describe a literature with many examples of focus groups conducted with incarcerated individuals: to identify smoking cessation intervention needs (Richmond, Butler, et al., 2009); to identify perceptions of prison health care delivery (Plugge, Douglas & Fitzpatrick, 2008); and to evaluate a prison-based drug treatment program (Swartz & Lurigio, 1999). Moreover, you learn that focus groups have been conducted with prison staff to identify changes in a prison-based therapeutic community (Linhorst, et al., 2001); to identify needs for a prison-based substance-abuse treatment program

---

Box 4.1 Focus Groups as a Data Collection Technique

Kruger and Casey (2009) have written a usable and reader-friendly book describing how to develop and conduct focus groups. According to Kruger and Casey (2009):

"The purpose of a focus group is to listen and gather information. It is a way to better understand how people feel or think about an issue, product or service. Focus groups are used to gather opinions. Participants are selected because they have certain characteristics in common that relate to the topic of the focus group. The researcher creates a permissive environment in the focus group that encourages participants to share perceptions and points of view without pressuring participants to vote or teach consensus. And the researcher doesn't do just one focus group. The group discussion is conducted several times with similar types of participants so the researcher can identify trends and patterns in perceptions. Then careful and systematic analysis of the discussions provides clues and insights as to how a product, service, or opportunity is perceived by members of the groups" (p. 2).

To conduct a focus group, a series of questions must be created to explore the topic. The purpose is *not* to obtain consensus about a topic but to gain an understanding of the range of perceptions about the topic. For instance, to explore how to best adapt the content and structure of the WMR curriculum within a jail environment, a series of open-ended questions would need to be created and asked of all those whose work would overlap with WMR (including and especially those who would actually attend the WMR groups to address their mental health needs). Once focus groups are completed, digitalized recordings can be transcribed and analyzed with techniques described in chapter 2 of this book.

(Linhorst, Dirks-Linhorst, Bernsen, & Childrey, 2009); to understand perceptions of resident mental health (Nurse, Woodcock, & Ormsbyl, 2003); and to understand influences on prison psychiatric nursing (Doyle, 1999).

Finally, convinced of the relevance of focus group methods, the stakeholders commit to the aims and design.[1] The research plan is submitted to the regional corrections department for review. Their research ethics board approves the project. Now a rigorous engaged scholarship plan is in place to adapt WMR for use in jail settings.

You implement a double-layer, focus group design (Krueger & Casey, 2009). The first layer, or unit of analysis, involves two jails. The second unit of analysis identifies the composition of members (i.e., male residents, female residents, uniformed/security staff, and nonuniformed/

program staff). The proposed design enables collaborators to contrast adaptation recommendations within and across two institutions and differing stakeholder groups (Krueger & Casey, 2009; Yin, 1994). Also, by separating stakeholder groups (e.g., uniform vs. nonuniform staff; male vs. female residents) the design reduces power differentials within the institution. And by doing this (i.e., separating) we create group environments where participants feel more comfortable sharing thoughts and feelings (Krueger & Casey, 2009). You plan individual interviews with correction administrators; an individual interview, unlike focus groups, neutralizes power differentials in pyramid-structured organizations. Now you will use a thematic analytic strategy to identify (see chapter 2) needed adaptation themes, within and across units of analysis. And finally, you will pilot test the adaptations before initiating a formal roll out.

A Sampling Strategy

Now we're ready to design, in collaboration, a sampling and recruitment strategy. How many focus groups and individual interviews will take place at jail facilities? Which jails? Who should be invited to participate? How many jail facilities? Answers to these questions will depend upon the distribution of mentally ill in jail. Where, for example, are the largest numbers? The jail administrator who originally asked for assistance identifies two facilities in urban locations. A purposive sampling strategy is recommended so that the range of participant views is included (see Kruger & Casey, 2009). There are three major participant groups: inmate/client, uniform/security staff, nonuniform program staff. The design seeks conceptual saturation from each group; *saturation* refers to the point at which investigators have identified the range of themes and are no longer receiving new information (Krueger & Casey, 2009, p. 21). Krueger and Casey (2009) recommend five to ten participants as an ideal size for focus groups. Groups larger than ten may limit opportunities for individuals to participate. And a group too small (less than 5) may not collect a full range of ideas. Table 4.1 lists target potential sample sizes for recruitment.

The research stakeholders finalize the criteria for group participation:

- *Inmate/client*—incarcerated adults that have been identified as having a serious mental illness. Serious mental illness could be defined (see Draine, Wilson, Metraux, Hadley, & Evans, 2010) as a schizophrenia spectrum diagnosis (DSM-IV code 295.XX) or a

Table 4.1 Sampling for Focus Groups

Institution and Participant Type	Question Development Focus Groups	Individual Interviews	Adaptation Focus Groups (Postintervention)
Jail One			
Administrators		N = 4	
Female residents (incarcerated persons)	N = 5 to 8		N = 5 to10
Male residents (incarcerated persons)	N = 5 to 8		N = 5 to10
Uniform/security staff			N = 5 to10
Nonuniform/program staff			N = 5 to10
Jail Two			
Administrators		N = 4	
Male residents (incarcerated persons)	N = 5 to 8		N = 5 to10
Uniform/security staff			N = 5 to10
Nonuniform/program staff			N = 5 to10
Totals	N = 15 to 24	N = 8	N = 35 to 70

major affective disorder diagnosis (DSM-IV code 296.XX). Our practice experience along with our review of the literature (Abram & Teplin, 1991; James & Glaze, 2006) suggests that many participants may have comorbid diagnoses (e.g., substance and/or trauma diagnoses in addition to an affective or psychotic disorder). These individuals should be included so they can speak to issues specific to living with comorbid diagnoses within jail settings.

• *Uniform/security staff*—individuals employed by the correction facility who work directly with the inmate/client population.
• *Nonuniform/program staff*—individuals employed by the correction facility who hold supportive roles in mental health service delivery.

Stakeholders now choose an iterative sequential strategy (see Groleau, Zelkowitz, & Cabral, 2009) and decide that with this approach internal and external validity is addressed. By working with participants in creating questions, data we collect will more accurately reflect (i.e., internal validity) concerns of inmates, overseers, and policymakers. Second, by including settings that represent the range of clients with mental illnesses, we attend to external validity (i.e., if our proposed design were implemented at similar sites, we should find comparable results). We then assure internal validity by conducting three *Question Development Focus Groups* (for sampling details, see Table 4.1). The purpose of these is to ascertain the key sociocultural themes (e.g., mental illness representations, collective values, and experiences) specific to jailed individuals living with serious mental illness (Groleau et al., 2009). Specifically, we propose an unstructured format (1) that invites participants to share their experience of jail, mental illness, health, and services; and (2) that explores topics and questions related to WMR curriculum adaptations. We are now ready to audiorecord discussions cofacilitated by a PI and a trained peer consultant (i.e., someone with a history of serious mental illness and incarceration). After we complete the initial groups, we will identify emergent themes (see chapter 2) and with these craft meaningful questions for subsequent groups: *Adaptation Needs Focus Groups*, which explicitly address needed or desired WMR adaptations.

Now that we have the modified questions we are ready for the next iteration of data collection (i.e., called *Adaptation Needs Focus Groups*) among inmate-client and staff groups and individual administrators (see Table 4.1, sampling section). Here, our aim is to identify content, process, and WMR areas for adaptation. Our effort will now be to record and transcribe. Other than in-vivo follow-up probes to specific participant responses (i.e., to achieve clarification), we will ask the same questions in the same sequence across individuals, groups, and institutions. It is in this way that we will accomplish consistent data collection for more reliable cross-group comparisons (Ward & Atkins, 2002; Kruger & Casey 2009).

Focus group and interview audio recordings will be transcribed and loaded into ATLAS.ti. Using thematic analysis (see chapter 2) we will identify adaptation-related themes *within* and *across* stakeholder groups and institutions. The next analytic steps include (1) reading the entire focus group and interview transcripts (and listening to the recordings);

(2) in a second reading, identify all quotations that refer to WMR themes; (3) code each identified quotation by attaching a code name; in most instances create a code name using some of the respondent's actual words—called in-vivo, initial, or open coding; (4) compare quotations attached to a specific in-vivo code and determine which match the code you created (and with those that do not fit, either create a new code or attach it to another code that better fits the quotation); and finally; (5) compare and sort the in-vivo codes into higher level or umbrella codes. Moreover, we will assign two coders; they will independently follow steps 1, 2, 3; they will then compare findings and reconcile differences (Charmaz, 2006). Next, coders will independently conduct steps 4 and 5 and repeat the reconciliation process. Coding will continue until all data are accounted for and no new codes emerge.

The following are dimensional (i.e., umbrella) level themes (see chapter 2) that might be discovered if the engaged project were actually conducted: *structural* (Kohn et al., 2002); *didactic* (Kohn et al., 2002); and *content* (Wieder et al., 2006). Structural dimensions, for example, relate to procedural changes: length of session and number of topics covered per session (i.e., the "how" aspect of doing WMR groups). Didactic modifications include interactive methods in which WMR content is shared (i.e., the "who" aspect of doing WMR groups). Content dimensions include modifications to specific topics (i.e., the "what" aspect of doing WMR groups). Clinical modifications include the treatment concerns derived from other modifications; but in addition, they target particular clinical outcomes such as reducing trauma symptoms. And finally, your iteration process leads to an adapted WMR that should be field tested in the open system of jail facilities.

One might ask: When does the iteration process for adapting a practice model stop? The answer: never! While this unequivocal "no" may appear zealous and unrealistic, remember that professional practice always and necessarily unfolds in open systems, requiring iterative processes to capture cultural, economic, and political change. Equally important, implementation always produces new knowledge. And with new knowledge, we find our way back to model assumptions. Failing to do so would foreclose contributions that practice makes to theory and model development. Indeed, without *constant iterative processes* practitioners and researchers cannot coproduce knowledge. Engaged scholarship assures continuous two-way feedback!

In this chapter we have offered one data collection method (focus groups) and an analytic strategy (thematic analysis) for investigating a jail setting that would be likely to produce a PPG if implementation did not anticipate (1) the particularity of jails, (2) the nature of open systems. Of course, PPGs will inevitably be part of any context where models of practice are implemented with top-down mandates. We have illustrated how stakeholders could use an engaged scholarship approach. Otherwise, in disengaged scholarship, research is left to the experts, and practitioners' and clients' systems are treated as closed.

In sum, engaged scholarship assumes the inevitability of phenomenological practice gaps. While the EBP literature acknowledges the need for *positive variance* (i.e., varying EBP by implementation context), the question of why EBP models need adaptation to specific settings cannot be answered within the closed system ontology of positivism. Engaged scholarship encourages us to coproduce knowledge of implementation, especially when policymakers mandate the use of variables tested, models of practice. It is time for research participants to coproduce knowledge. It is time for practitioners to reject the premise that experts make knowledge and transfer it downward. Indeed, those downstream are imagined to be unproductive and passive agents consuming research knowledge tossed into the stream by others more capable. In the concluding chapter, we argue that stakeholders must be reflexive agents weighing the inputs and outputs of research as a two-way process. This reflexivity has seven components and each is embedded in the critical realist methodology described in chapter 1.

5

The Role of Reflexivity in Engaged Scholarship

We conclude this book by looking in detail at the concept reflexivity and how engaged scholarship research must account for its use in practice. Margaret Archer (2007, 2010c) asks us to consider how human reflexivity works. This is perhaps the single most important question for the whole of social work practice and research. Without reflexivity, how otherwise would engaged scholarship be conducted? Without reflexivity, how do agents change? How do researchers work alongside one another exploring, challenging, and revising as the work unfolds? How do habitual practices turn to emancipatory or empowering ones? How do organizations or individuals take up policy or therapeutic discourses or narratives and do something creative and novel with them?

Reflexivity, Archer argues, occurs in the first-person through internal conversation or dialogue that uses language, emotion, sensation, and image. And while most acknowledge "self-talk" and can describe it, there is little research on how "internal conversations" mediate between our personal and ultimate concerns and social contexts, that is, between our internal and external worlds (Clarke, 2008). It is in the course of our internal conversations, moreover, that agency in the world is made possible and we gain control. Archer aims to understand how particular courses of action, what she calls projects, are determined through several modes of reflexive deliberation. We all engage in practical projects, social work practitioners (and researchers) and clients, and these projects are subjectively produced in relation to our objective circumstances. In short, we transform our subjective concerns into projects. And it is in this everyday and especially complex tension that we practice social work, that is, between our subjects' (and our own) practical projects and their objective conditions or between what some in philosophy and social science call *agency* and *structure*. Moreover, it is in this relationship that we come to understand what we (and our clients) *actually do*.

What is meant by reflexivity? This has been widely discussed in the social work literature and reviewed by D'Cruz and colleagues (2007). For our purposes, reflexivity refers to our human capacity to consider ourselves in relation to our contexts; and our contexts in relation to ourselves (Archer, 2010a, 2010b, 2010c; Clarke, 2008; Sayer, 2010, pp. 108–122, Sayer, 2011, pp. 116–117; White, Fook & Gardner, 2006).[1] This occurs through the "'internal conversations' we all hold about our personal concerns (what we care about most) and how to realize them in a social order that is not of our making or choosing. Through these inner deliberations and the courses of action they define, we exert some governance over our own social lives" (Archer, 2007). Archer, in her 2003 study and her more recent elaboration (2011), describes four modes of internal conversation or reflexivity. It is through these internal conversations, moreover, that individuals locate themselves in social life. First, she describes "communicative reflection," a mode where before engaging in action, individuals *turn to others* for the completion or confirmation of their internal conversation. These are conversations about the self and personal projects that reach completion through externalization or projection toward others and through conversation with familiar, similar others, limiting their worlds to the immediate social surround and along with it their social mobility. In this mode, "what to do, how to act, and, ultimately, who to be, are held open to the dialogical influences of those with whom they share their concerns. In other words, the membrane between the life of the mind and the life of the group is highly permeable and there is regular two-way trafficking between them" (Archer, 2003, p. 167). In the second mode, "autonomous reflection," there is independent, sustained, and complete internal dialogue that leads to direct action. In this mode of reflection, individuals are less likely to be influenced by those around them. Moreover, they have clear strategies toward constraints and enablements, thus making possible changes in their social position and modification of new positions in pursuit of their concerns (p. 207, p. 93). In the third mode, "meta-reflection," like the second, there is self-directive internal conversation based in and measured against strongly held values. Added to it, however, is critical reflection about internal conversation and social criticism. As the term suggests, metareflexives, as Archer calls them, reflect on their own reflections. In this mode, with social criticism, individuals are prepared to pay the price for subversion and to relinquish the benefits of inclusion and upward or lateral mobility. In each of these modes, Archer argues that agents are active and in different ways make contributions to social stability and change. They achieve power over and governance of their own lives.

Finally, there is "fractured reflection," a mode distinguished by the absence of purposeful internal conversation, escalating anguish, and bewilderment. Individuals in this mode are passive agents who enjoy no such governance, but instead are people to whom things happen. In each mode, researchers, practitioners, and clients may work with different modes of reflexivity and establish distinctive interpersonal modus vivendi. And it is through internal conversations, within existing or potential social contexts, that individuals consider how best to realize personal concerns. Each mode of reflexivity, moreover, entails a different posture toward society or very different relationships to structural constraints and enablements. We argue here that engaged research considers seven positions when thinking about reflexivity and that genuine *engagement requires autonomous reflexivity*: (1) personal (or standpoint), (2) ontological, (3) epistemological, (4) methodological, (5) theoretical (analytic), (6) normative, and (7) representational. Cutting across each of these *positions*, we find one or another of Archer's modes of reflection. In the first position, *personal*, researchers reflect "upon the ways in which our own values, experiences, interests, beliefs, political commitments, wider aims in life and social identities have shaped the research" (Willig, 2001, p. 10). In this *recursive process*, moreover, researchers are affected and transformed. *Personal reflexivity* requires attention to the meanings produced between researchers and their participants and "acknowledgment of the impossibility of remaining 'outside of' one's subject matter . . . to explore the ways in which a researcher's involvement with a particular study influences, acts upon and informs such research" (Nightingale & Cromby, 1999, p. 228).[2]

D'Cruz and her colleagues (2007), in their thorough review of the literature in social work on reflexivity, identified three types of personal reflection. The first regards reflexivity as an individual's considered response to an immediate context and making choices for further direction. Archer would describe this as autonomous reflection. This variation is concerned with the ability of individuals to process information and create knowledge to guide life choices, and has implications for the role of researchers and the relationships between social workers and clients; social and political factors are downplayed (p. 76). Their second type defines reflexivity as an individual's self-critical approach that questions how knowledge is generated and further, how relations of power operate (p. 77). The third treats reflexivity as concerned with the part that emotions play in the social work process (p. 75).

Bourdieu offers social workers another way of thinking about D'Cruz, Gillingham, and Melendez's characterizations of practice reflection. He argues that a truly reflexive practice requires that researchers/workers be at all times aware of and attentive to the effects of their own subject positioning (i.e., roles as researchers) and how their own internalized structures potentially produce distortions or bias. For Bourdieu this requires a sociology/anthropology of social work: a way of being fully present as a researcher with continual reflection on dispositions (i.e., what Bourdieu called *habitus*) and the myriad ways that institutional training shape the worker and researcher habitus (Floersch, 2002). In this reflexive mode, social workers/practitioners must monitor the potential of attributing their own characteristics to the people, events, and objects they study.[3]

Thus, it is in this personal position that we as researchers can monitor the myriad ways that our research is influenced by our habitus. Moreover, it is not sufficient for social work researchers to reflect on the proper steps in the research process (i.e., formulating the research aims and questions, recruitment and sampling, data collection and data analytic strategies). We must also observe and control the influence of our social position on this very process of selection. In the social work literature, terms such as reflexivity and reflectivity are used to refer to such kinds of thinking. Typically, *reflection* tends to be something we do after the fact; this is what Schön (1983) calls "reflection-on-action." Schön (1983), not unlike Bourdieu, differentiates "reflection-*on*-action" from "reflection-*in*-action," explaining "reflection-*in*-action" as the practitioner's experience of simultaneously reflecting on practice while in the very act of practicing. In social work, the term *reflexivity* is often used to denote "reflection-in-action." In sum, it is through our internal conversations that researchers manage emergent and unpredictable features of a given practice situation.

In personal reflection we would also include what Bourdieu and others have called the *scholastic fallacy*. Here, researchers must guard against the often unconscious tendency to assign (i.e., based upon their training and methodology) "systematicity" to objects of practice and study when it is not present. For example, researchers may see or imagine that workers or clients are following unambiguous rules or strategies when they are not; or when they are following rules and procedures they always do so in indeterminate and unstated ways. Moreover, when we do this we fail to see the many ways that worlds of practice are always unstable, uncertain, and unsettled in open systems. Finally, it is possible that in *personal reflection*, both researcher and practitioner (and clients) may be engaged in what Archer describes as *communicative reflection*. Here, both parties fail to fully engage with the research, as they *turn to others* for the completion or confirmation of their internal conversation (i.e., academic peers, agency heads, promotion and tenure expectations, peer providers, other mental health consumers, etc.). You will recall that these are internal conversations that reach completion through externalization or projection toward others and through conversation with familiar others, thus limiting their understandings to the immediacy of their social surround and with those most familiar to them. However, also in the personal position, one might expect to find what Archer calls *autonomous reflection*, where the internal conversation leads to effective and direct action, with clear strategies regarding constraining and enabling mechanisms, and less influence from the social surround.

For us, the second position, *epistemological reflexivity*, raises a very different set of questions about the limits and potential imposed by our ways of knowing. For example, do we see causality as the regular association among events or as more complex and related to causal mechanisms operating in open systems? Positivism, along with many of its associated methods (i.e., research techniques, statistics, regression analysis), for example, might cause us (i.e., practitioners, researchers, clients) to misrecognize (i.e., perhaps in the communicative or fractured mode of reflection) what is important about an object of study. We might, for example, look for statistical associations between poverty and gender, or poverty and crime; time and time again we will find a disproportionate number of single mothers in poverty. One could even predict that where there is poverty, more women will be suffering. These associations, however, require explanation. As argued in chapter 1, no amount of association explains how and why two things (e.g., poverty and gender) appear together in time. The failure to recognize the limitations of these kinds of explanatory accounts has led to terrible and unforgivable errors (e.g., scientific racism, which postulated a statistical association between race and culture or later between race and IQ). Likewise, with strong forms of social constructivism (or anti-essentialism) we may confuse the construction of a thing with its construal (see chapter 1 for discussion of this distinction). To be unaware of our epistemological positions also puts us at risk of confusing *what is* with how we know what is (i.e., what Bhaskar calls the epistemic fallacy), or of reducing what we know to how we know it (e.g., if we can see it, it must be, or it exists because we can measure it). There is yet another challenge posed by epistemological reflection and that relates to how we adopt (if we adopt) the standpoints of others (i.e., woman, people of color, gays, and lesbians). And while we may find that our differences or standpoints are incommensurable, research arbitrage can and should be used to explore them. Although differences may not be surmountable and should even be encouraged, research partnerships can still be formed with the express purpose of recognizing the differences and using them to deepen our understandings of what matters most to people. There are no doubt times when researchers and practitioners (and clients) are in the communicative mode of epistemological reflexivity. Take, for example, our current debate (especially in England and the United States) about the efficacy of anti-depressant medication (Kirsch et al. 2008), where it has been shown that psychiatrists continue to prescribe drugs despite evidence that the placebo effect is greater than the actual drug.

In the third position, *ontological reflexivity,* we think about the things that we take to be "real" or "knowable." Some, such as behaviorists, do not acknowledge the importance or "reality" of an internal, mental life. Again, one might consider those who are overcommitted to biology (i.e., practitioners, researchers, and clients) as the exclusive basis of mental illness as existing in the ontological communicative mode: they conform to the social expectations and worlds around them (e.g., to standards set by the pharmaceutical industry and the randomized control trial). Extreme behaviorism, or empiricism, seriously limits what can be known to what can be seen or measured. Evidence-based practice, for example, focuses almost entirely on behavioral outcomes—behaviors or actions (see chapter 1 for discussion of problems with behavioral outcomes approach) that can be seen or measured. Ontological questions have important implications for research, practice, and understanding. If, for example, we take dreams or the unconscious to be mere fictions (or beyond comprehension or as simple actions of the brain), or lacking meaning altogether, what part of the human experience may be left out? And the same could be said for many other aspects of the human experience beyond our conscious awareness or capacity to measure in observational terms.

In the fourth position, *methodological reflexivity,* the researcher and participants must ask questions about how the research design and methods (i.e., techniques, surveys, interviews, focus groups) place limits on the kinds of data collected (and approaches) and thus exclude some things from being seen or understood. How, for example, might data have been collected using different techniques (e.g., ethnography, observation, surveys)? And why was one choice made over another? With some methods we will capture the participant and researcher points of view. With others, voices are silenced and sometimes excluded. In this book we have argued for *engaged scholarship* and for methods that allow all stakeholders to join in a conversation about the limits and potential of competing methods and understandings of the research process. Some methods clearly preclude arbitrage. Others impose methods without consideration of even the basic rights of others (i.e., dosing children with medication without assent or consent or experimenting with prisoners). Methods can be used to empower—especially where researchers seek engagement.

In the fifth position, we consider *analytic (or theoretical)* choices. Here, for example, we ask questions about how the data are to be analyzed and how, by making choices, other options are excluded, elided, or never considered. And with different theories and analytic choices we may see things that others might altogether ignore (i.e., perhaps the things that make the most difference or the things that truly matter). For example, we may choose a theory about social class that allows us to see how wealth is differently distributed based upon ownership and control. Or we may choose to limit our understanding of economic inequality by focusing instead on rational choice theory: people are poor because they make bad choices, or people are sick because they fail to listen to our public health messages. Among other things, these theories all assume that when we do things we do them with awareness (Clarke & Hoggett, 2009), and this is a very dangerous assumption.

In the sixth position, *normative reflexivity*, unlike the personal, we explore the complex and inevitable dynamic relationship between fact and value (Sayer, 2011, pp. 24–29). It is impossible to conduct value-free research, for two reasons. First, it is a logical impossibility. Such an assertion (i.e., that we can have a value-free science) requires that we make a value claim—that there can be value-free research. Second, with every question posed we make value statements. For example, when medical sociologists choose to research medical compliance or medication adherence, they are making a value choice. They are making a choice, in most instances, to explore the factors that will influence patient compliance (Conrad, 1992). One is often left to wonder about the values that drive all compliance research and how researchers may sometimes wittingly and unwittingly collude in oppressive forms of surveillance and control. And the medical sociologists' values are always in some particular interest: economic, political, professional, personal; these interests in some way, however minor—often unexpressed, unrecognized, or misrecognized—may serve the medical industrial complex or the pharmaceutical industry. Others may make choices to study the same phenomenon but with different and competing values. With engaged scholarship, one must continuously explore value differences among all stakeholders.

Finally, there is the *representational position* (Sayer, 2011, pp. 1–22; Todd & Nind, 2011). In this position, we face choices about how we talk or write about our research participants (Steinmetz, 2004, pp. 380–381). Anthropologists (e.g., Marcus & Fischer, 1999) and feminist scholars (e.g., Mulvey, 1975) have made invaluable contributions to our understanding of modes of representation. When we focus our representational strategies, for example, on one scene or character and not another, what are the consequences for those we study? Do we use the first or third person, for example? And what is the effect of using the third person when we talk to or about our subjects? Modes of representation, however, go well beyond rhetorical choices (Parton, 2008). They may involve unfair or inaccurate representations, fundamental failures of recognition (Honneth, 1996; Houston, 2008) and various forms of exclusion. Indeed, just as research is a complex and sometimes messy process, so are the choices we make about how best to represent our findings. Do we reduce our subjects to tables and charts? Do they become mere data points? And in adopting certain rhetorical strategies do we subject our research subjects to shame, exposure, and manipulation? And should we not reflect with our engaged partners on how findings might be used and to what ends? How do we give them voice and for what purposes? And what role do they play in decisions about representation? Finally, there are questions about how knowledge should be distributed. Should the distribution of research findings be left entirely to the whims of publishers, journals, and editors? And how should our research partners participate in decisions about modes of distribution? Should the knowledge be free and available to all of our research partners, and if not, why not?

We have illustrated in this book how engaged scholarship, critical realism, and qualitative methods can be used to investigate how the emergent properties of self (internal) and society (external) shape the situations in which we find ourselves and thus have the capacity to serve as constraints and enablements. These powers (social constraints and enablements), however, must be set into motion (activated) by agents. Therefore, engaged scholarship explores how researchers and practitioners, by virtue of their reflective powers, activate research projects.

CONCLUSION

Research detached from practice is disconnected from what is real, what is open, what can be experienced, and what is possible in human activity (Aram & Salipante, 2003; Van de Ven, 2007). We have argued, moreover, that the more one believes in an artificial distinction between *fact* and *value* (i.e., is and ought), the more one is removed not only from the actual world of practice but also from the things that matter most to people (Sayer, 2011). And the more we imagine (i.e., especially using methods that allow the imagination to follow positivism) that a separation between the two is possible, the less likely we are to grasp the true— subjective and objective—conditions of human suffering. Hannah Arendt has argued that through our wrestling with theory in practice, we become human and effective, and that we produce possibilities for human emancipation, democracy, and well-being (Arendt, 1963, 1978, 1981, 1998, 2006).

We have argued that it is not only effectiveness that guides our research actions and activities: we act according to prescribed political, moral, and ethical imperatives, not just in our self-interest or to maximize our opportunities and minimize our losses. Social work research is not only meant to challenge social institutions, policy, and practice. Research must tell us more than how things came to be and why. It must also give us a sense of how things ought to be in the ethics of caring (Flyvbjerg, 2001; Gray, 2008; Held, 2006, Sayer, 2007; Webb, 2006, pp. 210–234). Social work's critique of injustice, racism, or heterosexism, for example, requires that knowledge be generated to address institutionally generated false beliefs. Social work, moreover, is also committed to understanding and producing knowledge about how human needs are to be met and how, why, and when they are thwarted. And it is through knowledge that we learn something about the functions performed by false beliefs. And because of this, social work does not subscribe to a purely "objective" world, free from concept and value (Houston, 2005; Sayer, 2007). Knowledge produced in social work is always connected to the social worlds we inhabit and cannot be understood independently of the social actors (i.e., workers and clients, researchers and research subjects) involved in producing knowledge. Unlike the natural sciences, unlike electrons (i.e., brute facts), social entities (i.e., institutional facts) do not exist independent of the activities that govern them. The value-dependent nature of social work knowledge, however, must not be construed to mean that reality is simply produced with our concepts (see chapter 1).

In this book we have argued that social workers and researchers should collaboratively coproduce knowledge (Bourdieu & Wacquant, 1992: 39–42; Houston, 2005, p. 15). Engaged scholarship makes at least four assumptions about social work research: (1) Actors, networks, professional organizations, and licensing bodies assign significance to particular practice activities or actions. Practice is not limited to what social workers do (i.e., their activities) but also to the myriad ways practices are valorized, configured, and made significant and meaningful (Rouse, 1996, p. 133). (2) The contexts or fields within which practice unfolds are prescribed. And how we study these has enormous consequences for understanding what social workers actually do.[4] (3) The standards for conduct and action that circumscribe, limit, and enable practice among all professions matter (Abbott, 1988). For example, for many and complex reasons (e.g., forms of resistance, competing theories, personal, unconscious), social workers often depart from standard or prescribed practice. (4) Because professional practice exists in a creative tension with models or theories of practice (i.e., open systems), neither practice nor theory is reducible to one another (Stern, 2003, p. 187). This raises questions about why, when, how, and where practice guidelines are followed and the roles played by these guidelines in reproducing various forms or methods of practice (Floersch, 2004, 1997, 2002a). In short, social work is faced not only with asking questions about what it means to follow a given practice convention or guideline. We must also address what following a specific guideline achieves (Fay, 1975, pp. 29–41). Rarely, if ever, are the norms of practice derivative, that is, they are not a mutually understood, intentional, or consciously shared belief or value (Archer, 2010, pp. 123–144). Nor can practices be described as statistical averages; we *conform to practice* and our conformity shapes not only our practices but also our identities as social workers.

Social worker actions are not random and thus imponderable.[5] There are clear patterns and regularities to social worker action. Thus, the research methods we use should be aimed at understanding the ways these emerge, vary, and change. At the same time, however, because social work unfolds in open systems (i.e., homes and families, neighborhoods, communities, hospitals, and schools, where many mutually interacting causal mechanisms are at work) workers improvise, engage in novel action, and depart from recognized routines; they are versatile in different settings and often change action swiftly and unpredictably as they adapt to setting specific demands and client realities. Rarely is it the case that social worker and client interactions are stable and coordinated, mutually understood, or reciprocal. Moreover, while conscious, rational decision making is one way workers do this, not all actions are rationally or consciously considered or executed; nor is all social worker action oriented toward defined ends (Clarke & Hoggett, 2009; Archer, 2010b, 2010c).[6]

In sum, social work has two basic orientations toward understanding and studying practice. The first addresses the central significance of subjective experience for client, practitioner, and researcher. This orientation gives emphasis to the viewpoints of all participants and their subjective understandings and meaning making of mental health interventions, such as psychotropic treatment (illustrated in chapter 2). The second is aimed at understanding the enactment or performance of social

work activities (illustrated in chapter 3). Here, emphasis is on social conduct, that is, on how social workers act, how their actions change, what
forms their actions take and the outcomes of their actions (illustrated in
chapter 4). Both orientations have conscious and unconscious dimensions, tacit and implicit dimensions (Fook, 2002b; Hollway & Jefferson,
2000). And while neither is dominant they both depend on our habits,
impulses, emotions, intuitions, our values and desires (Smart, 2007).
Many who focus on tacit knowledge in practice focus on the subjective
experience of workers with the aim of reducing the effects of subjectivity
on practice outcomes (see Fook, 2002c, for a discussion of this). Others
focus on the role of subjectivity as a necessary and creative aspect of practice (Floersch, 2000). Both orientations mean that the role of reflexivity
in practice and research must be understood as an essential feature of
open systems. In sum, an open system includes the way social workers,
researchers, and clients *reflexively* coproduce knowledge under the
umbrella of engaged scholarship.

Appendix

 Ohio Mental Health Consumer Outcomes System
Adult Consumer Form

Today's Date ___ ___ / ___ ___ / ___ ___ ___ ___

Name _____

Date of Birth ___ ___ / ___ ___ / ___ ___ ___ ___

Gender (check one): Male ☐   Female ☐

Agency Use Only

Client's Medical Record Number

_____

We are very interested in how you are doing, and how our services may or may not be helping you. Please answer all of the questions below, then give the questionnaire to your case manager or another staff person at the mental health agency.

Part 1

Below are some questions about how satisfied you are with various aspects of your life in *the past 6 months*. For each question, checkmark ☑ the answer that best describes how you feel.

How do you feel about:

1. The amount of friendship in your life?
- ☐ Terrible
- ☐ Mostly dissatisfied
- ☐ Equally satisfied/dissatisfied
- ☐ Mostly satisfied
- ☐ Very pleased

2. The amount of money you get?
- ☐ Terrible
- ☐ Mostly dissatisfied
- ☐ Equally satisfied/dissatisfied
- ☐ Mostly satisfied
- ☐ Very pleased

3. How comfortable and well-off you are financially?
- ☐ Terrible
- ☐ Mostly dissatisfied
- ☐ Equally satisfied/dissatisfied
- ☐ Mostly satisfied
- ☐ Very pleased

4. How much money you have to spend for fun?
- ☐ Terrible
- ☐ Mostly dissatisfied
- ☐ Equally satisfied/dissatisfied
- ☐ Mostly satisfied
- ☐ Very pleased

5. The amount of meaningful activity in your life (such as work, school, volunteer activity, leisure activity)?
- ☐ Terrible
- ☐ Mostly dissatisfied
- ☐ Equally satisfied/dissatisfied
- ☐ Mostly satisfied
- ☐ Very pleased

6. The amount of freedom you have?
- ☐ Terrible
- ☐ Mostly dissatisfied
- ☐ Equally satisfied/dissatisfied
- ☐ Mostly satisfied
- ☐ Very pleased

7. The way you and your family act toward each other?
- ☐ Terrible
- ☐ Mostly dissatisfied
- ☐ Equally satisfied/dissatisfied
- ☐ Mostly satisfied
- ☐ Very pleased
- ☐ Does not apply

Please turn to the next page →

8. Your personal safety?

- [ ] Terrible
- [ ] Mostly dissatisfied
- [ ] Equally satisfied/dissatisfied
- [ ] Mostly satisfied
- [ ] Very pleased

9. The neighborhood in which you live?

- [ ] Terrible
- [ ] Mostly dissatisfied
- [ ] Equally satisfied/dissatisfied
- [ ] Mostly satisfied
- [ ] Very pleased

10. Your housing/living arrangements?

- [ ] Terrible
- [ ] Mostly dissatisfied
- [ ] Equally satisfied/dissatisfied
- [ ] Mostly satisfied
- [ ] Very pleased

11. Your health in general?

- [ ] Terrible
- [ ] Mostly dissatisfied
- [ ] Equally satisfied/dissatisfied
- [ ] Mostly satisfied
- [ ] Very pleased

12. How often do you have the opportunity to spend time with people you really like?

- [ ] Never
- [ ] Seldom/rarely
- [ ] Sometimes
- [ ] Often
- [ ] Always

Part 2

The next few items ask you about your health and medications *within the past 6 months.*

13. How often does your physical condition interfere with your day-to-day functioning?

- [ ] Never
- [ ] Seldom/rarely
- [ ] Sometimes
- [ ] Often
- [ ] Always

14. Concerns about my medications (such as side effects, dosage, type of medication) are addressed:

- [ ] Never
- [ ] Seldom/rarely
- [ ] Sometimes
- [ ] Often
- [ ] Always
- [ ] Not applicable/no medications

The next two items deal with how you have been treated by other people.

15. I have been treated with dignity and respect at this agency.

- [ ] Never
- [ ] Seldom/rarely
- [ ] Sometimes
- [ ] Often
- [ ] Always

16. How often do you feel threatened by people's reactions to your mental health problems?

- [ ] Never
- [ ] Seldom/rarely
- [ ] Sometimes
- [ ] Often
- [ ] Always

Part 3

The following questions ask you about how much you were distressed or bothered by some things *during the last seven days*. Please mark the answer that best describes how you feel.

During the past 7 days, about how much were you distressed or bothered by:

17. Nervousness or shakiness inside

- [ ] Not at all
- [ ] A little bit
- [ ] Some
- [ ] Quite a bit
- [ ] Extremely

Please turn to the next page ➜

18. Being suddenly scared for no reason

☐ Not at all
☐ A little bit
☐ Some
☐ Quite a bit
☐ Extremely

19. Feeling fearful

☐ Not at all
☐ A little bit
☐ Some
☐ Quite a bit
☐ Extremely

20. Feeling tense or keyed up

☐ Not at all
☐ A little bit
☐ Some
☐ Quite a bit
☐ Extremely

21. Spells of terror or panic

☐ Not at all
☐ A little bit
☐ Some
☐ Quite a bit
☐ Extremely

22. Feeling so restless you couldn't sit still

☐ Not at all
☐ A little bit
☐ Some
☐ Quite a bit
☐ Extremely

23. Heavy feelings in arms or legs

☐ Not at all
☐ A little bit
☐ Some
☐ Quite a bit
☐ Extremely

24. Feeling afraid to go out of your home alone

☐ Not at all
☐ A little bit
☐ Some
☐ Quite a bit
☐ Extremely

25. Feeling of worthlessness

☐ Not at all
☐ A little bit
☐ Some
☐ Quite a bit
☐ Extremely

26. Feeling lonely even when you are with people

☐ Not at all
☐ A little bit
☐ Some
☐ Quite a bit
☐ Extremely

27. Feeling weak in parts of your body

☐ Not at all
☐ A little bit
☐ Some
☐ Quite a bit
☐ Extremely

28. Feeling blue

☐ Not at all
☐ A little bit
☐ Some
☐ Quite a bit
☐ Extremely

29. Feeling lonely

☐ Not at all
☐ A little bit
☐ Some
☐ Quite a bit
☐ Extremely

30. Feeling no interest in things

☐ Not at all
☐ A little bit
☐ Some
☐ Quite a bit
☐ Extremely

31. Feeling afraid in open spaces or on the streets

☐ Not at all
☐ A little bit
☐ Some
☐ Quite a bit
☐ Extremely

Please turn to the next page →

32. How often can you tell when mental or emotional problems are about to occur?

☐ Never
☐ Seldom/rarely
☐ Sometimes
☐ Often
☐ Always

33. When you can tell, how often can you take care of the problems before they become worse?

☐ Never
☐ Seldom/rarely
☐ Sometimes
☐ Often
☐ Always

Part 4

Below are several statements relating to one's view about life and having to make decisions. Please check the response that is closest to how you feel about the statement. Check the word or words that best describes how you feel now.

34. I can pretty much determine what will happen in my life.

☐ Strongly agree
☐ Agree
☐ Disagree
☐ Strongly Disagree

35. People are limited only by what they think is possible.

☐ Strongly agree
☐ Agree
☐ Disagree
☐ Strongly Disagree

36. People have more power if they join together as a group.

☐ Strongly agree
☐ Agree
☐ Disagree
☐ Strongly Disagree

37. Getting angry about something never helps.

☐ Strongly agree
☐ Agree
☐ Disagree
☐ Strongly Disagree

38. I have a positive attitude toward myself.

☐ Strongly agree
☐ Agree
☐ Disagree
☐ Strongly Disagree

39. I am usually confident about the decisions I make.

☐ Strongly agree
☐ Agree
☐ Disagree
☐ Strongly Disagree

40. People have no right to get angry just because they don't like something.

☐ Strongly agree
☐ Agree
☐ Disagree
☐ Strongly Disagree

41. Most of the misfortunes in my life were due to bad luck.

☐ Strongly agree
☐ Agree
☐ Disagree
☐ Strongly Disagree

42. I see myself as a capable person.

☐ Strongly agree
☐ Agree
☐ Disagree
☐ Strongly Disagree

43. Making waves never gets you anywhere.

☐ Strongly agree
☐ Agree
☐ Disagree
☐ Strongly Disagree

Please turn to the next page ➜

44. People working together can have an effect on their community.

☐ Strongly agree
☐ Agree
☐ Disagree
☐ Strongly Disagree

45. I am often able to overcome barriers.

☐ Strongly agree
☐ Agree
☐ Disagree
☐ Strongly Disagree

46. I am generally optimistic about the future.

☐ Strongly agree
☐ Agree
☐ Disagree
☐ Strongly Disagree

47. When I make plans, I am almost certain to make them work.

☐ Strongly agree
☐ Agree
☐ Disagree
☐ Strongly Disagree

48. Getting angry about something is often the first step toward changing it.

☐ Strongly agree
☐ Agree
☐ Disagree
☐ Strongly Disagree

49. Usually I feel alone.

☐ Strongly agree
☐ Agree
☐ Disagree
☐ Strongly Disagree

50. Experts are in the best position to decide what people should do or learn.

☐ Strongly agree
☐ Agree
☐ Disagree
☐ Strongly Disagree

51. I am able to do things as well as most other people.

☐ Strongly agree
☐ Agree
☐ Disagree
☐ Strongly Disagree

52. I generally accomplish what I set out to do.

☐ Strongly agree
☐ Agree
☐ Disagree
☐ Strongly Disagree

53. People should try to live their lives the way they want to.

☐ Strongly agree
☐ Agree
☐ Disagree
☐ Strongly Disagree

54. You can't fight city hall (authority).

☐ Strongly agree
☐ Agree
☐ Disagree
☐ Strongly Disagree

55. I feel powerless most of the time.

☐ Strongly agree
☐ Agree
☐ Disagree
☐ Strongly Disagree

56. When I am unsure about something, I usually go along with the rest of the group.

☐ Strongly agree
☐ Agree
☐ Disagree
☐ Strongly Disagree

57. I feel I am a person of worth, at least on an equal basis with others.

☐ Strongly agree
☐ Agree
☐ Disagree
☐ Strongly Disagree

Please turn to the next page →

58. People have a right to make their own decisions, even if they are bad ones.

- ☐ Strongly agree
- ☐ Agree
- ☐ Disagree
- ☐ Strongly Disagree

59. I feel I have a number of good qualities.

- ☐ Strongly agree
- ☐ Agree
- ☐ Disagree
- ☐ Strongly Disagree

60. Very often a problem can be solved by taking action.

- ☐ Strongly agree
- ☐ Agree
- ☐ Disagree
- ☐ Strongly Disagree

61. Working with others in my community can help to change things for the better.

- ☐ Strongly agree
- ☐ Agree
- ☐ Disagree
- ☐ Strongly Disagree

Part 5

Please tell us some things about yourself.

62. What was the last school grade you completed?

- ☐ Less than 1st grade
- ☐ 1st grade
- ☐ 2nd grade
- ☐ 3rd grade
- ☐ 4th grade
- ☐ 5th grade
- ☐ 6th grade
- ☐ 7th grade
- ☐ 8th grade
- ☐ 9th grade
- ☐ 10th grade
- ☐ 11th grade
- ☐ High school diploma/GED
- ☐ Trade/Tech school
- ☐ Some college
- ☐ 2 yr college/Associate degree
- ☐ 4 yr college/Undergraduate degree
- ☐ Graduate school courses
- ☐ Graduate degree
- ☐ Post-graduate studies
- ☐ Further special studies

63. Race (check all that apply):

- ☐ White
- ☐ Native American/Pacific Islander
- ☐ Black/African American
- ☐ Hispanic/Latino
- ☐ Asian
- ☐ Other _____

64. What is your marital status?

- ☐ Never married
- ☐ Married
- ☐ Separated
- ☐ Divorced
- ☐ Widowed
- ☐ Living together

65. What is your current living situation?

- ☐ Your own house/apartment
- ☐ Friend's home
- ☐ Relative's home
- ☐ Supervised group living
- ☐ Supervised apartment
- ☐ Boarding home
- ☐ Crisis residential
- ☐ Child foster care
- ☐ Adult foster care
- ☐ Intermediate care facility
- ☐ Skilled nursing facility
- ☐ Respite care
- ☐ MR intermediate care facility
- ☐ Licensed MR facility
- ☐ State MR institution
- ☐ State MH institution
- ☐ Hospital
- ☐ Correctional facility
- ☐ Homeless
- ☐ Rest home
- ☐ Other _____

66. What is your employment status?

- ☐ Employed full time
- ☐ Employed part time
- ☐ Sheltered employment
- ☐ Unemployed
- ☐ Student
- ☐ Homemaker
- ☐ Retired
- ☐ Disabled
- ☐ Inmate of institution

67. Are you in treatment because you want to be?

- ☐ Yes
- ☐ No

Please stop here. Thanks!

Glossary

Action Research Sometimes called participatory action research, this is a mode of relating to research subjects (i.e., not as objects) and of involving them in the research process. Action research is also aimed at producing change in social systems and is a mode of political engagement alongside research.

Actual, Real, Empirical These are terms used by critical realists to understand the structured nature of reality.

Agency/Structure Widely discussed and debated in the social sciences and philosophy, these terms refer to how individuals, as social actors, relate to macro processes and social structures (i.e., states, economies, social classes) and how social structures limit or determine social action. These terms also refer to the degrees of autonomy that social actors have in relationship to determinate social structures and how actors and actions are transformed by structure and in turn transform structure.

Arbitrage An engaged scholarship strategy of describing and identifying different and similar methodological dimensions (i.e., ontology, epistemology, theory, and values) and research methods (i.e., design, sampling, data collection, and data analysis).

Behaviorism A theory and method of clinical practice that assumes that human action can be explained without reference to the mind or internal mental states. Behaviorism assumes that mental concepts in practice and in science should be replaced with behavioral ones.

Brute Fact Objects of science that refer to entities such as structures, causal powers, and mechanisms that are independent from observation. Critical realists call this the "intransitive" realm.

Closed System Refers to experimental or environmental closure, where factors or variables are contained and controlled by researchers or practitioners (i.e., in laboratories).

Common Sense explanations that depend on sensory inputs and offer simple accounts of the world based upon what is seen, heard, or felt. Common sense refers to our everyday ways of understanding the world "the proof of the pudding is in the eating."

Contingent (Contingency) In open systems, since events are not predetermined, they depend on continually changing conditions. Contingency is usually contrasted with necessity. For example, for water to exist, you must (i.e., necessary for) have hydrogen and oxygen atoms. This is not a contingent condition.

Critical Realism A philosophy of social science that argues for the material presence of the social and natural world and assumes that the material presence exists outside of our knowledge of it. It discovers the deeper structures and relations that are not directly observable but lie behind the surface of social reality. Critical realism formulates an ontology that is capable of describing a world where change is possible.

Different but Interdependent Posits that methodological assumptions are sometimes incommensurable and when they are, it is not sufficient to argue that different assumptions lead to equally valid knowledge claims "my perspective is different, but since its equal to yours I can autonomously produce knowledge." Instead, engaged scholarship directs research partners to openly discuss methodological differences and similarities, and through arbitrage acknowledge that dissension is part of knowledge production. An equal but autonomous perspective leads to parallel universes in which research is conducted independently.

Downward Causation A type of causation that includes emergence and a stratified reality, e.g., each of these—body, brain, mind, self, and identity—exist in a stratified reality; each emerges from the other, and each may act back (i.e., downward) on lower levels to produce new configurations or structures.

Downward Conflation The reduction of the mind and mental states to social forces, discourses, or narratives. The mind, for example, has no emergent powers and is completely dependent on social forces.

Downward Transfer This is a one-way knowledge transfer, from the expert to the practitioner or client, from the knowledge producer to those who use knowledge.

Empiricism An epistemology that claims that the real and knowable (ontological) is only that which lends itself to direct observation or empirical investigation. Radical behaviorism is a form of empiricism.

Engaged Scholarship A form of research that includes multiple stakeholders in defining the aim, designing the study, and analyzing the data. It includes the arbitrage of ontological and epistemological differences that involve each phase of research.

Epistemic Fallacy Reducing what we know to how we know it. Statements about being are interpreted as statements about knowledge. *Behaviorism* is a good example. For behaviorists, observable behavior and events (i.e., human actions) are emphasized at the expense of unobserved (i.e., unobservable mental states, schemas, drives, unconscious states, dreams, etc.).

Epistemology Refers in the philosophy of science to how we make knowledge claims. The criterion utilized for making a truth claim. Sometimes theory of knowledge.

Equal but Autonomous Knowledge Assumes that different ways of knowing (i.e., ontology and epistemology) can be paired with proper contexts (i.e., practice with the subjective and research with the objective) and therefore should have equal explanatory power. Engaged scholarship strives for different but interdependent coproduction.

Essentialism The philosophical assumption that any kind of social or psychological entity (i.e., gender, sexuality, social class, and ethnicity) has properties that can be precisely defined or described. These entities are given, irreducible, and have a single definition or meaning.

Ethnography A research method wherein researchers collect data while in the natural environment of the object of study (e.g., neighborhood, clinic, household, organization, community, hospital, school, gangs, etc.).

Evidence-Based Practice Aims to apply the best available evidence gained from positivist methodology to clinical decision making. It assigns practical value to the strength of evidence so that some diagnostic systems and treatments (including lack of treatment) are given preference over others.

Experience-Near Refers to everyday life experience that is characterized in the first person. For example "After taking my anti-anxiety medication, I feel relieved." "I am searching for words to describe how I feel."

Fact/Value A false dichotomy in science that assumes some facts are objective and some are subjective or value-laden.

Fidelity In evidence-based clinical practice, an implementation assumption that requires practitioners to follow a manual of prescribed actions. It means being loyal to the practice.

Habitus Pierre Bourdieu, a French sociologist, used this concept to talk about the many ways that we embody social conventions (i.e., norms, habits). For example, our linguistic habits, our habits of eating, our interactional patterns, are all forms of habitus.

In Vivo Latin for "within the living"; refers in social science research to data collection that takes places in real time, live, and within the worlds of research subjects or partners.

Incommensurable The assumption that ontologies and epistemologies are unequal and irreconcilable; in short, because of different assumptions, in engaged scholarship partners agree to disagree.

Institutional Ethnography A research method similar to ethnography; however, institutional ethnography, developed by sociologist Dorothy Smith, describes a detailed account of institutional processes that structure and organize everyday experience.

Emergence For critical realism (and others in the philosophy of social science) this concept describes the powers and liabilities possessed by objects and the relationships among them. The mind, for example, emerges from the brain, which emerges from the body.

Institutional Fact A concept that refers to phenomenon whose existence is dependent on external social structures; these facts do not have an independent material presence, as do brute facts.

Knowledge Coproduction Knowledge produced in engaged scholarship projects by research partners using arbitrage.

Mechanism (Causal Mechanism) In critical realism, mechanism refers to unobservable phenomenon that requires theory to posit its powers to produce effects.

Method Refers to sampling techniques, data collection techniques, and data analytic techniques.

Methodology In social science, the ontological and epistemological assumptions guiding every research decision: aims, questions, design, including method choices.

Ontology Refers in science to assumptions about what exists, what we take to be knowable or real.

Open Systems In critical realism, events are not predetermined and depend therefore on all the conditions, observable and unobservable, that a given environment or context produces. The latter means that attempts to close are arbitrary.

Phenomenological Practice Gap (PPG) Explores the role of our experience in coming to know phenomena in our various worlds of practice, that is, between the knower, the practitioner and the known, the client. And it assumes that the theory or model of practice will never perfectly fit the world of practice, therefore a gap, of some size, will always exist.

Phenomenology The study of structures of consciousness as experienced from the first-person point of view.

Positive Variance A term used in evidence-based research implementation to describe how some contexts require variations in application.

Positivism The dominant methodology in the social sciences. It assumes closed systems and the identification of variables that can be isolated and with statistical methods shown to be correlated or predictive.

Primary Data Collection Data directly observed or collected by the researcher.

Reductionism There are different types of reductionism social, biological. In social reduction (Margaret Archer calls this "downward conflation"), the individual, agency, or individual action is reduced to the social conditions for the action. With biological reduction, the individual or social world is reduced to the genes, the brain, or the body. Critical realists argue that reducing one level of stratified reality to another erases the power and liabilities of the various levels of reality. For example, the mind becomes a function of the brain.

Reflexivity A concept that refers to different modes of self-reflection in research personal, ontological, epistemological, methodological, theoretical, representative, and normative.

Relevance Versus Rigor Rigor is often privileged in positivist research and refers to how stringently the methods are applied. Relevance is often subordinated to rigor. A project might be rigorous but not relevant to practice and to what matters most to people.

Scholastic Fallacy Means guarding against the often unconscious tendency to assign (i.e., based upon their modes of training and methodology) "systematicity" to objects of your research and practice when it is not present. For example, researchers may see or imagine that workers or clients are following unambiguous rules or strategies when they are not; or when they are following rules and procedures they always do so in indeterminate and unstated ways.

Social Constructivism Assumes that phenomena are socially constructed; objects of social science have no material presence independent of thought. There are strong and weak forms of constructivism. Some argue that there is no object world independent of our thoughts about it. Gravity, for the strong constructivist, exists only in thought, not in reality. Gravity, in short, is not a **brute fact.**

Standpoint Theory A methodological position for analyzing objects of study that endeavors to develop an epistemology for effective knowledge that starts with the insight of a person's particular experience, context, or standpoint. It is often attributed to feminist theorists.

Variables-Based Research Research methodology that assumes closed systems and utilizes the assumptions of positivism, including the central assumption that independent variables predict dependent ones.

Notes

Introduction

[1] Deborah Padgett, in her book, *Qualitative Methods in Social Work Research* (2008), borrows from critical realism the idea of "open system" but confuses open systems with the hermeneutic circle. Padgett writes, "qualitative research is predicated on an 'open systems' assumption where the observational (and the observer) is part of the study itself (Manicas & Secord, 1982). In contrast, quantitative research favors a closed (or controlled) system approach in which every effort is made to neutralize the effects of observational context (including the observer)" (Padgett, 2008, p. 2). The hermeneutic circle is an interpretative process that begins with how one relates a work's parts to the work as a whole.

Chapter 1

[1] Some have argued that we have traded rigor for relevance, that is, as our methods and training in methods (quantitative and qualitative) have supplanted practice training and practice methods, we've seen a steady decline in relevance. Here's another way of seeing this: with the growing emphasis on statistics and methodology in graduate education, there's been a steady decline in clinical training and these skills must now be acquired postgraduate. And with increasing emphasis on methods, especially in doctoral education, we have paid less and less attention to the skills necessary to supervise students.

[2] This is sometimes called empiricism. Empiricism is a way of knowing the world that gives exclusive emphasis to sensory experience. Empiricists argue that we can only know the world through our direct experience of it. "The proof of the

pudding is in the eating." For example, for the empiricist, dreams (and other invisible mental activities) are unknowable because they cannot be directly observed or experienced in a sensory way.

[3] Yet while our capacity to observe (i.e., personal and reflective as well as technology-driven) may increase our confidence in what we *believe* to exist, the existence of the things we observe does not depend on our observations (we will have more to say about the concept-dependent nature of our knowledge later). In short, Tyshawn will go on having an earache whether we observe it or not; the earache and underlying structures (i.e., the toxins enabled by the bacteria, the structures unique to his particular ear, and the structured conditions of living) exist independent of our observations. The same can be said for many of the events and phenomena social workers face in everyday practice and research.

[4] In his work, John Searle, a philosopher of mind, distinguishes brute from institutional facts.

[5] Searle, J. (1995). *The construction of social reality*. New York: Free Press.

[6] Yet there are often times when institutions attempt to impose their own understanding of brute facts to distort reality. Think, for example, of Galileo's struggle with the Church when in 1633 he argued that the Earth goes around the Sun. 346 years later Pope John Paul (1979) admitted that the institution had distorted the facts and that Galileo had been wrongly accused. In more recent times some have argued that the HIV virus does not cause AIDS. Others, also influenced by powerful ideological and political forces, argue that the causes of mental illness are to be found solely in neurotransmitters or in structures of the brain. And not too long ago there was widespread psychiatric consensus that homosexuality was a disease. In sum, powerful institutions (e.g., the Church, biopsychiatry, the pharmaceutical industry) have much at stake in what is accepted, or not, as brute facts, often with lethal consequences.

[7] Vakharia, K., Shapiro, N., & Bhattacharyya, N. (2010). Demographic disparities among children with frequent ear infections in the United States. *The Laryngoscope*. 120, 8. 1667 DOI: 10.1002/lary.20961

[8] There are several kinds of reductionism. First, there is scientism. This form of reductionism assumes that the methods used in the physical sciences can and should be applied to the human sciences (e.g., psychology, sociology, social work). There is also naturalism. This assumes that what we study, that is, the things we study in the physical or natural sciences, are not unlike the events, circumstances, and so forth that we study in the human sciences and thus should be studied using the same methods. Biological reductionism is a form of naturalism: it reduces human events, circumstances, behaviors, emotions, and thought to the function of nerve cells, hormones, or brain structures.

[9] In social work research, Stanley Houston (2005) offers the very best discussion of open systems. See in particular his article, Philosophy, theory and method in

social work: Challenging empiricism's claim on evidence-based practice. *Journal of Social Work, 5*(1), 7–20.

[10] Even Foucault finally returned to some notion of structure in his discussion of the self, especially when he realized that agential resistance is "predicated upon a self which has been violated, knows it, and can do something about it." Yet his early work precluded precisely this. In order to account for why power can be resisted, and thus to retain his own critical stance toward it, he has to reintroduce premises about the natural desires of people, which means withdrawing the earlier view that humanity is in no respect an entity—in place of a being, one of whose properties is to resist those things done to it that are contrary to its nature (Archer, 2000, pp. 32–33).

[11] "In none of these cases is the power something that can be exercised arbitrarily; it depends on the structure of the 'agent,' and can be exercised only in certain conditions" (Collier, 1981, p. 8).

[12] In psychology (i.e., James Garbarino, 1999, 2001) and social work (Rapp & Goscha, 2006) two concepts have emerged, without theoretical location, to describe these countervailing forces, strengths, and resilience. These concepts, both meant to describe protective forces in the external environment, might also be seen as countervailing forces. As countervailing forces, they create the possibility of same internal working model producing multiple outcomes.

[13] Stanley Lieberson and Freda Lynn write in their 2002 *Annual Review* article about the limits of prediction in sociology: "In our estimation, it is the fact that sociology's notion of prediction and deduction from theory is based on the classical physics model in which determinism seems to work pretty well, but that most natural sciences have a much more modest goal. As a consequence, we are again trying to do something that we have no business expecting to be able to do, at least in a world of complex influences that are not restrained as they would be in a true experiment. This again leads to unrealistic goals and forced efforts to have tests of predictability that are not appropriate, as well as criticisms from those dubious about the possibility of sociology being a science because they implicitly use a standard from classical physics rather than a more realistic standard of how it works in the wider set of sciences. Ironically, in the case of prediction, this is difficult in almost all of the natural sciences, given that they work with probabilistic situations. Indeed, there are parts of physics that have the same problem" (Lieberson & Lynn, 2002, p. 10).

[14] For social work researchers and practitioners one of the most important and recent works demonstrating these complex dynamics is to be found in a work compiled by Shonkoff and Phillips, 2000, *From Neurons to Neighborhoods: The Science of Early Childhood Development,* published jointly by the National Academies of Science and the National Institute of Medicine.

[15] Hedstrom and Ylikoski have recently published a review, Causal mechanisms in the social sciences, *Annual Review of Sociology, 36,* 49–67.

[16] In the social constructivist critique of psychoanalytic understandings of development, embodied, natural selves have been entirely elided (James et al., 1998, pp. 20–21). This is true, as well, in Vygotsky's understanding of development, where the "private is always posterior to the public, and, until the public has been internalized, we cannot begin to talk about privatization."

[17] This, similarly, was a turn made by both Habermas and Lacan in their surprisingly comparable efforts to obviate Freud's "distinction between thing-representation and word-representations: both are subsumed under the larger category of the signifier, and the distinct nature of images, as opposed to words is lost" (Whitebook, 1995, p. 181).

[18] Anthropologists and some sociologists have made a cottage industry using social constructivism to critique Western nosology (i.e., diagnostic systems and classifications, DSM) in mental health. They almost inevitably confuse construal with construction and by so doing create enormous conceptual difficulties in the discussion of causality.

[19] Adolph Grunbaum can be counted among the more vociferous critics of psychoanalytic theory in this regard. He argues that the weakest link is to be found in what he calls "contamination." "The analyst shapes the patient's material from the beginning of an analysis, by verbal interpretations and by more implicit means of influence and suggestion."

[20] This is also true but in a different way for positivists or behaviorists who altogether dismiss the operation of unobserved or unobservable causal mechanism (e.g., Crews' famous attack on psychoanalysis, Grunbaum, etc.).

[21] See Fook et al. (2006) for thorough integration and discussion of these debates.

[22] See Jerry Floersch's essay, Reading the case record: The oral and written narratives of social workers (2000), for detailed discussion of how social scientists mistakenly assume that the case record accurately reflects actual practice. Among other things, he argues that the case record often deliberately distorts the everyday practice of workers. He explores the many and sometimes contradictory reasons for writing records and the reasons for distorting or withholding information.

[23] In this book we argue something very different, so we will not spend a great deal of time further exploring the many debates and ways that scholars and philosophers have seen, exploited, and debated these different assumptions (i.e., ontological and epistemological) between qualitative and quantitative methods (Bryman, 1984; Hammersley, 2000; Houston, 2005, pp. 8–12; Qureshi, 2004). Some see qualitative methods as useful starting places for research to clarify or explore questions or clear ground for the use of "real" and more

thorough, "rigorous" methods. Here, qualitative methods are largely in the service of quantitative methods as handmaidens. The philosopher John Locke once described himself as an under laborer, as a philosopher clearing the brush or preparing the way for others to do the "real" research. This might be one way to describe how some see qualitative methods and methodologists (Bryman, 2008; Magill, 2002, p. 109; Steinmetz, 2004). For others, quantitative and qualitative are *incommensurable* (Sale, Lohfeld & Brazil, 2002; Steinmetz, 2004). This can mean several things. It can mean that *qualitative* and *quantitative* refer to different realities (i.e., incommensurable realities), that is, as methods to be used to explore fundamentally different kinds of things. Some, for example, might argue that qualitative methods are most appropriate and perhaps the only means to explore *subjective experience* or practice as it unfolds in real time, specific settings, or contexts. This would of course mean that *quantitative* methods are used to understand phenomena out of context, out of time or history or environment. And this would be an especially untenable argument. One could easily imagine using statistical techniques to explore some aspects, but not all, of subjective experience.

[24] Sociologists and anthropologists (along with many in social work and psychology) use ethnographic methods to explore events, activities, and experience as they unfold in natural settings over time. In ethnography, the researcher engages in face-to-face interaction with participants for the purpose of eliciting the experience-near.

[25] For a very long time many assumed that the Earth was the center of the universe. Some call this the geocentric or Ptolemaic view, and it was supported by many important philosophers: for example Aristotle and Ptolemy. If one trusts only one's eyes, it is easy to see how this conclusion can be drawn. First, the sun, the stars, and the planets appear to revolve around the Earth, each day, leaving the observer with the impression that the earth is at the center. Second, from the perspective of the observer on Earth, it appears that the planet does not move: it is stable, fixed, solid, unmoving, at rest. Galileo challenged this view and in 1616 was sentenced to a lifetime under house arrest.

[26] Social work has many and competing epistemologies. Some practitioners and researchers, for example, would not consider the possibility of there being invisible mental states (schemas, dreams, drives) with the causal powers to produce real and enduring effects. Behaviorists, for example, subscribe to this notion. Others might subscribe to strict forms of rationalism (sometimes called idealism) and logical or linguistic ways of knowing.

[27] Empiricism, however, should never be confused with empirical. Empirical refers to the things we study (e.g., mental events and behaviors, emotions, bacteria, cells, etc.), whereas empiricism refers to a restricted and limited way of knowing those things, that is, exclusively through our sensory experience and apparatus.

[28] It should be noted here that few in contemporary psychology doubt the existence of the unconscious. What remains controversial is the nature of unconscious (Horowtiz, 1997; Stein, 1997).

[29] Today, with the rise of cognitive science, behaviorism has been superseded by more sophisticated understandings of mind and personhood (Cavell, 2006; Clarke, 2008; Lahire, 2011, pp. 79–80; Smith, 2010).

[30] It should be noted that even where behaviorism was not the explicit model of practice, behavioral outcomes were often used as the measure of success and imposed on other models of practice.

[31] Manualized treatments require erasure of the uniqueness of each therapeutic encounter; the application of outcomes-based rules across diverse cases; elimination of tacit knowledge (the type of knowledge that in most cases is employed by expert practitioners) (Dreyfus and Dreyfus, 1986; Dunne 1993; Sayer, 2011).

[32] In 1973, Joel Fisher, a social work researcher, wrote an article, "Is social case work effective: A review," in which he challenges social work to examine its "unscientific practices."

[33] It is a very interesting but not well-explored fact that anthropology (cultural and social anthropology) has not been dominated by the variables approach (Stocking, 1998, pp. 81–87).

[34] See Jeanne Marsh (2004) for discussion of how behaviorism in social work was established and promoted.

[35] The shift in social work to a more uniform understanding of what counted as science (variables approach or positivism), however, began in earnest only in the 1970s, many years after similar moves in sociology, political science, and psychology (see Steinmetz, 2005a, for discussion of historical dynamics in the social sciences more generally). But it happened without doubt in similar ways (Mattini & Moore, 2004, pp. 55–73, Thyer, 2004, pp. 74–87). Variables research came to dominate the major journals and new journals, textbooks, and professional associations; the faculty in the leading departments; and the major funding streams. Steinmetz writes similarly of the development of positivism within sociology, "Without some intellectual diversity, such as disagreements on epistemology, methodology, and theory, there would be no raw materials that strategies of domination could sink their claws into and wield as weapons of differentiation or distinction" (Steinmetz, 2005a, p. 115). Social work, however, lacking clear disciplinary affiliations and a theory base, made a radical and decisive turn to methodology (mostly variables based) as means of establishing legitimacy and of assuring researchers a place at the table (see Andrew Sayer, 2011, and George Steinmetz, 2005a, 2005b, for very important and interesting discussions of how disciplinarity limits our capacities to offer causal accounts of events in open systems). Finally, social work also embraced scientism; according to this view,

because the objects of study in the human and the natural sciences are equivalent, their methods must also be shared (Denzin & Lincoln, 2000, pp. 7–10; Houston, 2005, p. 7; Steinmetz, 2005a). The latter has meant that in social work events, objects, mental life, and various practices have been treated as brute facts whose identity is somehow unrelated to the many and complex ways clients and workers think about and interpret them (Thyer, 2004, pp. 74–87).

Chapter 2

[1] This is an ontological claim that Paul Ricoeur makes.
[2] In this tradition, the human experience is defined by meaning-making capacities and interpretation.
[3] We used ATLAS.ti. to make the links. However, because the hyperlink is a more complicated tool, we chose not to describe it in this book. You can, of course, try it on your own. A cut and paste method, using any word processing software, works too, if you don't want to learn another software function.
[4] However, bench scientist, pharmaceutical salesman, and FDA officials, for example, are never involved at this level of reality.

Chapter 3

[1] See chapter 1 for discussion of critical realist understanding of how and when narratives or discourses are activated.
[2] This strategy, as suggested by its name, results from your use of one participant who suggests yet another potential participant or interviewee, thus snowballing until you have many participants.

Chapter 4

[1] Remember, however, the purpose of arbitrage is not to force consensus: arbitrage is designed to examine conceptual and practice differences. In this case, policymakers, jail staff, clinicians, and clients all have different needs and each group values different outcomes. Thus, engaged scholarship requires a design that does not foreclose on any one group and it recognizes that some differences cannot be reconciled in one project. Stakeholders must agree to disagree in principle but they must also agree and take action to iteratively collect data and reload each new project with the findings from the previous. With iteratively new aims, design, and data, it is likely that some disagreements will dissolve.

Chapter 5

[1] Graham Clarke (2008) offers a very compelling argument about the limits of Archer's account of how we come to have, in the first instance, our capacities for internal conversation.

[2] This is often referred to as the hermeneutic circle.

[3] Finlay (2002), in her examination of the reflexive experiences of qualitative researchers across various research traditions, identified five variants of reflexivity: (1) Introspection—the examining of one's own experiences and personal meanings; insights can emerge from personal introspection which then form the basis of a more generalized understanding and interpretations; reflections are assumed to provide data regarding the social/emotional world of participants (p. 214); (2) Inter-subjective reflection—the mutual meanings emerging within the research relationship [between participant and researcher] via the situated and negotiated nature of the research encounter (p. 215); (3) Mutual collaboration—purposive reflexive dialogue between participants/co-researchers and researchers that occurs minimally at data analysis and evaluation, in which there are cycles of sharing, honing and refining interpretations in response to the dialogue (p. 218); (4) Social critique—situating such purposive dialogues within a theoretical framework about the social construction of power at the micro and macro levels (p. 222); (5) Discursive deconstruction—making explicit the dynamic, multiple meanings embedded in language used, and considering how that impacts on modes of presentation (p. 222).

[4] Here, the knowledge of the practitioner is conflated with that of the client. Moreover, acceptance of the discursive and situated nature of knowledge does not require acceptance of the notion that its referents lack essential qualities. For some, because our clients come to share our concepts, ipso facto, they are seen or understood as the produced effect of our concepts or discourse. Anthropologists, sociologists (especially those working within the sociology and anthropology of science), historians of clinical practice and social work (Kunzel, 1993; Gordon, 1994; Lunbeck, 1994; Odem, 1995; Summerson Carr, 2010), and narrative therapists in clinical social work and cognate fields (especially those inspired by Foucault) argue that clinical work (pathologizing, classifying, disciplining, marginalizing, dominating) produces client subjectivity or even invents madness.

[5] See Ira Cohen's essay, "Theories of Action and Praxis," chapter 3, 1996, in *The Blackwell Companion to Social Theory*, edited by Bryan Turner.

[6] Much of the history of social work has been written as if workers engage in action within the structure of a telos, that is, with an end point in mind. See chapter 1.

References

Abbott, A. (1988). *The system of professions: An essay on the division of expert labor.* Chicago: University of Chicago Press.

Abbott, A. (2004). The idea of outcome in U.S. sociology. In G. Steinmetz (Ed.), *The politics of method in the social sciences: Positivism and its epistemological others* (pp. 393–426). Durham: Duke University Press.

Abram, K. M., & Teplin, L. A. (1991). Co-occurring disorders among mentally ill jail detainees: Implications for public policy. *American Psychologist, 46,* 1036–1045.

Agar, M. H. (1996). *The professional stranger: An informal introduction to ethnography* (2nd ed.). San Diego: Academic Press.

Alegria, M., & McGuire, T. (2003). Rethinking a universal framework in the psychiatric symptom-disorder relationship. *Journal of Health and Social Behavior, 44*(3), 257–274.

Allen, D., Gilchrist, L., Brown, L., & Cox, G. (1994). One system, many perspectives: Stakeholders and mental health system evaluation. *Evaluation and Program Planning, 17*(1), 47–51.

Aram, J. D., & Salipante Jr, P. F. (2003). Bridging scholarship in management: Epistemological reflections. *British Journal of Management, 14*(3), 189–205.

Archer, M. (1995). *Realist social theory: The morphogenetic approach.* Cambridge: Cambridge University Press.

Archer, M. (2000). *Being human: The problem of agency.* Cambridge: Cambridge University Press.

Archer, M. (2003). *Structure, agency and the internal conversation.* Cambridge: Cambridge University Press.

Archer, M. S. (2007). *Making our way through the world: Human reflexivity and social mobility.* Cambridge: Cambridge University Press.

Archer, M. S. (2010a). *Conversations about reflexivity*. Abingdon, Oxon; New York: Routledge.

Archer, M. S. (2010b). Morphogenesis versus structuration: On combining structure and action. 1982. *The British Journal of Sociology, 61* Suppl 1, 225–252. doi:10.1111/j.1468–4446.2009.01245.x

Archer, M. S. (2010c). Routine, reflexivity, and realism. *Sociological Theory, 28*(3), 272–303.

Arendt, H. (1978). *The life of the mind* (1st ed.). New York: Harcourt Brace Jovanovich.

Arendt, H. (1981). *The life of the mind* (1 Harve/HBJ ed.). New York: Harcourt Brace Jovanovich.

Arendt, H. (1998). *The human condition* (2nd ed.). Chicago: University of Chicago Press.

Arendt, H. (2006; 1963). *Eichmann in Jerusalem: A report on the banality of evil.* New York: Penguin Books.

Arnd-Caddigan, M., & Pozzuto, R. (2008). Types of knowledge, forms of practice. *The Qualitative Report, 13*(1), 61–77.

Azevedo, J. (1997). *Mapping reality: An evolutionary realist methodology for the natural and social sciences.* Albany: State University of New York Press.

Backer, T.E. (2001) Finding the balance: Program fidelity and adaptation in substance abuse prevention. A State-of-the-Art Review. Rockville, MD: US Department of Health and Human Service, Center for Substance Abuse Prevention.

Barrett, L. F. (2009). The future of psychology: Connecting mind to brain. *Perspectives on Psychological Science, 4*(4), 326.

Bauer, R. L., Morgan, R. D., & Mandracchia, J. T. (2011). Offenders with severe and persistent mental illness. In T. J. Fagan, & R. K. Ax (Eds.), *Correctional mental health: From theory to best practice* (pp. 189–212). Thousand Oaks, CA: Sage Publications.

Bellefeuille, G. & Ricks, F. (2010). Relational inquiry: A child and youth care approach to research. *Children and Youth Services Review, 32*, 1235–1241.

Berlin, S. B., & Marsh, J. C. (1993). *Informing practice decisions.* Chicago: Prentice Hall.

Bernal, G., Bonilla, J., & Bellido, C. (1995). Ecological validity and cultural sensitivity for outcome research: Issues for cultural adaptation and development of psychosocial treatments with hispanics. *Journal of Abnormal Child Psychology, 23*(1), 2367–2382.

Bhaskar, R. (1975). *A realist theory of science* Leeds: Leeds Books.

Bhaskar, R. (1986). *Scientific realism and human emancipation.* London: Verson.

Bhaskar, R. (1998). *The possibility of naturalism: A philosophical critique of the contemporary human sciences.* London: Routledge.

Bhaskar, R. (2008). *Dialectic: The pulse of freedom*. London; New York: Routledge.

Bourdieu, P. (1977). *Outline of a theory of practice*. Cambridge: Cambridge University Press.

Bourdieu, P., & Wacquant, L. J. D. (1992). *An invitation to reflexive sociology*. Chicago: University of Chicago Press.

Boyatzis, R. E. (1998). *Transforming qualitative information: Thematic analysis and code development*. Thousand Oaks, CA.: Sage Publications.

Boyer, E. L. (1990). *Scholarship reconsidered: Priorities of the professoriate*. Princeton, NJ: Carnegie Foundation for the Advancement of Teaching.

Bradbury, H., & Reason, P. (2003). Action research: An opportunity for revitalizing research purposes and practices. *Qualitative Social Work, 2*(2), 155–175.

Braslow, J. (1997). *Mental ills and bodily cures*. Berkeley, CA: University of California Press.

Braun, V., & Clarke, V. (2006). Using thematic analysis in psychology. *Qualitative Research in Psychology, 3*(2), 77–101.

Breen, L. J., & Darlaston-Jones, D. (2010). Moving beyond the enduring dominance of positivism in psychological research: Implications for psychology in Australia. *Australian Psychologist, 45*(1), 67–76.

Brooks, P. (1992). *Reading for the plot design and intention in narrative*. Cambridge, MA: Harvard University Press.

Bryman, A. (1984). The debate about quantitative and qualitative research: A question of method or epistemology? *The British Journal of Sociology, 35*(1), 75–92.

Bryman, A. (2008). *Social research methods* (Third ed.). Oxford: Oxford University Press.

Bullock, W. A., O'Rourke, M., & Smith, M. K. (2005). Implementing illness management & recovery in mental health practices and agencies. *Family Therapy Magazine, 4*(3), 32–36.

Bullock, W. A., Sage, J., Hupp, D., O'Rourke, M., & Smith, M. K. (August, 2007). *Development and evaluation of the wellness management and recovery (WMR) program*. Unpublished manuscript.

Campbell, M. (2006). Institutional ethnography and experience as data. In D. Smith (Ed.), *Institutional ethnography as practice* (pp. 91–108). Toronto: Altimira Press.

Campbell, M., & Gregor, F. (2002). *Mapping social relations: A primer in doing institutional ethnography*. Aurora, ON: Garamond Press.

Carter, Bob. (2000). *Realism and racism: Concepts of race in sociology*. London: Routledge.

Cavell, M. (2006). *Becoming a subject: Reflections in philosophy and psychoanalysis*. Oxford: Oxford University Press.

Cha, T., Kuo, E., Marsh, J. C., & Kvieskien , G. (2006). Useful knowledge for social work practice. *Social Work & Society, 4*(1), 111–122.

Charmaz, K. (2006). *Constructing grounded theory: A practical guide through qualitative analysis.* London: Sage Publications Ltd.

Charmaz, K. (2008) Grounded Theory as an Emergent Method. In S. N. Hesse-Biberand & P. Leavy (eds) Handbook of Emergent Methods, pp. 155–170. New York: Guilford Press.

Charmaz, K. C. (1990). Discovering chronic illness: Using grounded theory. *Social Science and Medicine, 30*(11), 1161–1172

Clarke, G. (2008). Notes on the origins of "Personal relations theory" in aspects of social thinking of the scottish enlightenment. *Psychoanalysis, Culture & Society, 13*(3), 325–334.

Clarke, G. (2011). On: The narcissism of minor differences. *The International Journal of Psychoanalysis, 92*(1), 231–233.

Clarke, S. (2006). Theory and practice: Psychoanalytic sociology as psycho-social studies. *Sociology, 40*(6), 1153–1169.

Clarke, S., & Hoggett, P. (2009). *Researching beneath the surface.* London: Karnac.

Clarke, S., Hahn, H., & Hoggett, P. (2008). *Object relations and social relations: The implications of the relational turn in psychoanalysis.* London: Karnac Books.

Collier, A. (1994). *Critical realism: An introduction to roy bhaskar's philosophy.* London: Verso.

Conrad, P. (1985). The meaning of medications: Another look at compliance. *Social Science & Medicine, 20*(1), 29–37.

Conrad, P. (1992). Medicalization and social control. *Annual Review of Sociology,*18, 209–32.

Cooper, W. O., Arbogast, P. G., Ding, H., Hickson, G. B., Fuchs, D. C., & Ray, W. A. (2006). Trends in prescribing of antipsychotic medications for us children. *Ambulatory Pediatrics, 6*(2), 79–83.

Cromby, J. (2004). Between constructionism and neuroscience. *Theory & Psychology, 14*(6), 797–821.

D'Cruz, H., Gillingham, P., & Melendez, S. (2007). Reflexivity, its meanings and relevance for social work: A critical review of the literature. *The British Journal of Social Work, 37*(1), 73–90.

Danermark, B., Ekstrom, M., Jakobsen, L., & Karlsson, J. C. (2002). *Explaining society: Critical realism in the social sciences.* London: Routledge.

David, M. (2003). The politics of communication, information technology, local knowledge, and social exclusion. *Telematics and Informatics, 20*, 235–253.

DeMontigny, G. (2005). *Social working: An ethnography of front-line practice.* Toronto: University of Toronto Press.

DeVault, M. & McCoy, L. (2006). Institutional Ethnography: Using Interviews to Investigate Ruling Relations. In D. Smith (Ed.), *Institutional Ethnography as Practice* (pp. 15–44). Toronto: Rowman & Littlefield Publishers, Inc.

DeVault, M. L. (1999). Institutional ethnography: A strategy for feminist inquiry. In *Liberating method: Feminism and social research* (pp. 46–54). Philadelphia: Temple University Press.

Dennett, D. C. (1992). The Self as a Center of Narrative Gravity, in F. S. Kessel, P. M.Cole and D. L. Johnson (eds) *Self and Consciousness: Multiple Perspectives*. Hillsdale, NJ: Erlbaum.

Dennett, D. C. (1993). *Consciousness explained*. Harmondsworth, UK: Penguin.

Denzin, N. K., & Lincoln, Y. S. (2000). The discipline and practice of qualitative research. In N. Denzin K., & Y. Lincoln S. (Eds.), *Handbook of qualitative research* (pp. 1–28). Thousand Oaks, CA: Sage Publications.

Doll, W. E. (2008). Chaos and complexity. In L. Givens (Ed.), *The sage encyclopedia of qualitative methods* (1st ed.). Thousand Oaks, CA: Sage Publications.

Doyle, J. (1999). A qualitative study of factors influencing psychiatric nurse practice in Australian prisons. *Perspectives in Psychiatric Care, 35*(1), 29–35.

Draine, J., Wilson, A. B., Metraux, S., Hadley, T., & Evans, A. C. (2010). The impact of mental illness status on the length of jail detention and legal mechanism of jail release. *Psychiatric Services, 61*(5), 458–462.

Dreyfus, H. (1986). *Mind over machine*. New York: Free Press.

Ekstrom, S. R. (2004). The mind beyond our immediate awareness: Freudian, jungian, and cognitive models of the unconscious. *Journal of Analytical Psychology, 49*(5), 657–682.

Elder-Vass, D. (2007a). Luhmann and emergentism. *Philosophy of the Social Sciences, 37*(4), 408.

Elder-Vass, D. (2007a). A method for social ontology: Iterating ontology and social research. *Journal of Critical Realism, 6*(2), 226–249.

Elder-Vass, D. (2007b). Social structure and social relations. *Journal for the Theory of Social Behaviour, 37*(4), 463–477.

Elder-Vass, D. (2010). The causal power of discourse. *Journal for the Theory of Social Behaviour, 41*(2)143–160.

Emirbayer, M., & Williams, E. M. (2005). Bourdieu and social work. *Social Service Review,79*(4), 689–724.

Fay, B. (1975). *Social theory and political practice*. London: Allen & Unwin.

Fay, B. (1976). *Social theory and political practice*. New York: Holmes & Meier.

Fay, B. (1987). *Critical social science: Liberation and its limits*. Ithaca, NY: Cornell University Press.

Ferguson, H. (2008). Liquid social work: Welfare interventions as mobile practices. *British Journal of Social Work, 38*(3), 561–579.

Finlay, L. (2002). Negotiating the swamp: The opportunity and challenge of reflexivity in research practice. *Qualitative Research, 2*(2), 209–230. doi:10.1177/146879410200200205

Fischer, J. (1973). Is casework effective? A review. *Social Work, 18*(1), 5–20.

Fischer, J. (1978). Does anything work? *Journal of Social Service Research, 1*(13), 215–243.

Fischer, J. (1981). The social work revolution. *Social Work, 26*(3), 199–207.

Floersch, J. (2000). Reading the case record: The oral and written narratives of social work. *Social Services Review, 74*(2), 169–192.

Floersch, J. (2002). *Meds, money, and manners: The case management of severe mental illness.* New York: Columbia University Press.

Floersch, J. (2004). A method for investigating practitioner use of theory in practice. *Qualitative Social Work, 3*(2), 161–177.

Floersch, J., Longhofer, J., Kranke, D., & Townsend, L. (2010). Integrating thematic, grounded theory, and narrative analysis: A case study of adolescent psychotropic treatment. *Qualitative Social Work, 9,* 407–425.

Floersch, J., Townsend, L., Longhofer, J., Munson, M., Winbush, V., Kranke, D., Faber,R., Thomas, J., Jenkins, J. H. and Findling, R. (2009). Adolescent experience of psychotropic treatment, *Transcultural Psychiatry, 46*(1): 157–179.

Flyvbjerg, B. (2001). *Making social science matter: Why social science fails and how it can succeed again.* Cambridge: Cambridge University Press.

Fook, J. (2002a). *Social work: Critical theory and practice.* Thousand Oaks, CA: Sage Publications.

Fook, J. (2002b). Theorizing from practice: Towards an inclusive approach for social work research. *Qualitative Social Work, 1*(1), 79–95. doi:10.1177/147332500200100106

Fook, J. (2002c). Theorizing from practice. *Qualitative Social Work, 1*(1), 79–95.

Fook, J., & Askeland, G. A. (2006). The "critical" in critical reflection. In J. Fook, S. White & F. Gardner (Eds.), *Critical reflection in health and social work* (pp. 40–54). Berkshire, UK: Open University Press.

Fook, J., & Gardner, F. (2007). *Practising critical reflection: A resource handbook.* Maidenhead, UK: Open University Press.

Fook, J., Ryan, M., & Hawkins, L. (1997). Towards a theory of social work expertise. *British Journal of Social Work, 27*(3), 399–417.

Fook, J., White, S., & Gardner, F. (2006). Critical reflection: A review of contemporary literature and understandings. In S. White, J. Fook & F. Gardner (Eds.), *Critical reflection in health and social care.* New York: McGraw Hill.

Fraser, H. (2004). Doing narrative research: Analyzing personal stories line by line. *Qualitative Social Work, 3*(2), 179–201.

Fraser, N., & Honneth, A. (2003). *Redistribution or recognition?: A political-philosophical exchange*. London, UK: Verso books.

Freeman, W. (2000). Consciousness, intentionality and causality. In R. Nunez, & W. J. Freeman (Eds.), *Reclaiming cognition: The primacy of action, intention and emotion* (pp. 143–172). Exeter, UK: Imprint Academic.

Freire, E. S. (2006). Randomized controlled clinical trial in psychotherapy research: An epistemological controversy. *Journal of Humanistic Psychology, 46*(3), 323–335.

Froggett, L. (2002). *Love, hate and welfare: Psychosocial approaches to policy and practice*. Bristol, UK: Policy Press.

Froggett, L., & Chamberlayne, P. (2004). Narratives of social enterprise. *Qualitative Social Work, 3*(1), 61.

Gabriel, B., Bromberg, E., Vandenbovenkamp, P. Kornblith, A. and Luzatto, P. (2000). Art therapy with adult bone marrow transplant patients in isolation: A pilot study, *Psycho-Oncology 10*(2), 114–123.

Garro, L. C. (2000). Cultural meaning, explanations of illness, and the development of comparative frameworks. *Ethnology, 39*(4), 305–334.

Glaser, B. G. and Strauss, A. L. (1965) *Awareness of Dying*. New York: Aldine Publishing.

Gray, M. (1995). The ethical implications of current theoretical developments in social work. *British Journal of Social Work, 25*(1), 55.

Gray, M., & Mcdonald, C. (2006). Pursuing good practice? *Journal of Social Work, 6*(1), 7–20.

Gray, M., Plath, D., & Webb, S. A. (2009). *Evidence-based social work: A critical stance*. New York: Routledge.

Groleau, D., Kirmayer, L., & Young, A. (2006). The McGill Illness Narrative Interview (MINI): An interview schedule to explore different meanings and modes of reasoning related to illness experience. *Transcultural Psychiatry, 43*(4), 697–717.

Groleau, D., Zelkowitz, P., & Cabral, I. E. (2009). Enhancing generalizability: Moving from an intimate to a political voice. *Qualitative Health Research, 19*(416), 426.

Hallberg, L. R. M. (2006). The "core category" of grounded theory: Making constant comparisons. *International Journal of Qualitative Studies on Health and Well-being, 1*(3), 141–148.

Hammersley, M. (2000). *Evidence-based practice in education and the contribution of educational research*. Thousand Oaks, CA: Sage Publications.

Hardwick, L., Worsley, A. (2011). The invisibility of practitioner research. *Practice, 23*(3), 135–146.

Haskell, Robert E. (2009). Unconscious linguistic referents to race: Analysis and methodological frameworks. *Discourse and Society, 20*(1), 59–84.

Hasson-Ohayon, I., Roe, D., & Kravetz, S. (2007). A randomized controlled trial of the effectiveness of the Illness Management and Recovery program. *Psychiatric Services, 58*(11), 1461–1466.

Healy, D. (2004). *The creation of psychopharmacology.* Cambridge, MA.: Harvard University Press.

Healy, D. (2009). Trussed in evidence? Ambiguities at the interface between clinical evidence and clinical practice. *Transcultural Psychiatry, 46*(1), 5–15.

Hedström, P., & Ylikoski, P. (2010). Causal mechanisms in the social sciences. *Annual Review of Sociology, 36,* 49–67.

Heineman, M. B. (1981). The obsolete scientific imperative in social work research. *The Social Service Review, 55*(3), 371–397.

Herman, D. (2007). *The Cambridge companion to narrative.* Cambridge: Cambridge University Press.

Hibberd, F. J. (2008). Synchronic emergent powers in critical realism's account of mind. *International Association of Critical Realism, Annual Conference,* London, England. 1–8.

Hibberd, F. J. (2001). Gergen's social constructionism, logical positivism and the continuity of error. *Theory & Psychology, 11*(3), 297–321.

Hollway, W., & Jefferson, T. (2000). *Doing qualitative research differently: Free association, narrative and the interview method.* Thousand Oaks, CA: Sage Publications.

Honneth, A. (1996). *The struggle for recognition: The moral grammar of social conflicts.* Cambridge, MA.: The MIT Press.

Horwitz, A. V., & Wakefield, J. C. (2007). *The loss of sadness: How psychiatry transformed normal sorrow into depressive disorder.* New York: Oxford University Press.

Houston, S. (2003). Establishing virtue in social work: A response to mcbeath and webb. *British Journal of Social Work, 33*(6), 819–824.

Houston, S. (2005). Philosophy, theory and method in social work. *Journal of Social Work, 5*(1), 7–20.

Houston, S. (2008). Beyond homo economicus: Recognition, self-realization and social work. *British Journal of Social Work, 40*(3) 841–857. doi:10.1093/bjsw/bcn026

Houston, S. (2010). Prising open the black box: Critical realism, action research and social work. *Qualitative Social Work, 9*(1), 73–91.

Hoy, J. (2008). *Outcomes and Incomes: Implementing a Mental Health Recovery Measure in a Medical Model World* (Doctoral dissertation). Available from OhioLink ETD Center. (Document number: 1207019285).

Huff, A. S. (2000). 1999 presidential address: changes in organizational knowledge production. *Academy of Management Review, 25*(2), 288–293.

Hwang, W. C. (2009). The formative method for adapting psychotherapy (FMAP): A community-based developmental approach to culturally adapting therapy. *Professional Psychology, Research, and Practice, 40*(4), 369–377.

James, A., Jenks, C., & Prout, A. (1998). *Theorizing childhood.* Williston, VT: Teachers College Press.

James, D. J., & Glaze, L. E. (2006). *Mental health problems of prison and jail inmates (bureau of justice statistics special report NCJ 213600).* Washington, DC: Department of Justice.

Jenkins, J. H. (1997). Subjective experience of persistent psychiatric disorder: Schizophrenia and depression among us latinos and euro-americans. *British Journal of Psychiatry, 170*: 20–25.

Jenkins J. H., Strauss, M. E., Carpenter, E. A., Miller, D., Floersch, J. and Sajatovic, M. (2005). Subjective experience of recovery from schizophrenia-related disorders and atypical antipsychotics. *The International Journal Social Psychiatry, 51*(3): 211–227.

Kandel, E. (2005). *Psychiatry, psychoanalysis, and the new biology of mind.* Arlington, VA: American Psychiatric Publishing.

Kanter, J. (1989). Clinical case management: Definition, principles, components. *Psychiatric Services, 40*(4), 361.

Karp, D. A. (1996). *Speaking of sadness: Depression, disconnection, and the meanings of illness.* New York: Oxford University Press.

Kaufman, J., Birmaher, B., Brent, D., Rao, U., Flynn, C., Moreci, P., Williamson, D., & Ryan, N. (1997). Schedule for affective disorders and schizophrenia for school-age children-present and lifetime version (K-SADS-PL): Initial reliability and validity data. *Journal of the American Academy of Child and Adolescent Psychiatry, 36*(7), 980–988.

Kazi, M. (2003). Realist evaluation for practice. *British Journal of Social Work, 33*(6), 803–818.

Keat, R., & Urry, J. (1982). *Social theory as science* (2nd ed.). London & Boston: Routledge & Kegan Paul.

Keat, R., & Urry, J. (2011). *Social theory as science.* London: Routledge.

Kelly, J. A., Heckman, T. G., Stevenson, L. Y., Williams, P. N., Ertl, T., Hays, R. B., Leonard N.R., O'Donnell, L., Terry, M.A., Sogolow, E.D., Neumann, M. S. (2000). Transfer of research-based HIV prevention interventions to community service providers: Fidelity and adaptation. *AIDS Education and Prevention, 12*(5 suppl), 87–98.

Kirk, S. A., & Fischer, J. (1976). Do social workers understand research? *Journal of Education for Social Work, 12*(1), 63–70.

Kirk, S. A., & Kutchins, H. (1992). *The selling of DSM: The rhetoric of science in psychiatry.* New York: Aldine de Gruyter.

Kirmayer, L. J. (2005). Culture, context and experience in psychiatric diagnosis. *Psychopathology, 38*(4), 192–196.

Kirsch, I., Brett, D., Huedo-Medina, T., Scoboria, A., Moore, T, & Johnson, B. (2008). Initial severity and antidepressant benefits: A meta-analysis of data submitted to the food and drug administration. *PLoS Medicine,* 5(2), DOI: 10.1371/journal.pmed.0050045

Kleinman, A. (1988). *The illness narratives: Suffering, healing, and the human condition.* New York: Basic Books.

Kohn, L. P., Oden, T., Munoz, R. F., Robinson, A., & Leavitt, D. (2002). Adapted cognitive behavioral group therapy for depressed low-income african american women. *Community Mental Health Journal, 38*(6), 497–504.

Kondrat, M. E. (1992). Reclaiming the practical: Formal and substantive rationality in social work practice. *Social Service Review, 66*(2), 237–255.

Kondrat, M. E. (1995). Concept, act, and interest in professional practice: Implications of an empowerment perspective. *The Social Service Review, 69*(3), 405–428.

Kondrat, M. E. (2002). Actor-centered social work: Re-visioning "person-in-enviromnent" through a critical theory lens. *Social Work, 47*(4), 435–449.

Krueger, R. A., & Casey, M. A. (2009). *Focus groups: A practical guide for applied research* (4th ed.) Thousand Oaks, CA: Sage Publications.

Kulkarni, S. P., Baldwin, S., Lightstone, A. S., Gelberg, L., & Diamant, A. L. (2010). Is incarceration a contributor to health disparities? Access to care of formerly incarcerated adults. *Journal of Community Health, 35,* 268–274.

Kuzel, A. J., & Like, R. C. (1991). Standards of trustworthiness for qualitative studies in primary care. In P. G. Norton, M. Stewart, F. Tudiver, M. J. Bass & E. V. Dunn (Eds.), *Primary care research: Traditional and innovative approaches* (pp. 138–158). Thousand Oaks, CA: Sage Publications.

Kvale, S., & Brinkmann, S. (2008). *InterViews: Learning the craft of qualitative research interviewing* (2nd ed.). Thousand Oaks, CA: Sage Publications.

Lacasse, J. R., & Gomory, T. (2003). Is graduate social work education promoting a critical approach to mental health practice? *Journal of Social Work Education, 39*(3), 383–410.

Lahire, B. (2011). *The plural actor* (D. Fernbach Trans.). Cambridge, UK: Polity Press.

Lanphear, B. P., Byrd, R. S., Auinger, P., & Hall, C. B. (1997). Increasing prevalence of recurrent otitis media among children in the United States. *Pediatrics, 99*(3), doi:10.1542/peds.99.3.e1

Lawson, T. (1997). *Economics and reality.* London: Routledge Press.

Layder, D. (1997). *Modern social theory: Key debates and new directions.* London: Routledge.

Lewontin, R. C. (1993). *The doctrine of DNA: Biology as ideology.* Harmondsworth: Penguin.

Lewontin, R. C. (2001). It ain't necessarily so: The dream of the human genome and other illusions. *New York Review of Books.*

Linhorst, D. M., Dirks-Linhorst, P. A., Bernsen, H. L., & Childrey, J. (2009). The development and implementation of jail-based substance abuse treatment program. *Journal of Social Work Practice in the Addictions, 9,* 91–112.

Linhorst, D. M., Knight, K., Johnston, J. S., & Trickey, M. (2001). Situational influences on the implementation of a prison-based therapeutic community. *The Prison Journal, 81*(4), 436–453.

Litaker, D., Tomolo, A., Liberatore, V., Stange, K., & Aron, D. (2006). Using complexity theory to build interventions that improve health care delivery in primary care. *Journal of General Internal Medicine, 21,* S30–S34.

Longhofer, J., & Floersch, J. (2010). Desire and disappointment: Adolescent psychotropic treatment and adherence. *Anthropology and Medicine, 17*(2), 159–172.

Longhofer, J, Floersch, J., and Janis H. Jenkins. (2003). The social grid of community medication management. *The American Journal of Orthopsychiatry, 73*(1), 24–34.

Longhofer, J., Kubek, P., Floersch, J. (2010). *On being and having a case manager: A relational approach to recovery in mental health.* New York: Columbia University Press.

Longhofer, J., and Floersch, J. (2004). The phenomenological practice gap: Practice guidelines, evaluation, and clinical judgment. *Qualitative Social Work, 3*(4), 483–486.

Manicas, P. T. (2006). *A realist philosophy of social science: Explanation and understanding.* Cambridge: Cambridge University Press.

Marcus, G., & Fischer. (1999). *Anthropology as cultural critique: An experimental moment in the human sciences.* Chicago: University of Chicago Press.

Marsh, J. (2002a). Learning from clients. *Social Work, 47*(4), 341–344.

Marsh, J. (2002b). Using knowledge about knowledge utilization. *Social Work, 47*(2), 101–104.

Marsh, J. (2004). Theory-driven vs. theory-free research in empirical social work practice. In H. Briggs E., & T. Rzepnicki L. (Eds.), *Using evidence in social work practice: Behavioral perspectives* (20–350). Chicago: Lyceum Books.

Martin, E. (2007). *Bipolar expeditions: Mania and depression in american culture.* Princeton, NJ: Princeton University Press.

Mattaini, M., & Moore, S. (2004). Ecobehavioral social work. In *Using evidence in social work practice* (pp. 55–73). Chicago: Lyceum Books.

Mattingly, C. (1998). *Healing dramas and clinical plots: The narrative structure of experience.* Cambridge, UK: Cambridge University Press.

Maxwell, J. A. (2004). Reemergent scientism, postmodernism, and dialogue across differences. *Qualitative Inquiry, 10*(1), 35–41.

McBeath, G., & Webb, S. A. (2002). Virtue ethics and social work: Being lucky, realistic, and not doing ones duty. *British Journal of Social Work, 32*(8), 1015.

McCoy, L. (1995). Activating the photographic text. In M. Campbell, & A. Manicom (Eds.), *Knowledge, experience, and ruling relations: Studies in the social organization of knowledge*. Toronto, ON: University of Toronto Press.

McCoy, L. (2006). Keeping the institution in view: Working with interview accounts of everyday experiences. In D. Smith (Ed.), *Institutional ethnography as practice* (pp. 109–128). Toronto, ON: Altimira Press.

McCracken, S. G., & Marsh, J. C. (2008). Practitioner expertise in evidence-based practice decision making. *Research on Social Work Practice, 18*(4), 301.

McNeece, C. A., & Thyer, B. A. (2004). Evidence-based practice and social work. *Journal of Evidence-Based Social Work, 1*(1), 7–25.

Meinert, R. G., Pardeck, J. T., & Kreuger, L. (2000). *Social work: Seeking relevancy in the twenty-first century*. Binghampton, NY: Hawthorne Press.

Minton, T. D., & Sabol, W. J. (2009). *Jail inmates at midyear 2008-statistical tables (bureau of justice statistics special report NCJ 225709)*. Washington, DC: Department of Justice.

Moerman, M. (2002). *Meaning, Medicine and the placebo effect*. Cambridge, UK: Cambridge University Press.

Moll, I. (2004). Psychology, biology and social relations. *Journal of Critical Realism, 3*(1), 49–76.

Moreno, C., Gonzalo, L., Blanco, C., Jiang, H., Schmidt, A., & Olfson, M. (2007). National trends in the outpatient diagnosis and treatment of bipolar disorder in youth. *Archives of General Psychiatry, 64*(9): 1032–1039.

Mosse, D. (2003). Good policy is unimplementable? Reflections on the ethnography of aid policy and practice. *EIDOS Workshop on Order and Disjuncture: The Organization of Aid and Development*, London. 26–28.

Mueser, K. T., Corrigan, P. W., Hilton, D. W., Tanzman, B., Schaub, A., Gingerich, S., Essock, S. M., Tarrier, N., Morey, B., Vogel-Scibilia, S., & Herz, M. I. (2002). Illness Management and Recovery: A review of the research. *Psychiatric Services, 53*(10), 1272–1284.

Mueser, K.T., Meyer, P. S., Penn, D. L., Clancy, R., Clancy, D. M., & Salyers, M. P. (2006). The illness management and recovery program: Rational, development, and preliminary findings. *Schizophrenia Bulletin, 32*(Suppl. 1), S32–S43.

Mulvey, L. (1975). Visual pleasure and narrative cinema. *Screen, 16*(3), 6–18.

Natasi, B., Varjas, K., Schensul, S., Tudor, K., Schensul, J., & Ratnayake, P. (2000). The participatory intervention model: A framework for conceptualizing and promoting intervention acceptability. *School Psychology Quarterly, 15*(2), 207–232.

Neisser, U. (1994). Self-narratives: True and False, In U. Neisser and R. Fivush (Eds.) The *Remembering Self*. New York: Cambridge University Press.

Nellhaus, T. (2004). From embodiment to agency: Cognitive science, critical realism, and communication frameworks. *Journal of Critical Realism, 3*(1), 103–132.

No Child Left Behind Act of 2001: H.R. 1—107th Congress. (2001). In GovTrack. us (database of federal legislation). Retrieved March 28, 2011, from http://www.govtrack.us/congress/bill.xpd?bill=h107–1

Nurse, J., Woodcock, P., & Ormsby, J. (2003). Influence of environmental factors on mental health within prisons: Focus group study. *British Medical Journal,* *327*(7413), 480–485.

Ohio Department of Mental Health1. (2002). *History of the outcomes initiative.* *Retrieved from:.*http://www.mh.state.oh.us/iniatives/outcomes/hist.html

Ohio Department of Mental Health2. (2002). *Consumer outcomes incentive grant report.* Retrieved from: http://www.mh.state.oh.us/initiatives/outcomes/outcomes.html

Ohio Department of Mental Health3. (2002). *Highlights of the initial statewide report of the consumer outcomes system. Retrieved from*: http://www.mh.state.oh.us/iniatives/outcomes/duseinitrpsm.html

Ohio Department of Mental Health1. (2002). *Outcomes pilot evaluation. Retrieved from:* http://www.mh.state.oh.us/initiatives/outcomes/histoipeval.html

Oktay, J. (2012). *Grounded theory.* New York: Oxford University Press.

Olfson, M., Marcus, S. C., & Weissman, M. M. (2002). National trends in the use of psychotropic medications by children. *Journal of the American Academy of Child &Adolescent Psychiatry, 41*(5), 514–521.

Oliver, C. (2011). Critical realist grounded theory: A new approach for social work research. *British Journal of Social Work,* published online May 22, 2011, doi:10.1093/bjsw/bcr061.

Padgett, D.K. (2008). *Qualitative methods in social work research* (2nd ed.). Thousand Oaks, CA: Sage Publications.

Parton, N. (2008). Changes in the form of knowledge in social work: From the 'social' to the 'informational'? *British Journal of Social Work, 38,* 253–269.

Patton, M. Q. (2002). *Qualitative research and evaluation methods* (3rd ed.). Thousand Oaks, CA: Sage Publications.

Pellauer, D. (2007). *Ricoeur: A Guide for the perplexed.* London: Continuum International Publishing Group.

Pence, E. (2001). Safety for battered women in a textually mediated legal system. *Studies in Cultures, Organizations and Societies, 7*(2), 199–229.

Pettigrew, A. (1997). What is a Processual Analysis? *Scandinavian Journal of Management, 13,* 337–348.

Pettigrew, A. M. (2001). Management research after modernism. *British Journal of Management, 12*(02), S61.

Plugge, E., Douglas, N., & Fitzpatrick, R. (2008). Patients, prisoners, or people? Women prisoners' experiences of primary care in prison: A qualitative study. *The British Journal of General Practice, 58*(554), 630–636.

Postle, B. R. (2006). Working memory as an emergent property of the mind and brain. *Neuroscience, 139*(1), 23–38.

Putnam, H. (2002). *The collapse of the fact/value dichotomy and other essays.* Cambridge, MA: Harvard University Press.

Qureshi, H. (2004). Evidence in policy and practice. *Journal of Social Work, 4*(1), 7–23.

Richmond, R., Butler, T., Wilhelm, K., Wodak, A., Cunningham, M., & Anderson, I. (2009). Tobacco in prisons: A focus group study. *Tobacco Control, 18*(176), 182.

Riessman, C. K. (2008). *Narrative Methods for the Human Sciences.* Thousand Oaks, CA: Sage Publications.

Riessman, C. K. and Quinney L. (2005). Narrative in social work: A critical review. *Qualitative Social Work 4(4). 391–412.*

Ron, A. (2002). Regression analysis and the philosophy of social science: A critical realist view. *Journal of Critical Realism, 1*(1), 119–142.

Rosen, A. (1994). Knowledge use in direct practice. *The Social Service Review, 68*(4), 561–577.

Rosen, A. (2003). Evidence-based social work practice: Challenges and promise. *Social Work Research, 27*(4), 197–208.

Rosenfeld, R. M., & Bluestone, C. D. (2003). *Evidence-based otitis media.* Philadelphia: B.C. Decker.

Rossiter, A. (2011). Unsettled social work: The challenge of levinas's ethics. *British Journal of Social Work, 41*(5), 980–995.

Roth, D. (2005). The Ohio Mental Health Consumer Outcomes System. In T. Campbell-Orde, J. Chamberlin, J. Carpenter, & H. Leff (Eds.), *Measuring the Promise: a Compendium of Recovery Measures* (Volume II), (pp. 42–49). Cambridge: Evaluation Center @ HSRI.

Rotter, M., McQuistion, H. L., Broner, N., & Steinbacher, M. (2005). The impact of the "Incarceration culture" on reentry for adults with mental illness: A training and group treatment model. *Psychiatric Services, 56*(3), 265–267.

Rouse, J. (1996). *Engaging science: How to understand its practices philosophically.* Cornell: Cornell University Press.

Ryan, Marie-Laure (2007). Toward a Definition of Narrative, In D. Herman (Ed.) *The Cambridge Companion to Narrative,* (pp. 22–35). Cambridge: Cambridge University Press.

Sale, J. E. M., Lohfeld, L. H., & Brazil, K. (2002). Revisiting the quantitative-qualitative debate: Implications for mixed-methods research. *Quality and Quantity, 36*(1), 43–53.

Sawyer, R. K. (2001). Emergence in sociology: Contemporary philosophy of mind and some implications for sociological theory. *American Journal of Sociology, 107*(3), 551–585.

Sayer, A. (1992). *Method in social science: A realist approach* (2nd ed.). London: Routledge Press.

Sayer, A. (1997). Essentialism, social constructionism, and beyond. *The Sociological Review, 45*(3), 453–487.

Sayer, A. (2000). *Realism and Social Science.* Thousand Oaks, CA: Sage Publications.

Sayer, A. (2007). Understanding why anything matters: Needy being, flourishing and suffering. In J. Frauley, & F. Pearce (Eds.), *Critical realism and the social sciences: Heterodox elaborations* (pp. 240–257). Toronto: University of Toronto Press.

Sayer, R. A. (2010). *Method in social science: A realist approach* (Rev 2 ed.). New York: Routledge.

Sayer, R. A. (2011). *Why things matter to people: Social science, values and ethical life.* Cambridge, UK: Cambridge University Press.

Schafer, R. (1992) *Retelling a Life.* New York: Basic Books.

Schultze, U., & Boland, R. J. (2000). Knowledge management technology and the reproduction of knowledge work practices. *Journal of Strategic Information Systems, 9,* 193–212.

Schön, D. A. (1983). *The reflective practitioner: How professionals think in action.* New York: Basic books.

Seidman, I. (2006). *Interviewing as qualitative research* (3rd ed.). New York: Teachers College Press.

Senge, P., & Scharmer, O. (2001). Community action research: Learning as a community of practitioners, consultants and researchers. In P. Reason, & H. Bradbury (Eds.), *Handbook of action research.* London: Sage Publications.

Shaffer, D., Gould, M. S., Brasic, J., Ambrosini, P., Fisher, P., Bird, H., & Aluwahlia, S. (1983). A children's global assessment scale (CGAS). *Archives of General Psychiatry, 40*(11): 1228–1231.

Shaw, I. (2011). *Evaluating in Practice.* Burlington, VT: Ashgate Publishing Company.

Shaw, I., Gould, N. (2001). *Qualitative social work research.* London: Sage Publications.

Shedler, J. (2010). The efficacy of psychodynamic psychotherapy. *American Psychologist, 65*(2), 98–109.

Shonkoff, J. P., & Phillips, D. (2000). *From neurons to neighborhoods: The science of early childhood development.* Washington, D.C.: National Academies Press.

Smart, C. (2007). *Personal life: New directions in sociological thinking.* Cambridge, UK: Polity Press.

Smith, C. (2010). *What is a person? Rethinking humanity, social life, and the moral good from the person up.* Chicago: University Of Chicago Press.

Smith, D. (1987). The limits of positivism in social work research. *The British Journal of Social Work, 17*(4), 401–416.

Smith, D. (2005). *Institutional ethnography: A sociology for people.* Toronto: AltaMira Press.

Smith, D. (2006). *Institutional ethnography as practice.* Toronto: AltaMira Press.

Smith, D. E. (1987). *The everyday world as problematic: A feminist sociology.* Boston: Northeastern University Press.

Smith, D. E. (1999). *Writing the social: Critique, theory, and investigations.* Toronto: University of Toronto Press.

Smith, D. H. (2007). Controversies in childhood bipolar disorders. *The Canadian Journal of Psychiatry, 52*(7), 407–408.

Solomon, J., Card, J. J., & Malow, R. M. (2006). Adapting efficacious interventions: Advancing translational research in HIV prevention. *Evaluation and the Health Professions, 29*(2), 162–194.

Specht, H., & Courtney, M. E. (1995). *Unfaithful angels: How social work has abandoned its mission.* New York: Free Press.

Stahl, R., & Shdaimah, C. (2008). Collaboration between community advocates and academic researchers: Scientific advocacy or political research? *British Journal of Social Work, 38*(8), 1610–1629

Starkey, K., & Madan, P. (2001). Bridging the relevance gap: Aligning stakeholders in the future of management research. *British Journal of Management, 12*, S3–S26.

Steinmetz, G. (2004). Odious comparisons: Incommensurability, the case study, and "small n's" in sociology. *Sociological Theory, 22*(3), 371–400.

Steinmetz, G. (2005a). The genealogy of a positivist haunting: Comparing prewar and postwar us sociology. *Boundary, 32*(2), 109.

Steinmetz, G. (2005b). *The politics of method in the human sciences: Positivism and its epistemological others.* Durham, NC: Duke University Press.

Steinmetz, G. (2006). Bourdieu's disavowal of lacan: Psychoanalytic theory and the concepts of "habitus" and "symbolic capital." *Constellations, 13*(4), 445–464.

Steinmetz, G. (2007). Transdisciplinarity as a nonimperial encounter: For an open sociology. *Thesis Eleven, 91*(1), 48.

Stern, D. G. (2003). The practical turn. In S. P. Turner & P. A. Roth (Eds.), *The Blackwell Guide to the Philosophy of the Social Sciences* (pp. 185–206). Blackwell Publishing Ltd.

Stern, L., & Kirmayer, L. (2004). Knowledge structures in illness narratives: Development and reliability of a coding scheme. *Transcultural Psychiatry, 41*(1), 130–142.

Strauss, A. and Corbin, J. (1994). Grounded Theory Methodology: An Overview, in N. K. Denzin and Y. S. Lincoln (eds) *Handbook of Qualitative Research*, (pp. 273–285). Thousand Oaks, CA: Sage Publications.

Stuart, C., & Whitmore, E. (2006). Using reflexivity in a research methods course: Bridging the gap between research and practice. In J. Fook, S. White & F. Garnder (Eds.), *Critical reflection in health and social care* (pp. 156–171). Berkshire, UK: Open University Press.

Summerson-Carr, E. (2010). *Scripting addiction: The politics of therapeutic talk and american sobriety.* Princeton: Princeton University Press.

Swartz, J. A., & Lurigio, A. J. (1999). Final thoughts on IMPACT: A federally funded, jail-based, drug-user-treatment program. *Substance use & Misuse, 34*(6), 887–906.

Szöllösi-Janze, M. (2001). *Science in the third reich.* New York: Berg.

Thomas, C. P., Conrad P., Casler R., & Goodman, E. (2006). Trends in the use of psychotropic medications among adolescents, 1994 to 2001. *Psychiatric Services, 57*, 63–69.

Thyer, B. (1995). Promoting an empiricist agenda within the human services: An ethical and humanistic imperative. *Journal of Behavior Therapy and Experimental Psychiatry, 26*(2), 93–98.

Thyer, B. (2001). What is the role of theory in research on social work practice? *Journal of Social Work Education, 37*(1), 9–25.

Thyer, B. (2004). Science and evidence-based social work practice. In H. E. Briggs, & T. L. Rzepnicki (Eds.), *Using evidence in social work practice* (pp. 74–89). Chicago: Lyceum Press.

Thyer, B. (2008). The quest for evidence-based practice? We are all positivists! *Research on Social Work Practice, 18*(4), 339–345.

Thyer, B., & Sowers-Hoag, K. M. (1988). Behavior therapy for separation anxiety disorder. *Behavior Modification, 12*(2), 205.

Todd, L., & Nind, M. (2011). (Editorial) Giving voice in educational research. *International Journal of Research and Method in Education, 34*(2), 115–116.

Townsend, E. (1998). *Good intentions overruled: A critique of empowerment in the routine organization of mental health services.* Toronto: University of Toronto Press.

Tranfield, D., & Starkey, K. (1998). The nature, Social Organization and Promotion of Management Research: Towards Policy. *British Journal of Management, 9*(4), 341–353.

Vakharia, K. T., Shapiro, N. L., & Bhattacharyya, N. (2010). Demographic disparities among children with frequent ear infections in the united states. *Laryngoscope, 120*, 1667–1670.

Valenstein, E. S. (2002a). *Blaming the brain: The truth about drugs and mental health.* New York: Free Press.

Valenstein, E. S. (2002b). The discovery of chemical neurotransmitters. *Brain and Cognition, 49*(1), 73–95.

Van De Ven, A. H., & Johnson, P. E. (2006). Knowledge for theory and practice. *Academy of Management Review, 31*(4), 802–821.

Van Maanen, J. (1988). *Tales of the field.* Chicago: University of Chicago Press.

Van Manen, M. (1995). On the epistemology of reflective practice. *Teachers and Teaching: Theory and Practice, 1*(1), 33–50.

Van Manen, M. (1998). Modalities of body experience in illness and health. *Qualitative Health Research, 8*(1), 7–24.

Van Manen, M. (2007). Phenomenology of practice. *Phenomenology & Practice, 1*(1), 11–30.

Van Manen, M., & Li, S. (2002). The pathic principle of pedagogical language. *Teaching and Teacher Education, 18*(2), 215–224.

Van de Ven, A. H. (2007). *Engaged scholarship: A guide for organizational and social research.* New York: Oxford University Press.

Verhaeghe, P. (2004). *On being normal and other disorders: A manual for clinical psychodiagnostics.* New York: Other Press.

Vollmer, F. (2005). The narrative self, *Journal for the Theory of Social Behavior, 35*(2): 189–205.

Wakefield, J. C. (1995). When an irresistible epistemology meets an immovable ontology. *Social Work Research, 19*(1), 9–17.

Ward, H., & Atkins, J. (2002, September). *From their lives: A manual on how to conduct focus groups of low-income parents.* University of Southern Maine: Institute for Child and Family Policy of the Edmund S. Muskie School of Public Service, Institute for Child and Family Policy.

Webb, S. A. (2001). Some considerations on the validity of evidence-based practice in social work. *British Journal of Social Work, 31*(1), 57–79.

Webb, S. A. (2006). *Social work in a risk society.* London: Palgrave Macmillan.

Webb, S. A., & Mcbeath, G. B. (1989). A political critique of kantian ethics in social work. *British Journal of Social Work, 19*(1), 491–506.

Wedel, J., Shore, C., Feldman, G., & Lathrop, S. (2005). Toward an anthropology of public policy. *Annals of the American Academy of Political and Social Science, 600*(1), 30–51.

Wells, K. (2011). *Narrative inquiry.* Oxford: Oxford University Press.

Werner, A. (2004). *A guide to implementation research.* Washington D.C.: Urban Institute Press.

White, S., & Stancombe, J. (2003). *Clinical judgment in the health and welfare professions: Extending the evidence base.* Maidenhead, UK: Open University Press.

White, S., Fook, J., & Gardner, F. (2006). Critical reflection: A review of contemporary literature and understandings. In S. White, J. Fook & F. Gardner (Eds.), *Critical reflection in health and social care* (pp. 3–20). Maidenhead, England: Open University Press.

Whitebook, J. (1995). *Perversion and utopia: A study in psychoanalysis and critical theory.* Boston: MIT Press.

Wieder, B. L., Lutz, W. J., & Boyle, P. (2006). Adapting integrated dual disorders treatment for in-patient settings. *Journal of Dual Diagnosis, 2*(1), 101–107.

Wilkinson, M. (2004). The mind–brain relationship: The emergent self. *Journal of Analytical Psychology, 49*(1), 83–101.

Will, D. (1980). Psychoanalysis as a human science. *British Journal of Medical Psychology, 53*(3), 201–211.

Will, D. (1983). Transcendental realism and the scientificity of psychoanalysis: A reply to recent criticism. *British Journal of Medical Psychology, 56*(4), 371–378.

Will, D. (1984). The progeny of positivism: The maudsley school and Anti Psychiatry. *British Journal of Psychotherapy, 1*(1), 50–67.

Will, D. (1986). Psychoanalysis and the new philosophy of science. *International Review of Psycho-Analysis, 13*, 163–173.

Williams, S. (1999). Is anybody there? critical realism, chronic illness and the isability debate. *Sociology of Health & Illness, 21*(6), 797–819.

Williams, S. (2000a). Chronic illness as biographical disruption or biographical disruption as chronic illness? Reflections on a core concept. *Sociology of Health & Illness, 22*(1), 40–67.

Williams, S. (2000b). Reason, emotion and embodiment: Is "mental" health a contradiction in terms? *Sociology of Health & Illness, 22*(5), 559–581.

Williams, S. (2003). Beyond meaning, discourse and the empirical world: Critical realist reflections on health. *Social Theory and Health, 1*(1), 42–71.

Williams, S. (2006). Medical sociology and the biological body: Where are we now and where do we go from here? *Health: An Interdisciplinary Journal for the Social Study of Health, Illness and Medicine, 10*(1), 5–30.

Willig, C. (2001). *Introducing qualitative research in psychology: Adventures in theory and method.* Philadelphia, PA: Open University Press.

Wong, I. C., Murray, M. L., Camilleri-Novak, D. and Stephens, P. (2004). Increased Prescribing Trends of Paediatric Psychotropic Medications. *Archives of Disease in Childhood, 89*(12), 1131–1132.

Yin, R. K. (1994). *Case study research: Design and methods* (2nd ed.). Thousand Oaks: Sage Publications.

Young, A. (1995). *The harmony of illusions: An ethnographic account of post-traumatic stress disorder.* Princeton, NJ: Princeton University Press.

Index

empowerment, 34, 66, 93, 110,
115–117, 121–122, 129
engaged scholarship, xii–xviii, 5–6, 10, 23,
30–34, 36–38, 64–69, 77, 81, 83,
89–91, 93, 105–106, 108, 123–125,
129–130, 132, 136–137, 139, 145,
146–148, 150, 169
entities, 5, 12, 28–29, 65, 95, 141,
148–149, 157
epistemic fallacy, 26, 144
epistemology, 6, 23, 26, 168
essence, 18–20
essentialism, 4, 15, 18, 20, 144
ethnography, xviii, 24–25, 40–41, 47, 81,
145, 167
institutional ethnography, 83–84,
86–88, 90–94, 103, 108
cultural ethnography, 88
evaluation, xii, xiv, 3, 26, 83–84,
115, 125, 131, 170
evidence-based practice, xi, xiii, xv, xviii,
23, 33–34, 83–84, 122–123, 125–130,
137, 144–145, 165
experience, x–xi, xvii–xviii, 3–6, 8–9,
14, 18–19, 21–26, 30–33, 35,
39–43, 46–49, 52–53, 75, 83, 85–87,
90, 91, 93–95, 102–108, 111,
113–119, 123–124, 126, 128–129,
134–135, 141–142, 145, 147,
149–150, 163–164, 167, 169–170
with medication, 64–68, 73–74, 77–80
subjectivity in, 4, 11, 14, 16, 22,
65, 67–68, 73, 140, 142, 147,
149–150, 167, 170
experience-near, 39–40, 167

feminist theory, 29, 146, 161
fidelity, 83
focus groups, 131–135, 145
foster care, 33, 79
fractured reflection, 141, 143
funding, 23, 92, 118, 168

gender 18, 20, 68, 143–144
inequalities of, 10
grounded theory, xviii, 31, 45, 47,
50–52, 61, 74–75, 105, 108, 116
guilt, 10, 35
GT. See grounded theory

habitus, 142
hallucination, 17
health insurance, 84, 96
hermeneutic unit, 54–55
heterosexuality. See sexuality
hierarchical organization, 14, 119–120
Hispanic populations, 130
histories, 9–10, 17, 21, 34–35, 68–70, 89,
126, 129, 135, 167–168, 170
homelessness, 27
homosexuality. See sexuality
hospitalization, x, 24–25, 50, 69–70, 149
housing, 103, 110
human development, 4, 16
hyperactivity. See attention-deficit
hyperactivity disorder

id, 19
identity, 13–14, 80, 141, 149, 169
ideographic approach, 29
illness, 10, 21, 25, 42, 67–70, 77, 79–80, 83
illness management and recovery,
127. See also Wellness
Management and Recovery
IMR. See illness management and recovery
incommensurability, xiii, xvi, 23–24,
80, 144, 167
individualized service plan.
See treatment planning
individuals, xvii, 3, 10, 15, 21, 28, 30,
37–38, 41, 52, 65–66, 78, 85, 87–88,
91, 95–96, 101, 105 106, 108, 119,
128, 131, 133–135, 139–142
infant determinism, 4
informed assent, 70
informed consent, 37, 70, 96, 98
institutional ethnography. See
ethnography
institutional facts, 77–79, 81, 85–86,
123–124, 126, 148, 164
institutional review board, 37, 41,
44, 57, 70, 92, 96
insulin shock therapy, 34
insurance. See also Medicaid; Medicare
health insurance, 96
insurance companies, 26, 84
interdependence. See difference vs.
interdependence
internal conversation. See self-talk

CPSIA information can be obtained at www.ICGtesting.com
Printed in the USA
BVOW041229090912

299832BV00005B/1/P